Certificate Stage

Module D

Tax Framework
(Finance Act 1998)

Revision Series

9213/F99

British Library Cataloguing-in-Publication Data

A catalogue record for this book is available from the British Library.

Published by AT Foulks Lynch Ltd
Number 4
The Griffin Centre
Staines Road
Feltham
Middlesex
TW14 0HS

ISBN 0 7483 3921 3

© AT Foulks Lynch Ltd, 1999

Acknowledgements

The past ACCA examination questions are the copyright of the Association of Chartered Certified Accountants. The answers to the questions from June 1994 onwards are the answers produced by the examiners themselves and are the copyright of the Association of Chartered Certified Accountants. The answers to the questions prior to June 1994 have been produced by AT Foulks Lynch Ltd.

We are grateful to the Chartered Institute of Management Accountants and the Institute of Chartered Accountants in England and Wales for permission to reproduce past examination questions. The answers have been prepared by AT Foulks Lynch Ltd.

CONTENTS

SCHEDULE A AND PERSONAL ALLOWANCES

Examiner plus - the examiner's official answers
Further questions on this topic from the real exams with the examiner's official answers.

SCHEDULE E

Examiner plus - the examiner's official answers
Further questions on this topic from the real exams with the examiner's official answers.

INCOME TAX – SCHEDULE D CASES I/II AND CAPITAL ALLOWANCES

Examiner plus - the examiner's official answers
Further questions on this topic from the real exams with the examiner's official answers.

NEW SYLLABUS EXAMINATIONS WITH THE EXAMINER'S OFFICIAL ANSWERS

JUNE 1994 EXAMINATION

DECEMBER 1994 EXAMINATION

PREFACE

The new edition of the ACCA Revision Series, published for the June and December 1999 examinations, contains a wealth of features to make your prospects of passing the exams even brighter.

Examiner Plus

This book contains all the new syllabus examinations from June 1994 up to and including December 1998, plus the examiner's official answers, set out in chronological order at the back of the book.

We have cross referenced all these questions to their topic headings in the contents pages so you can see at a glance what questions have been set on each syllabus area to date, topic by topic.

The inclusion of these questions and answers really does give students an unparalleled view of the way the new syllabus examinations are set and, even more importantly, a tremendous insight into the mind of the Examiner. The Examiner's answers are in some cases fairly lengthy and whilst the Examiner would not necessarily expect you to include all the points that his answers include, they do nevertheless give you an excellent insight into the sorts of things that the Examiner is looking for and will help you produce answers in line with the Examiner's thinking.

Other Features

Step by Step Answer Plans and *'Did you answer the question?'* checkpoints are fully explained on the following two pages.

Tutorial Notes

The answers to the new syllabus examinations are the answers written by the Examiner but we have of course updated them for the Finance Act 1998. This sometimes of course changes the nature of a question as changes in legislation since the question was originally set alter the way the question works. We have therefore included tutorial notes at various points in the answers to indicate any such changes or to highlight significant technical points that will help you understand the answer. The tutorial notes are clearly identified with the heading *Tutorial note*, the note being enclosed in brackets.

Topic Index

The topics covered in all the answers have been indexed. This means that you can easily access an answer relating to any topic which you want to consider by use of the index as well as by reference to the contents page at the front of the book.

The Revision Series also contains the following features:

- Practice questions and answers - a total bank of around 95 questions and answers

- An analysis of the new syllabus exams from June 1994 to December 1998

- Update notes to bring you up to date for new examinable documents and any changes to legislation as at 1st December 1998.

- The syllabus and format of the examination

- General Revision Guidance

- Examination Technique - an essential guide to ensure that you approach the examinations correctly

- Key Revision Topics

- Formulae and tables where appropriate

HOW TO USE THE ANSWER PLANS AND 'DID YOU ANSWER THE QUESTION?' CHECKPOINTS

STEP BY STEP ANSWER PLANS

A key feature in this year's Revision Series is the Step by Step Answer Plans, produced for all new syllabus exam questions from June 1995 to June 1998.

Students are always being told to plan their answers and this feature gives you positive assistance by showing you how you should plan your answer and the type of plan that you should produce before you attempt the question.

Of course, in the exam, your answer Plan can be less fully written than ours because you are writing it for yourself. We are producing an answer plan which communicates the details to you the student and therefore is of necessity much fuller. However, all the detail is there, written in a way which shows you the lines along which you should be thinking in order to produce the answer plan.

You will notice that the Answer Plans start and finish with the exhortation that you must make sure that you have read the question and that you are answering it correctly. Each time you write down the next step in the Answer Plan, you must ask yourself - 'Why am I including this step?' 'Is it relevant?' 'Is this what the Examiner has asked me to do and expected me to do?'

Help with the answer

In addition, if you really do get stuck with the question and cannot see how to approach it, you may find it helpful to turn to the answer page, **cover up the answer itself!,** and start to read the Answer Plan. This may trigger your memory such that you can then return to the question itself and gain all the benefit of doing the question properly without reference to the answer itself.

Practice makes perfect

Like all elements of examination technique the time to learn how to plan your answers is not in the examination itself. You have to practise them now - every time you produce an answer - so that when you come to the examination itself these answer plans will be second nature.

It is probably a good idea to sketch out your answer plans in the way we have produced them here (but remember they can be briefer) and then compare them swiftly to our Answer Plan at the back of the book (don't look at the answer itself at this stage!).

This may indicate that you have completely missed the point of the question or it might indicate one or two other areas that you might wish to explore.

Then, without having yet looked at the answer itself, start writing your answer proper and then compare that with the examiner's own answer.

'DID YOU ANSWER THE QUESTION?' CHECKPOINTS

This is another feature included in this year's edition of the Revision Series. They are included in the new syllabus exam answers from June 1995 to June 1998.

At various points of the answers, you will come across a box headed **'Did you answer the question',** followed by a brief note which shows you how the printed answer is answering the question and encourages you to make sure that your own answer has not wandered off the point or missed the point of the question completely.

This is an invaluable feature and it is a discipline you must develop as you practise answering questions. It is an area of examination technique that you must practise and practise again and again until it becomes second nature. How often do we read in an Examiner's report that candidates did not answer the question the Examiner had set but had simply answered the question that they wanted him to set or simply wandered off the point altogether? You must make sure that your answers do not fall into that particular trap and that they do rigorously follow the questions set.

A good way of practising this aspect of examination technique is to imagine an empty box headed up 'Did you answer the question?' at the end of the paragraph or paragraphs you are about to write on a particular topic. Try and imagine what you are going to write in that box; what are you going to say in that box which justifies the two or three paragraphs that you are about to write. If you can't imagine what you are going to put in that box, or when you imagine it you find that you are struggling to relate the next few paragraphs to the question, then think very hard before you start writing those paragraphs. Are they completely relevant? Why are you writing them? How are they relevant to the question?

You will find this 'imagining the box' a very useful way of focusing your mind on what you are writing and its relevance to the question.

SUMMARY

Use the two techniques together. They will help you to produce planned answers and they will help you make sure that your answers are focused very fully and carefully on the question the Examiner has actually set.

1 SYLLABUS AND EXAMINATION FORMAT

FORMAT OF THE EXAMINATION

	Number of marks
Section A: 3 compulsory questions	67
Section B: 3 (out of 5) questions of 11 marks each	33
	100

Section A will contain questions on Income Tax, Corporation Tax and Capital Gains Tax.

Time allowed: 3 hours

Tax rates and allowances will be given in the paper.

---

(1)   OVERVIEW OF THE TAX SYSTEM

    (a)   Structure and procedures of Inland Revenue and Customs & Excise.

    (b)   Duties and powers of the Inspector of Taxes and VAT offices.

    (c)   Returns.

    (d)   Schedular system of Income Tax.

    (e)   Assessments, due dates, interest on overdue tax, repayment supplement.

    (f)   Sources of information - statute, case law, statements of practice, VAT leaflets, extra-statutory concessions.

(2)   INCOME TAX ON EMPLOYEES AND UNINCORPORATED BUSINESSES

    (a)   Basis of assessment under Schedule E (including emoluments of office and pension).

    (b)   Benefits in kind.

    (c)   Lump sum receipts.

    (d)   PAYE system.

    (e)   Employees' incentive schemes.

    (f)   Principles and scope of Cases I and II of Schedule D.

    (g)   Rules basis and application of Cases I and II.

    (h)   Other sources including

          (i)   Schedule A
          (ii)   Schedule D Cases III and VI.

    (i)   Calculating tax liability.

    (j)   Minimising/deferring tax liability.

(3)   TAXATION OF CORPORATE BUSINESSES

The impact of Corporation Tax on the transactions and other activities of corporate taxpayers

    (a)   Principles and scope of Corporation Tax.

    (b)   Rules basis and application of Corporation Tax.

    (c)   Calculating the Corporation Tax due (excluding groups and consortia) on income and chargeable gains.

    (d)   Identifying and investigating areas of concern in the information on which the computation is based.

    (e)   Minimising/deferring tax liabilities by identifying/applying relevant exemptions, reliefs and allowances.

(4)   CHARGEABLE GAINS OF INDIVIDUALS AND CORPORATE TAXPAYERS

    (a)   Principles and scope.

    (b)   Rules basis and application.

    (c)   Calculating the tax due.

    (d)   Minimising/deferring tax liabilities by identifying/applying relevant exemptions, reliefs and allowances.

(5)   NATIONAL INSURANCE

The impact of National Insurance contributions on individuals.

(6)   SOCIAL SECURITY

Outline knowledge of main areas of benefit.

(7)   VALUE ADDED TAX

The principles and scope of Value Added Tax.

ANALYSIS OF PAST PAPERS

Topics	J94		D94		J95		D95		J96		D96		J97		D97		J98		D98	
Employed v self-employed aspects			7	○	7	○	7	○			7	○							5	○
IT/CGT adminsitration	7	○	7	●	2	■	7	●			5	○			8	○	6	○	6	○
IT computation	2/8	□ ○	2	□	2	□	2	□	2	□	2	□	2	□			2	□	2	□
PAs given as tax reducers	2/6	■ ○	2	■	2	■	2	■	2	■	2 8	■ ●	2	■	7	○	2	■	2	■
Pension plan contributions relief	8	○	7	●			2/7	■ ●	8	○	2 8	■ ●	2	■			2	■		
Sch A computations			5	○	2	□			1	■			7	○			8	○	2	■
Sch E benefits in kind	2	□	2	■	2	□	2	□	2	□	2 8	■ ●	8	○	2	□	2	■		
ABAs	5	○																		
Capital allowances for plant and machinery	1/2	■ ■	2/6	□ ●	1	□			5/6	● ●	2 1	□ ■	1 2	■ ■			1 2 5	■ ■ ●	1	■
Farmers' averaging for Sch DI	5	○																		
IBAs	1	■	1/2	■ ■	1	□			2	□			1	■			5	○	1	■
Loss relief for sole traders	5	●									6	○			5	○			7	○
Partnership profits and losses					8	○									6	○				
Profit adjustment for Sch DI	2	□	7	●	6	○	7	●									7	○		
Sch DI basis periods	2	□	2/6	□ ○	5	○	7/8	● ○	6	○	2	□	2	■			2	□	2	□
Terminal loss relief for sole traders			6	○					7	○										
Capital loss treatment	1/3	■ □			1	■	1	■												
CGT calculation					2	■	2	■	3	□	3	□	1 2	■ ■	3	■	2	■	3	■

Topics	J94	D94	J95	D95	J96	D96	J97	D97	J98	D98
CGT for part disposals				3 □						3 ■
Compensation proceeds and CGT				3 □						
Roll over/ hold over reliefs for CGT	3 □						3 □	3 □	3 □	
Inter spouse transfers for CGT				3 □					3 □	
Leases and CGT		3 □								3 ■
Retirement relief for CGT	3 □			3 □		3 □			3 □	
PPR for CGT			3 □					3 □		
Share pooling for CGT		3 □			3 □	3 □	3 □			3 ■
Share CGT treatment for takeovers/rights issues			3 □		3 □					3 ■
CGT taper reliefs								3 ■		
Loss relief for companies			1 ■	1 □		1 ■	1 ■	1 □	1 ■	
MCT computation (SCMR etc,)	1 □	1 □	1 □	1 □	1 □	1 □	1 □		1 □	1 □
Cash accounting/bad debt relief for VAT		4 ○	4 ●							
NIC for employers/employees		7 ●			6/7 ○ ●		5 ○	2 ■		8 ○
NIC for sole traders		7 ●			7 ●			2 ■		
PAYE system		8 ○				8 ○	6 ○			
Pay and file	7 ●			5 ○		5 ○				
VAT accounting and records			4 ○	4 ○		4 ○		4 ○	4 ○	
VAT penalties and appeals			4 ○		4 ○			4 ○		4 ●
VAT registration/deregistration	4 ○	4 ○						4 ●	4 ○	4 ○

Key

The number refers to the number of the question where this topic was examined in the exam.

Topics forming the whole or a substantial part of a question:

□   Compulsory   ○   Optional

Topics forming a non-substantial part of a question

■   Compulsory   ●   Optional

3 GENERAL REVISION GUIDANCE

PLANNING YOUR REVISION

What is revision?

Revision is the process by which you remind yourself of the material you have studied during your course, clarify any problem areas and bring your knowledge to a state where you can retrieve it and present it in a way that will satisfy the Examiners.

Revision is not a substitute for hard work earlier in the course. The syllabus for this paper is too large to be hastily 'crammed' a week or so before the examination. You should think of your revision as the final stage in your study of any topic. It can only be effective if you have already completed earlier stages.

Ideally, you should begin your revision shortly after you begin an examination course. At the end of every week and at the end of every month, you should review the topics you have covered. If you constantly consolidate your work and integrate revision into your normal pattern of study, you should find that the final period of revision - and the examination itself - are much less daunting.

If you are reading this revision text while you are still working through your course, we strongly suggest that you begin now to review the earlier work you did for this paper. Remember, the more times you return to a topic, the more confident you will become with it.

The main purpose of this book, however, is to help you to make the best use of the last few weeks before the examination. In this section we offer some suggestions for effective planning of your final revision and discuss some revision techniques which you may find helpful.

Planning your time

Most candidates find themselves in the position where they have less time than they would like to revise, particularly if they are taking several papers at one diet. The majority of people must balance their study with conflicting demands from work, family or other commitments.

It is impossible to give hard and fast rules about the amount of revision you should do. You should aim to start your final revision at least four weeks before your examination. If you finish your course work earlier than this, you would be well advised to take full advantage of the extra time available to you. The number of hours you spend revising each week will depend on many factors, including the number of papers you are sitting. You should probably aim to do a minimum of about six to eight hours a week for each paper.

In order to make best use of the revision time that you have, it is worth spending a little of it at the planning stage. We suggest that you begin by asking yourself two questions:

- How much time do I have available for revision?
- What do I need to cover during my revision?

Once you have answered these questions, you should be able to draw up a detailed timetable. We will now consider these questions in more detail.

How much time do I have available for revision?

Many people find it helpful to work out a regular weekly pattern for their revision. We suggest you use the time planning chart provided to do this. Your aim should be to construct a timetable that is sustainable over a period of several weeks.

Time planning chart

	Monday	Tuesday	Wednesday	Thursday	Friday	Saturday	Sunday
00.00							
01.00							
02.00							
03.00							
04.00							
05.00							
06.00							
07.00							
08.00							
09.00							
10.00							
11.00							
12.00							
13.00							
14.00							
15.00							
16.00							
17.00							
18.00							
19.00							
20.00							
21.00							
22.00							
23.00							

1   First, block out all the time that is **definitely unavailable** for revision. This will include the hours when you normally sleep, the time you are at work and any other regular and clear commitments.

2   Think about **other people's claims on your time**. If you have a family, or friends whom you see regularly, you may want to discuss your plans with them. People are likely to be flexible in the demands they make on you in the run-up to your examinations, especially if they are aware that you have considered their needs as well as your own. If you consult the individuals who are affected by your plans, you may find that they are surprisingly supportive, instead of being resentful of the extra time you are spending studying.

3   Next, give some thought to the times of day when you **work most effectively**. This differs very much from individual to individual. Some people can concentrate first thing in the morning. Others work best in the early evening, or last thing at night. Some people find their day-to-day work so demanding that they are unable to do anything extra during the week, but must concentrate their study time at weekends. Mark the times when you feel you could do your best work on the timetable. It is extremely

important to acknowledge your personal preferences here. If you ignore them, you may devise a timetable that is completely unrealistic and which you will not be able to adhere to.

4   Consider your **other commitments**. Everybody has certain tasks, from doing the washing to walking the dog, that must be performed on a regular basis. These tasks may not have to be done at a particular time, but you should take them into consideration when planning your schedule. You may be able to find more convenient times to get these jobs done, or be able to persuade other people to help you with them.

5   Now mark some time for **relaxation**. If your timetable is to be sustainable, it must include some time for you to build up your reserves. If your normal week does not include any regular physical activity, make sure that you include some in your revision timetable. A couple of hours spent in a sports centre or swimming pool each week will probably enhance your ability to concentrate.

6   Your timetable should now be taking shape. You can probably see obvious study sessions emerging. It is not advisable to work for too long at any one session. Most people find that they can only really concentrate for one or two hours at a time. If your study sessions are longer than this, you should split them up.

What do I need to cover during my revision?

Most candidates are more confident about some parts of the syllabus than others. Before you begin your revision, it is important to have an overview of where your strengths and weaknesses lie.

One way to do this is to take a sheet of paper and divide it into three columns. Mark the columns:

OK   Marginal   Not OK

or use similar headings to indicate how confident you are with a topic. Then go through the syllabus (reprinted in Section 1) and list the topics under the appropriate headings. Alternatively, you could use the list of key topics in Section 5 of this book to compile your overview. You might also find it useful to skim through the introductions or summaries to the textbook or workbooks you have used in your course. These should remind you of parts of the course that you found particularly easy or difficult at the time. You could also use some of the exercises and questions in the workbooks or textbooks, or some of the questions in this book, as a diagnostic aid to discover the areas where you need to work hardest.

It is also important to be aware which areas of the syllabus are so central to the subject that they are likely to be examined in every diet, and which are more obscure, and not likely to come up so frequently. Your textbooks, workbooks and lecture notes will help you here. Remember, the Examiner will be looking for broad coverage of the syllabus. There is no point in knowing one or two topics in exhaustive detail if you do so at the expense of the rest of the course.

Writing your revision timetable

You now have the information you need to write your timetable. You know how many weeks you have available, and the approximate amount of time that is available in each week.

You should stop all serious revision 48 hours before your examination. After this point, you may want to look back at your notes to refresh your memory, but you should not attempt to revise any new topics. A clear and rested brain is worth more than any extra facts you could memorise in this period.

Make one copy of this chart for each week you have available for revision.

Using your time planning chart, write in the times of your various study sessions during the week.

In the lower part of the chart, write in the topics that you will cover in each of these sessions.

Example of a revision timetable

Revision timetable Week beginning:							
	Monday	Tuesday	Wednesday	Thursday	Friday	Saturday	Sunday
Study sessions							
Topics							

Some revision techniques

There should be two elements in your revision. You must **look back** to the work you have covered in the course and **look forward** to the examination. The techniques you use should reflect these two aspects of revision.

Revision should not be boring. It is useful to try a variety of techniques. You probably already have some revision techniques of your own and you may also like to try some of the techniques suggested here, if they are new to you. However, don't waste time with methods of revision which are not effective for you.

- Go through your lecture notes, textbook or workbooks and use a highlighter pen to mark important points.

- Produce a new set of summarised notes. This can be a useful way of re-absorbing information, but you must be careful to keep your notes concise, or you may find that you are simply reproducing work you have done before. It is helpful to use a different format for your notes.

- Make a collection of key words which remind you of the essential concepts of a topic.

- Reduce your notes to a set of key facts and definitions which you must memorise. Write them on cards which you can keep with you all the time.

- When you come across areas which you were unsure about first time around, rework relevant questions in your course materials, then study the answers in great detail.

- If there are isolated topics which you feel are completely beyond you, identify exactly what it is that you cannot understand and find someone (such as a lecturer or recent graduate) who can explain these points to you.

- Practise as many exam standard questions as you can. The best way to do this is to work to time, under exam conditions. You should always resist looking at the answer until you have finished.

- If you have come to rely on a word processor in your day-to-day work, you may have got out of the habit of writing at speed. It is well worth reviving this skill before you sit down in the examination hall: it is something you will need.

- If you have a plentiful supply of relevant questions, you could use them to practise planning answers, and then compare your notes with the answers provided. This is not a substitute for writing full answers, but can be helpful additional practice.

- Go back to questions you have already worked on during the course. This time, complete them under exam conditions, paying special attention to the layout and organisation of your answers. Then compare them in detail with the suggested answers and think about the ways in which your answer differs. This is a useful way of 'fine tuning' your technique.

- During your revision period, do make a conscious effort to identify situations which illustrate concepts and ideas that may arise in the examination. These situations could come from your own work, or from reading the business pages of the quality press. This technique will give you a new perspective on your studies and could also provide material which you can use in the examination.

4 EXAMINATION TECHNIQUES

THE EXAMINATION

This section is divided into two parts. The first part considers the practicalities of sitting the examination. If you have taken other ACCA examinations recently, you may find that everything here is familiar to you. The second part discusses some examination techniques which you may find useful.

The practicalities

What to take with you

You should make sure that you have:

- your ACCA registration card
- your ACCA registration docket.

You may also take to your desk:

- pens and pencils
- a ruler and slide rule
- a calculator
- charting template and geometrical instruments
- eraser and correction fluid.

You are not allowed to take rough paper into the examination.

If you take any last-minute notes with you to the examination hall, make sure these are not on your person. You should keep notes or books in your bag or briefcase, which you will be asked to leave at the side of the examination hall.

Although most examination halls will have a clock, it is advisable to wear a watch, just in case your view is obscured.

If your calculator is solar-powered, make sure it works in artificial light. Some examination halls are not particularly well-lit. If you use a battery-powered calculator, take some spare batteries with you. For obvious reasons, you may not use a calculator which has a graphic/word display memory. Calculators with printout facilities are not allowed because they could disturb other candidates.

Getting there

You should arrange to arrive at the examination hall at least half an hour before the examination is due to start. If the hall is a large one, the invigilator will start filling the hall half an hour before the starting time.

Make absolutely sure that you know how to get to the examination hall and how long it will take you. Check on parking or public transport. Leave yourself enough time so that you will not be anxious if the journey takes a little longer than you anticipated. Many people like to make a practice trip the day before their first examination.

At the examination hall

Examination halls differ greatly in size. Some only hold about ten candidates. Others can sit many hundreds of people. You may find that more than one examination is being taken at the hall at the same time, so don't panic if you hear people discussing a completely different subject from the one you have revised.

While you are waiting to go in, don't be put off by other people talking about how well, or badly, they have prepared for the examination.

You will be told when to come in to the examination hall. The desks are numbered. (Your number will be on your examination docket.) You will be asked to leave any bags at the side of the hall.

Inside the hall, the atmosphere will be extremely formal. The invigilator has certain things which he or she must tell candidates, often using a particular form of words. Listen carefully, in case there are any unexpected changes to the arrangements.

On your desk you will see a question paper and an answer booklet in which to write your answers. You will be told when to turn over the paper.

During the examination

You will have to leave your examination paper and answer booklet in the hall at the end of the examination. It is quite acceptable to write on your examination paper if it helps you to think about the questions. However, all workings should be in your answers. You may write any plans and notes in your answer booklet, as long as you cross them out afterwards.

If you require a new answer booklet, put your hand up and a supervisor will come and bring you one.

At various times during the examination, you will be told how much time you have left.

You should not need to leave the examination hall until the examination is finished. Put up your hand if you need to go to the toilet, and a supervisor will accompany you. If you feel unwell, put up your hand, and someone will come to your assistance. If you simply get up and walk out of the hall, you will not be allowed to reenter.

Before you finish, you must fill in the required information on the front of your answer booklet.

Examination techniques

Tackling Paper 7

This examination is divided into two sections. The first section contains three compulsory questions and is worth 67 marks. These marks will be allocated approximately as follows:

- corporation tax (25 marks)
- income tax (25 marks)
- capital gains tax (17 marks)

The second section will contain five questions, of which three must be answered. Each question will carry 11 marks. At least two questions in this second section will be computational.

In general, candidates appear to do better on computational questions and on questions which give a list of points for consideration where the structure of the answer is fairly obvious.

You will be given some tax rates and allowances on the paper. These are shown at the back of this book. You should be aware of what information you will, and will not, be provided with.

Your general strategy

You should spend the first ten minutes of the examination reading the paper. If you have a choice of question, decide which questions you will do. you must divide the time you spend on questions in proportion to the marks on offer. Don't be tempted to spend more time on a question you know a lot about, or one which you find particularly difficult. If a question has more than one part, you must complete each part.

On every question, the first marks are the easiest to gain. Even if things go wrong with your timing and you don't have time to complete a question properly, you will probably gain some marks by making a start.

Spend the last five minutes reading through your answers and making any additions or corrections.

You may answer written questions in any order you like. Some people start with their best question, to help them relax. Another strategy is to begin with your second best question, so that you are working even more effectively when you reach the question you are most confident about.

Once you have embarked on a question, you should try to stay with it, and not let your mind stray to other questions on the paper. You can only concentrate on one thing at once. However, if you get completely stuck with a question, leave space in your answer book and return to it later.

Answering the question

All Examiners say that the most frequent reason for failure in examinations, apart from basic lack of knowledge, is candidates' unwillingness to answer the question that the Examiner has asked. A great many people include every scrap of knowledge they have on a topic, just in case it is relevant. Stick to the question and tailor your answer to what you are asked. Pay particular attention to the verbs in the question.

You should be particularly wary if you come across a question which appears to be almost identical to one which you have practised during your revision. It probably isn't! Wishful thinking makes many people see the question they would like to see on the paper, not the one that is actually there. Read a question at least twice before you begin your answer. Underline key words on the question paper, if it helps focus your mind on what is required.

If you don't understand what a question is asking, state your assumptions. Even if you do not answer in precisely the way the Examiner hoped, you may be given some credit, if your assumptions are reasonable.

Presentation

You should do everything you can to make things easy for the marker. Although you will not be marked on your handwriting, the marker will find it easier to identify the points you have made if your answers are legible. The same applies to spelling and grammar. Use blue or black ink. The marker will be using red or green.

Use the margin to clearly identify which question, or part of a question, you are answering.

Start each answer on a new page. The order in which you answer the questions does not matter, but if a question has several parts, these parts should appear in the correct order in your answer book.

If there is the slightest doubt when an answer continues on another page, indicate to the marker that he or she must turn over. It is irritating for a marker to think he or she has reached the end of an answer, only to turn the page and find that the answer continues.

Use columnar layouts for computations. This will help you to avoid mistakes, and is easier to follow.

Use headings and numbered sentences if they help to show the structure of your answer. However, don't write your answers in one-word note form.

It is a good idea to make a rough plan of an answer before you begin to write. Do this in your answer booklet, but make sure you cross it out neatly afterwards. The marker needs to be clear whether he or she is looking at your rough notes, or the answer itself.

Computations

Before you begin a computation, you may find it helpful to jot down the stages you will go through. Cross out these notes afterwards.

It is essential to include all your workings and to indicate where they fit in to your answer. It is important that the marker can see where you got the figures in your answer from. Even if you make mistakes in your computations, you will be given credit for using a principle correctly, if it is clear from your workings and the structure of your answer.

If you spot an arithmetical error which has implications for figures later in your answer, it may not be worth spending a lot of time reworking your computation.

If you are asked to comment or make recommendations on a computation, you must do so. There are important marks to be gained here. Even if your computation contains mistakes, you may still gain marks if your reasoning is correct.

Use the layouts which you see in the answers given in this booklet and in model answers. A clear layout will help you avoid errors and will impress the marker.

Essay questions

You must plan an essay before you start writing. One technique is to quickly jot down any ideas which you think are relevant. Re-read the question and cross out any points in your notes which are not relevant. Then number your points. Remember to cross out your plan afterwards.

Your essay should have a clear structure. It should contain a brief introduction, a main section and a conclusion. Don't waste time by restating the question at the start of your essay.

Break your essay up into paragraphs. Use sub-headings and numbered sentences if they help show the structure of your answer.

Be concise. It is better to write a little about a lot of different points than a great deal about one or two points.

The Examiner will be looking for evidence that you have understood the syllabus and can apply your knowledge in new situations. You will also be expected to give opinions and make judgements. These should be based on reasoned and logical arguments.

Reports, memos and other documents

Some questions ask you to present your answer in the form of a report or a memo or other document. It is important that you use the correct format - there are easy marks to be gained here. Adopt the format used in sample questions, or use the format you are familiar with in your day-to-day work, as long as it contains all the essential elements.

You should also consider the audience for any document you are writing. How much do they know about the subject? What kind of information and recommendations are required? The Examiner will be looking for evidence that you can present your ideas in an appropriate form.

5 KEY REVISION TOPICS

The aim of this section is to provide you with a checklist of key information relating to this Paper. You should use it as a reminder of topics to be revised rather than as a summary of all you need to know. Aim to revise as many topics as possible because many of the questions in the exam draw on material from more than one section of the syllabus. You will get more out of this section if you read through Section 3, *General Revision Guidance*, first.

Some syllabus topics, in particular those which are only ever likely to appear in Section B - the choice part of the paper - may not appear on the following lists of Key Revision Topics. This is because we are encouraging you in Section 5 to concentrate on what is important. The questions in Sections 7 and 9 include all of the exam questions set since June 1994 and a large number of those set since 1990. Consequently you will meet questions in this book on topics which are not listed for Key Revision. Question 1 in Section 7 concerns General and Special Commissioners and is a case in point. Such questions will remind you that the following lists deliberately do not embrace the whole syllabus. If you can widen your revision to cover the fringes of the syllabus so much the better.

1 ADMINISTRATION

You must be familiar with the new system of Self Assessment, in particular:

- the dates for filing the return
- the pay days
- the payment of interest on unpaid/overpaid tax
- the liability for penalties and surcharges
- the procedure for a Revenue Enquiry.

You should also be aware of how the Pay and File system operates for corporation tax and how PAYE is used to collect tax from employees.

Refer to chapters 1 and 7 (PAYE) of the Lynchpin, and attempt all the questions shown under the heading of Administration on the contents page of this book.

2 SCHEDULE A AND PERSONAL ALLOWANCES

All income from property is assessable under Schedule A. You must be able to deal with the following topics:

- the 'business' basis of measuring net rents
- the basis of assessment
- the wear and tear allowance for furnished lettings
- the conditions and advantages of furnished holiday lettings
- rent a room relief
- the assessment of lease premiums.

Personal allowances is usually an essential element in most income tax computations and can be the topic of an exam question in its own right in Section B. You should have no hesitation in applying the following:

- the PA and the BPR as allowances against income
- the MCA, APA and WBA and maintenance payments as tax reducers (at 15%).

You should also know how allowances apply for:

- taxpayers over 65/75 for PA and MCA
- year of marriage/separation/death of a spouse.

Refer to chapters 3, 5 and 6 of the Lynchpin, and attempt all the questions shown under the heading of Schedule A and Personal Allowances on the contents page of this book.

3 SCHEDULE E

You should have a clear grasp of the following Schedule E rules:

- the definition of emoluments
- the date emoluments are 'received'
- relief for expenses
- the treatment of termination payments
- the (albeit imperfect) tests for distinguishing employed status from self-employed status
- exempt benefits in kind
- the basic difference in taxing benefits for 'lower paid' and 'higher paid' employees and directors
- the treatment of accommodation
- the special PIID rules for assessing
  - cars and fuel
  - vans
  - mobile phones
  - beneficial loans
  - use of/transfer of assets.

Refer to chapters 7 and 8 of the Lynchpin, and attempt all the questions shown under the heading of Schedule E on the contents page of this book.

4 INCOME TAX - SCHEDULE D CASES I/II AND CAPITAL ALLOWANCES

The following income tax aspects of taxing a trade can be expected to be frequently tested and should be thoroughly understood:

- the 'badges' of trade - (ie, practical tests for identifying whether a trade exists}
- the tax/NIC implications of being assessable under Sch DI versus Sch E
- the adjustment of profit - in particular the disallowing of expenses and the deduction of capital allowances
- the basis of assessment (ie, CYB) - in particular:
  - the opening year rules
  - the closing year rules and
  - the rules for allowing and assessing a change of accounting date
- the case law based definition of 'plant' for capital allowances

- the calculation of capital allowances on plant and machinery with particular attention to:
  - identifying the date of expenditure
  - the two year slot qualifying for FYA
  - the option for 'de-pooling' short life assets
  - pool cars/expensive cars
  - private use assets
  - restricted WDA/FYA rates for long life assets

- capital allowances for industrial buildings concentrating on:
  - the statute based definition of qualifying buildings
  - the 25% de minimis limit for non-qualifying parts
  - allowances for the first user
  - balancing adjustments on sale
  - allowances for the secondhand user
  - rules for dealing with industrial/non-industrial use
  - enhanced allowances for structures in EZs
  - modifications for allowing IBAs for hotels

- capital allowances on less important categories:
  - agricultural buildings
  - scientific research
  - patents
  - know-how.

Refer to chapters 9, 10 and 11 of the Lynchpin, and attempt all the questions shown under the heading of Income Tax - Schedule D Cases I/II and Capital Allowances on the contents page of this book.

5   PARTNERSHIP TAX

This topic was excluded from Paper 7 for several sittings before being reintroduced for the December 1997 sitting and onwards.

A partnership tax question should not be unduly difficult if you understand:

- how to allocate profits between partners (ie, according to their PSA for the period of account)

- how to deal with a change of PSA/composition of partnership

- how each partner is assessed as if he were a sole trader in respect of his allocated share of profit.

Other partnership aspects could be tested and are not difficult to master:

- the rules for allocating trading losses

- the individual partner's use of a loss on a 'soletrader' basis

- the individual partner's 'soletrader' liability for NIC

- the individual partner's CGT liability on his share of normally computed gains and losses on disposal of partnership assets.

Refer to chapter 13 of the Lynchpin, and attempt all the questions shown under the heading of Partnership Tax on the contents page of this book.

6   TRADING LOSSES

You should be able to identify the amount of a trading loss and be aware in particular that:

- trading losses automatically include capital allowances to the extent they are claimed
- special rules apply in the opening years
- a 'terminal' loss is put together in accordance with strict rules - learn them as you have no chance of guessing them correctly in the exam room!

You must be confident in using the following trading loss reliefs:

- S.385 - carrying the loss forward
- S.387 - carrying forward unrelieved business charges
- S.380 - using the loss against STI of current/previous year
- S.72 - FA91 extension of s.380 against capital gains
- S.381 - carrying back losses arising in the first 4 years
- S.388 - carrying back a 'terminal' loss.

If you are not told precisely which claim(s) to make in an exam question you must be prepared to make a sensible choice appropriate to the circumstances - eg, consider restricting a capital allowance claim to avoid wasting PAs.

Refer to chapter 12 of the Lynchpin, and attempt all the questions shown under the heading of Trading Losses on the contents page of this book.

7   PERSONAL TAX COMPUTATIONS

If you have worked through the above stages of Section 5 including the questions referred to you will have already revised most of the general rules for constructing a personal tax computation. In particular:

- Income, grossed up where received net, is shown conveniently as 'non-savings' or 'savings' income
- Charges are deducted before 'STI' and PAs are deducted after
- Losses under s.380/381 take priority over PAs but not over charges
- Income tax liability requires a precise knowledge of
    - the special rates to apply to savings income
    - the application of tax reducers
    - the relief for non-MIRAS mortgage interest
    - the need to include tax retained on charges
    - relief for tax deducted and payments on account
- A chargeable gain is treated as though it was extra income but only for deciding the rate(s) of CGT.

To consolidate these points refer now to chapters 2, 4, 5 and 6 of the Lynchpin, and attempt all the questions shown under the heading of Personal Tax Computations on the contents page of this book.

8   CAPITAL GAINS TAX

There is always one compulsory question on CGT and it can be tested as a part of another compulsory question and often also in Section B.

You should have a good working knowledge of the following background topics:

- Chargeable persons (ie, for paper 7 this is limited to individuals and companies)
- Chargeable assets (ie, learn the exempt list as otherwise it is chargeable)
- Chargeable disposals (eg, disposal on death is exempt)
- the basic computation including indexation allowance
- the relevance of the March 1982 value and 'global' rebasing
- how to compare cost/March 1982 results
- the valuation rules
- the definition of business assets for taper relief (for 1998/99 only such assets benefit from taper relief).

Some topics are marginally less important but should still be understood:

- the rules for connected persons
- no gain/no loss treatment for inter-spouse disposals
- claims for negligible value
- computations involving short lease disposals
- treatment of/relief for compensation proceeds
- EIS deferral relief
- Relief on incorporating a business.

Other topics are more important for exam purposes and should be thoroughly understood:

- the identification rules for share disposals, in particular

    - the post 5.4.98 matching rules for individual shareholders
    - the FA 1985 pool construction
    - the relevance of the 1982 holding
    - the impact of rights/bonus issues
    - the treatment of a take-over
    - 'small' treatment for rights sold 'nil-paid'

- part disposal computations

- interaction of gains/losses/taper relief/annual exemption

- relief for PPR

- Hold-over relief for gifts

- Roll-over/hold-over on replacement of business assets

- Retirement relief for soletrader or director etc of personal company

- Interaction of taper relief with exemptions/rollovers/deferrals.

Refer to chapters 14 to 21 of the Lynchpin, and attempt all the questions shown under the heading of Capital Gains Tax on the contents page of this book.

9   CORPORATION TAX

Question 1 in the exam is always a major compulsory question on corporation tax made up either actually or effectively of a number of interacting parts. For example, a detailed working on capital allowances may be needed before the amount of PCTCT and hence CT as required by the question can be computed. The question might actually ask for form CT61 details on income tax accounting thereby dispensing with the need to generate a separate IT working for the final CT computation.

Thus because corporation tax topics tend to be interdependent, in constructing a typical paper 7 answer it is important not to overlook any of the following:

- The areas where corporation tax differs from income tax in measuring amounts to assess:
    - no private use adjustment profit/capital allowance computations
    - quite separate rules for interest paid or received
    - no capital gains annual exemption or taper relief (but with indexation extending beyond April 1998)

- The PCTCT standard format

- IT quarterly accounting and its impact in calculating final CT liability

- The rates of CT especially in a 'straddle' situation (note FY1999 rates are known and might be used)

- The treatment of interest paid/received by a company (the examiner is particularly incensed by candidates who gross up bank interest - don't!)

- Apportioning PCTCT elements if the period of account is > 12 months

- The treatment of trading losses
    - S.393 (1) - carry forward of loss
    - S.393 (9) - carry forward of excess trading charges
    - S.393A (1)(a) - set against current profits before charges
    - S.393A (1)(b) - set against previous profits after trade charges
    - how the PCTCT standard layout is modified for losses
    - three year carry back for loss of last 12 months of trade

- the treatment of net capital losses for a company - only against future capital gains (such a simple point but tested in paper 7 over the years almost to exhaustion!).

Refer to chapter 22 to 24 of the Lynchpin, and attempt all the questions shown under the heading of Corporation Tax on the contents page of this book.

10   VALUE ADDED TAX AND NATIONAL INSURANCE

These topics appear in Section B of the paper - VAT is always tested in question 4 but NIC's appearance is less predictable. The questions on these taxes invariably represent easy marks. Don't forget that in Section B you have to choose three out of five and if you decide to leave VAT out of your revision you condemn yourself to three out of four. Leave out NIC as well and you may be down to no choice at all! Therefore, an understanding of the following topics could help you deal successfully with Section B.

VAT topics:

- registration - compulsory/voluntary
- de-registration - compulsory/voluntary
- supplies that are zero-rated
- supplies that are exempt
- expenses for which input tax irrecoverable
- input tax credit for a partially exempt trader
- the tax point of a supply
- the contents of a tax invoice
- records to be maintained
- VAT return contents

- penalty regime for
  - late registration
  - default surcharge
  - serious misdeclaration penalty
  - default interest
- cash accounting
- bad debt relief
- annual accounting
- appeals to VAT tribunal

NIC topics
- calculating for simple situations
  - Class 1 - employer's, employee's
  - Class 1A - employer's liability on company car/fuel
  - Class 2 - flat weekly rate for traders
  - Class 4 - 6% on 'band' trading profits computed as for income tax
- age exceptions
- collection arrangements

Refer to chapters 25 and 26 of the Lynchpin, and attempt all the questions shown under the heading of Value Added Tax and National Insurance on the contents page of this book.

UPDATES

Examinable documents

The ACCA Official Textbook and Revision Series for Paper 7 are fully up-to-date for the Finance Act 1998, which was enacted in July 1998.

This legislation is examinable in both June 1999 and December 1999.

The September 1998 issue of the ACCA Students' Newsletter carries a detailed article on the impact of the FA1998 on the tax papers for June and December 1999. You are strongly recommended to read it as a useful summary of topical issues. However, all of the guidance on syllabus exclusions etc had been available when the ATFL publications were updated for FA1998 so the article's contents have been fully taken into account in your study material.

Extra study material

We regret that a small section on the formulae which is applied when a business leases a car whose normal retail cost is greater than £12,000 has been inadvertently omitted from your textbook.

Please read the notes below as extra text for section 2.2 of Chapter 9 of your text.

We apologise for any inconvenience caused.

Leasing of cars

The rental charges payable for leasing a car are allowed on the basis of the normal adjustment principles - ie, disallow the private use portions.

However, if the car cost more than £12,000 when new the business use portion is reduced to the amount given in the following formula:

$$\text{Business portion of rental charge} \times \frac{£12,000 + \frac{1}{2}(\text{Cost of car} - £12,000)}{\text{Cost of car (when new)}}$$

Example

Roy enters into a leasing contract for a Turbo Saab car with an original cost of £30,000, paying £8,000 p.a. in rental charges. His business use amounts to 80%.

The annual allowable amount would be:

$$8,000 \times 80\% \times \frac{12,000 + \frac{1}{2}(30,000 - 12,000)}{30,000} = £4,480$$

(ie, disallow 8,000 - 4,480 = £3,520)

Note that if, instead, the vehicle was being acquired under a hire purchase agreement all of the business portion of the hire-purchase interest would be allowed. The car is treated instead as if the trader owned it from the start of the HP contract and capital allowances would be given (restricted for over £12,000 car) - see Chapter 10.

The point is illustrated in Question 5 (Roger Riviere) and Question 40 (Uranus Ltd).

7 PRACTICE QUESTIONS

---

1   GENERAL AND SPECIAL COMMISSIONERS

You are required:

(a)   to explain the duties, powers, necessary qualifications, remuneration, method of operation and method of appointment of both the General and Special Commissioners   **(9 marks)**

(b)   explain what further appeal(s) are open to the party who has lost an appeal before either body of Commissioners.   **(2 marks)**

      (Total: 11 marks)

      (ACCA Jun 92)

2   ARTHUR

Arthur owned a furnished house in a holiday resort which was available for commercial letting when not occupied by Arthur and his family.

In the tax year 1998/99 it was let for the following periods, no letting to the same person exceeding 30 days:

Month	Days
April	7
May	14
June	7
July	31
August	30 - occupied by Arthur
September	14

Apart from the above periods and two weeks in April when it was being decorated the house was available for letting throughout the tax year. The total rent received was £1,900 and the following expenditure was incurred:

	£
Insurance	250
Repairs and decorating	308
Water rates	160
Accountancy	60
Cleaning	480
Advertising	200
Interest on loan to purchase property	608
Replacement furniture	140

The annual allowance of 10% of rent (less water rates) has been agreed for wear and tear of furniture.

Arthur has also purchased two shops in the resort.

Shop 1. The annual rent was £3,000 on a tenant's repairing lease which expired on 30 June 1998. Arthur took advantage of the shop being empty to carry out repairs and decorating. The shop was let to another tenant on a five-year tenant's repairing lease at £4,000 per annum from 1 October 1998.

Shop 2. The shop was purchased on 10 April 1998 and required treatment for dry-rot. Arthur also undertook some normal re-decorating work before the shop was let on 1 October 1998 on a seven-year tenant's repairing lease at an annual rental of £6,000. A premium of £2,000 was received from the incoming tenant upon signing the lease on 1 October 1998.

The rent for both shops was due in advance on the usual calendar quarter days.

The following expenditure was incurred for 1998/99:

	Shop 1 £	*Shop 2* £
Insurance	190	300
Ground rent	10	40
Repairs and decorating	3,900 *(Note 1)*	5,000 *(Note 2)*
Accountancy	50	50
Advertising for tenant	100	100

Notes:

(1)   Includes £2,500 for re-roofing the shop following gale damage in February 1998. Because the roof had been badly maintained the insurance company refused to pay for the repair work.

(2)   Includes £3,000 for dry-rot remedial treatment which was present when the shop was bought in April 1998.

You are required to calculate the income assessable on Arthur for 1998/99 from the house and both shops and to show how any losses would be dealt with.   **(11 marks)**

(Pilot paper)

---

3   ALEXANDER AND SONIA

(a)   Emoluments from an office or employment are taxable under Schedule E.

You are required to explain the basis of assessment for Schedule E   **(5 marks)**

(b)   **You are required** to state how the taxable value of goods and services provided for employees is determined:

(i)   for employees earning less than £8,500 pa;
(ii)   for employees earning £8,500 pa and over.   **(2 marks)**

(c)   Alexander and Sonia, a married couple, permanently separated on 5 April 1998 and were divorced on 5 August 1998. They had one child, Nicholas. The court ordered Alexander to pay maintenance payments to both Sonia and Nicholas.

You are required to state the income tax treatment of such maintenance payments on the payer and on the recipient.   **(4 marks)**

(Total: 11 marks)

(ACCA Jun 92)

4   MICHAEL

Michael started in business as a hairdresser on 1 March 1996 and finished on 31 October 2002.

His profits, adjusted for taxation, were as follows:

	£
Period ended 30.4.97	15,000
Year ended 30.4.98	17,000
Year ended 30.4.99	12,000
Year ended 30.4.00	14,000
Year ended 30.4.01	18,000
Year ended 30.4.02	13,000
Period ended 31.10.02	3,000

You are required to calculate the assessable amounts for all relevant years, taking into account any relief which Michael is entitled to.

(9 marks)
(ACCA Dec 92)
(Pilot paper)

5   ROGER RIVIERE

Roger Riviere is a self-employed wholesale clothing distributor who commenced trading on 1 July 1996. His summarised accounts for the year ended 30 June 1998 are:

	£	£
Sales (1)		400,000
Opening stock (2)	40,000	
Purchases	224,000	
	264,000	
Closing stock (2)	(32,000)	232,000
Gross profit		168,000
Wages and national insurance (3)		52,605
Rent and business rates		31,060
Repairs and renewals (4)		3,490
Miscellaneous expenses (5)		665
Taxation (Roger's income tax)		15,590
Bad debts (6)		820
Legal expenses (7)		1,060
Depreciation		570
Lease rental on car (Roger's car) (8)		8,400
Loss on sale of office furniture		60
Deeds of covenant (9)		80
Transport costs		4,250
Interest (10)		990
Motor car running expenses (Roger's car) (11)		2,000
Premium on lease (12)		6,000
Lighting and heating		1,250
Sundry expenses (all allowable)		710
Re-location expenditure (13)		2,400
Net profit		36,000
		168,000

Figures in brackets refer to notes to the accounts.

Notes to accounts:

(1)   Sales include £500 reimbursed by Roger's family for clothing taken from stock. This reimbursement represented cost price.

(2)   Stock. The basis of both opening and closing stock valuations was 'lower of cost or market value' less a contingency reserve of 50% in view of the recession.

(3)   Wages. Included in wages are Roger's drawings of £50 per week, his national insurance contributions of £320 for the year and wages and national insurance contributions in respect of his wife totalling £11,750. His wife worked full-time in the business as a secretary.

(4)   Repairs and renewals. The charge includes £3,000 for fitting protective covers over the factory windows and doors to prevent burglary.

(5)   Miscellaneous expenses

	£
Theft of money by employee	65
Political donation to Green Party	100
Gifts of 100 'Riviere' calendars	500
	665

(6)   Bad debts:

	£	
Trade debt written off		720
Loan to former employee written off		250
Provision for bad debts (2% of debtors)	450	
Less: Opening provision	(600)	
		(150)
		820

(7)   Legal expenses:

	£
Defending action in respect of alleged faulty goods	330
Costs in connection with lease of new larger premises	250
Successful appeal against previous year's income tax assessment	200
Defending Roger in connection with speeding offence	190
Debt collection	90
	1,060

(8)   Lease rental on car. Roger's car was a BMW costing £30,000. The lease was entered into on 1 July 1996.

(9)   Deeds of covenant (payable for next 4 years) (gross amounts)

	£
Local children's hospital	50
Oxfam	30
	80

(10)   Interest

	£
Bank overdraft interest (business account)	1,020
Interest on overdue tax	130
Interest credited on National Savings Bank ordinary account *(see note 14)*	(160)
	990

(11)   Motor car running expenses. One-third of Roger's mileage is private. Included in the charge is £65 for a speeding fine incurred by Roger whilst delivering goods to a customer.

(12)   Premium on lease. The premium was for a lease of six years.

(13)   Re-location expenditure. The expenditure was incurred in transferring the business to new and larger premises.

(14)   National Savings Bank, ordinary account. The account had been opened on 1 May 1996 and interest had been credited as follows:

	£
31 December 1996	110
31 December 1997	160
31 December 1998	180

The following information is provided:

(1)   Capital allowances for the year to 30 June 1998 are £480.

(2)   Roger was born on 8 April 1965 and always pays the maximum permitted personal pension contribution.

(3)   Roger and his wife have a joint mortgage on their home of £50,000. The interest estimated to be payable for 1998/99 is £4,250 (gross). The MIRAS arrangements apply.

(4)   Roger and his wife have agreed that Roger will claim all the married couple's allowance in 1998/99.

You are required:

(a)   to prepare a profit adjustment statement in respect of the accounting period to 30 June 1998 showing the 1998/99 Schedule Case I adjusted profit.   **(13 marks)**

(b)   to calculate the Class 4 national insurance contributions payable for 1998/99 (using the data provided).   **(1 mark)**

(c)   to prepare an estimate for Roger of the income tax liability for 1998/99 and to advise him when the tax will become due for payment.   **(8 marks)**

           (Total: 22 marks)

           (Pilot paper)

6   CHANGE OF ACCOUNTING DATE

(a)   Which conditions must be met for a change of accounting date to be valid?

(4 marks)

(b)   What is the consequence of the conditions not being met?

(1 mark)

(c)   Cordelia, a sole trader commenced trading on 1 July 1995 and has always made up her accounts to 30 June. She decides to change her accounting date to 30 September.

She is undecided whether to make up accounts for the 3 month period to 30 September 1998 or for the 15 month period to 30 September 1999.

Cordelia's tax adjusted profits are as follows:

	£
Year ended 30 June 1998	48,000
Three months to 30 September 1998	15,000
Year ended 30 September 1999	60,000
Cordelia's overlap profits on commencement were	£12,000

The overlap profits were for a period of 9 months.

You are required to show Cordelia's Schedule D I assessments for 1998/99 and 1999/00 on the assumption that

(i)   she prepares accounts for 3 months to 30 September 1998
(ii)   she prepares accounts for 15 months to 30 September 1999

and gives the appropriate notice to the Inland Revenue.

(7 marks)
(Total: 12 marks)

7   DOMINIC AND JUSTIN

Dominic and Justin commenced in partnership on 1 July 1996 and decided to produce their accounts to 30 June annually. On 1 January 1998, Simon joined the partnership.

The partnership's accounts show the following adjusted profits:

	£
Year ended 30 June 1997	10,000
Year ended 30 June 1998	13,500
Year ended 30 June 1999	18,000

You are required to show the amounts assessable on the individual partners for all the years affected by the above information, assuming that profits are shared equally.

(11 marks)

8   HECTOR, ZAZA AND KIKI

Hector, Zaza and Kiki commenced in partnership on 1 May 1997, sharing profits in the ratio 5:3:2. The partnership agreement provides for interest on capital at a rate of 6% on the following balances:

Hector £20,000, Zaza £18,000, Kiki £22,000

The agreement also provides for salaries of £8,000 to Hector and £10,000 to Zaza.

The partnership's adjusted profit prior to capital allowances for the accounts year ended 31 December 1998 was £35,000 and the capital allowances have been agreed at £3,400.

All the partners are single. Neither Hector nor Zaza has any other income or outgoings. Kiki is in full-time employment as an accountant, earning a salary of £30,000 per annum. She only works part-time for the partnership. Her personal allowance is initially set against her income from employment, which also uses her full basic rate band.

The partnership pays a charitable deed of covenant of £5,000 (gross) per annum.

You are required to compute the tax liability for each of the partners for 1998/99. **(11 marks)**

Ignore national insurance contributions.

---

9 BERT AND HAROLD

Bert and Harold commenced trading after 5 April 1994. Their accounts for the year ended 30 September 1998 show an adjusted trading profit of £16,500.

Bert and Harold changed their profit-sharing arrangement on 1 July 1998. The old profit-sharing arrangement applies until 30 June 1998, and the new arrangement applies from 1 July 1998.

	Bert	*Harold*
Old arrangement:		
Salaries pa	£3,000	£2,000
Share of balance	3/5	2/5
New arrangement:		
Salaries pa	£6,000	£4,000
Share of balance	2/3	1/3

The partnership made a loan of £10,000 to Harold's nephew who pays interest of 9% annually. This interest is received on 1 June and 1 December.

You are required to:

(a) show the time apportionment of the 1998/99 Schedule DI income;
(b) show the allocation of the Schedule DI income;
(c) show the allocation of the partnership loan interest. **(11 marks)**

---

10 KEVIN WINTERBURN

Kevin Winterburn started trading as a builder in May 1996. His agreed Case I profit for the year ended 31 December 1998 was £15,000. In the year ended 31 December 1999 Kevin expects to incur a trading loss which is likely to be agreed at £20,000 for income tax purposes. On 17 July 1998 he sold some land which resulted in an assessable capital gain after indexation of £7,100. The land was not a business asset for taper relief purposes.

His wife, Susan, to whom Kevin has been married for five years, is headmistress at a girls' boarding school. The following information is provided:

(1) Susan's remuneration for the year ended 5 April 1999 was £25,000.

(2)   She is also provided with a house where she is required to live by her employers for the better performance of her duties. The gross annual value of the house, which is owned by the school was £1,000. The house cost £70,000 in 1997.

(3)   In the tax year ended 5 April 1999, the school paid £1,500 for gas, electricity and decorating in respect of the house.

(4)   The school also provided Susan with a new 1300cc company car costing £7,000 on 6 October 1998. No car had been provided previously. The running costs of the car, including all petrol, were £800 to 5 April 1999. The total mileage in the period was 4,000, of which 1,000 was on school business.

(5)   Susan sold some shares on 12 April 1998 resulting in an assessable capital gain after indexation of £3,000.

Kevin and Susan had a joint account with a UK bank. The interest credited on 31 December 1998 was £1,000.

You are required:

(a)   to calculate the tax liabilities of

    (i)   Kevin, and
    (ii)   Susan,

for 1998/99. You should assume that any elections which may reduce the overall tax liability are made but you should state the nature of the elections;   **(16 marks)**

(b)   to state how advantage might have been taken of any unused allowances, exemptions or reliefs.

(1 mark)
(Total: 17 marks)
(ACCA June 91)

---

11   DAWN WARR

Dawn Warr, who is unmarried, has been in business since 1 May 1996 running a small private educational centre, specialising in modern language teaching. Her adjusted tax profits, before capital allowances, have been:

	£
Year ended 30 April 1997	15,000
Year ended 30 April 1998	12,000
Period to 30 September 1998	9,000

The following purchases were made during the year ended 30 April 1997

	£
Plant and machinery	3,200
Car (used by Dawn and private use agreed at 75%)	5,600
Car (used by Dawn's assistant and private use agreed at 50%)	4,000

On 1 June 1997 new recording equipment was purchased for £1,000.

On 1 January 1998 Dawn traded in her car for a new one. She paid £4,800 and was allowed a £3,000 cash allowance on the existing car. Private use remained at 75%.

On 6 May 1998 new furniture costing £500 was purchased.

On 30 September 1998 all the business assets were sold for the following amounts

	£
Plant and machinery (all less than cost)	2,500
Dawn's car	6,000
Dawn's assistant's car	2,000

On 30 September 1998 Dawn closed the business and on 1 October 1998, her thirtieth birthday, took up a job as regional manager with a firm of travel agents specialising in European holidays. Her salary was £24,000 per annum payable monthly in arrears. She was provided with a new 1,600 cc car, on commencement of her new job, which cost £9,750. In 1998/99 she did 12,000 miles in her company car, of which 1,000 were private. All running costs, including private petrol, were paid for by Dawn's employers. Details of other income and outgoings are

(1)   Dawn's employers did not have a pension scheme and she decided to pay the maximum amount permissible under the personal pension plan rules, relative to her employment.

(2)   Interest on a deposit account with Barlloyd Bank. The account had been opened in 1995 and interest was credited as follows:

31 December 1997	£300
31 December 1998	£491

(3)   Interest on a NSB ordinary account, which was opened in May 1996 and closed in May 1999. Interest had been credited as follows:

31 December 1996	£189
31 December 1997	£190
31 December 1998	£199
31 May 1999	£120

(4)   Dawn had a mortgage on her house for £20,000. Interest of £1,400 (gross) was paid in 1998/99 under the MIRAS arrangements.

(5)   Dawn had entered into a charitable deed of covenant with the local church of £77 per annum (net) on 8 April 1998 for ten years.

(6)   Dawn realised capital gains of £21,000 in 1998/99 (after indexation but before annual exemption). Taper relief was not available.

You are required:

(a)   to calculate the assessable amounts, for the tax years 1996/97, 1997/98 and 1998/99 of Dawn's business profits.   **(15 marks)**

(b)   to calculate the income tax and tax on chargeable gains payable for the tax year 1998/99. **(11 marks)**
(Total: 26 marks)
(ACCA Jun 92)

---

12   JOSHUA WREKIN

Joshua Wrekin retired from his job as technical director with Wenlock Engineers Ltd on 30 April 1998, his 65th birthday. He received an ex-gratia payment from his employers of £27,250 plus his company car which was valued at £6,500. The Revenue accept that this is a termination payment (assessable under S148) and not a payment under an unapproved retirement benefit arrangement.

His monthly salary, payable on the last day of the month was £2,775. The car was a 2500cc, BMW costing £18,500 when first provided for Joshua in January 1995. The business mileage in April 1998 was 120. The running costs of the car for April 1998 were £400, including approximately half of the petrol used for Joshua's private motoring. Wenlock Engineers Ltd paid Joshua's subscription to BUPA, a private health insurance company, of £42 for the month of April 1998.

Joshua decided to use his engineering skills and business contacts as a self-employed consultant. He commenced on 1 May 1998 and made up his first accounts to 30 April 1999. He did not qualify for enterprise allowance. His summarised accounts for the first period of trading were:

	£	£	£
Consultancy fees			27,510
Reference books - *Note 1*		300	
Wife's wages as secretary - *Note 2*		4,200	
Car expenses - *Note 3*			
Depreciation	1,600		
Petrol and oil	1,500		
Servicing	200		
AA subscription	60		
Replacement tyres	150		
Insurance	1,000		
		4,510	
Depreciation of furniture and equipment		250	
Rent of office		7,000	
Premium payment for lease - *Note 4*		2,500	
Office running costs		1,500	
			(20,260)
Net profit			7,250

Notes:

(1)   The reference books were purchased in May 1998.

(2)   Wife's wages of £350 were paid on the last day of the month and accepted by the Revenue as being at a commercial rate.

(3)   The BMW was used in the business. Joshua's business mileage in the period covered by the first set of accounts was 20,000 and his private mileage was 2,000. This proportion is expected to apply for future periods.

(4)   The lease was for 10 years from 1 May 1998.

(5)   Capital purchases were made as follows:

		£
May 1998	Office furniture	1,000
May 1998	Computer/word processor	1,500
June 1998	Photocopier	920
June 1999	New telephone and fax system	1,088

No election was to be made to treat any of the assets purchased as 'short-life' assets.

Joshua estimates that the profits adjusted for tax purposes but before deducting capital allowances, for the years ending 30 April 2000 and 2001 will be £10,000 and £15,000 respectively.

Joshua's wife, Brenda, had purchased a life annuity from an insurance company on her 65th birthday during 1997 which paid her £100 a month. The income element has been agreed with the Revenue at £50. She received £1,752 interest from the Northern Shires Building Society on 31 December 1998 and paid £924 (net) to a national charity under a four-year deed of covenant on 1 January each year.

Joshua received National Insurance Retirement Pension of £4,082 for the year 1998/99 and both he and Brenda began paying private medical insurance of £40 each per month on 1 May 1998.

You are required:

(a) to calculate the Schedule D Case II assessable amounts for the first three tax years in respect of Joshua's business; **(13 marks)**

(b) to calculate the income tax liability of Joshua for 1998/99, and **(9 marks)**

(c) to calculate the income tax liability of Brenda for 1998/99. **(8 marks)**
(Total: 30 marks)
(ACCA Dec 91)

13 MAURICE THISTLETHWAITE

Maurice Thistlethwaite, aged 53, is a research chemist with Pulsating Paints Ltd His wife Marjorie, aged 52, is a teacher with North Shires County Council. Details of their income and outgoings for the year ended 5 April 1999 were:

(1) Gross salaries

Maurice	£23,500
Marjorie	£17,000

Maurice paid 5% of his salary to an approved pension scheme and Marjorie paid 6% of her salary to the teachers pension scheme.

(2) Pulsating Paints Ltd paid a private health insurance benefit for Maurice of £375 and also provided him with a new 1,500 cc car costing £11,600 on 6 November 1998. His total mileage from that date to 5 April 1999 was 8,000 miles, of which 1,000 were on business. The company paid all running costs of the car (£1,200) including Maurice's private petrol.

(3) Maurice paid £81 to a professional body of which he was a member and Marjorie paid £50 to her teaching union. Marjorie also had to purchase an academic gown during the year at the request of her employer. This cost £75.

(4) Marjorie made free-standing additional voluntary contributions to a UK life assurance company of £900 (after relief for basic rate income tax).

(5) On 1 May 1996 Maurice began performing as a magician at local charities and social clubs. It had been agreed with the Inland Revenue to treat the income as trading income and adjusted profits for the year ended 31 December 1998 had been agreed as £1,973.

Out of this income Maurice had paid the maximum amount to a personal pension scheme.

(6) Maurice and Marjorie had joint accounts with the Barland Bank plc on which interest of £3,000 was paid and with the Barchester and Bognor Building Society on which interest of £4,000 was paid.

(7)   Investments in UK companies were held in joint names and dividends of £3,733 were received.

(8)   Mortgage interest of £800 (gross) was paid in respect of a loan on the family home. The mortgage was a joint one with both spouses paying one half of the interest. The interest payments were made under the MIRAS arrangements.

(9)   Following the sale of investments during the year, profits of £13,700 had been computed for chargeable gains purposes. The investments had been held in joint names.

(10)   Maurice had entered into deeds of covenant as follows

    (a)   with his daughter Antonia on 25 August 1994 for £2,000 per annum (gross). Antonia is a full-time student at London University

    (b)   with the local parish church on 25 April 1995 for £250 per annum (net after income tax).

You are required to calculate the income tax liability and tax on chargeable gains payable for 1998/99 by Mr and Mrs Thistlethwaite.

                                                       (20 marks)
                                                     (ACCA Dec 90)

---

14   ANGELA

(a)   On 31 March 1999, her 58th birthday, Angela sold all her shares in Scott Stockings Ltd, a manufacturing company.

    (1)   Holdings of ordinary shares in the company were held as follows:

Angela	15
Michael, Angela's husband	15
Martin, Angela's brother	15
Raquel, Michael's sister	10
Yvonne, Angela's cousin	15
Charles, Angela's uncle	15
David, Angela's uncle	15
	100%

    (2)   Angela had been a full-time working officer of the company for the last six years and had owned 15% of the shares for the last eight years.

    (3)   The capital gain, after indexation but before taper relief, was £290,000.

    (4)   The market values of the company's assets on 31 March 1999 were:

	£'000
Land and buildings	2,000
Plant and machinery*	1,000
Goodwill	500
Investments in gilt-edged securities	250
Net current assets	1,500
	5,250

    * All items of plant and machinery have a market value of more than £6,000.

You are required to calculate Angela's assessable capital gain for 1998/99, assuming no other disposals of chargeable assets in the year. **(10 marks)**

(b)   Victor had the following transactions in the ordinary shares of Victorious Vulcanising plc, a quoted company.

	No of shares	*Total amount*
		£
1.8.78 Bought	600	7,200
1.4.87 Bought	1,000	11,000
1.9.89 (1 for 2 rights) Bought	800	4,800
1.8.98 Sold	2,100	45,150

The value per share on 31 March 1982 was £8.

You are required to calculate Victor's capital gain for 1998/99 before the annual exemption.

(11 marks)
(Total: 21 marks)
(ACCA Dec 92)

---

15   KATHLEEN

(a)   In October 1998 Kathleen had her 57th birthday and decided to retire immediately from her 'personal' company. She had two children, Corinne and Stephen, to whom she gave all her shares in the company in equal shares. In October 1998 the total value of the shares was £1,050,000. The shares had cost £250,000 in September 1981 and were valued at £200,000 in March 1982. Kathleen had been a full-time working director in the company since October 1993. The company did not own any 'non-business' chargeable assets.

No election has been made or will be made, to have all pre-31 March 1982 acquisitions re-based to 31 March 1982: S35(5) TCGA 1992.

You are required:

(i)   to calculate the capital gain (before annual exemption) assessable on Kathleen for 1998/99; and **(6 marks)**

(ii)   to explain the present and future consequences of a joint election made by Kathleen, Corinne and Stephen to 'hold-over' any capital gain. **(2 marks)**

(b)   Ranek Innovators Ltd sold a factory in November 1998 for £200,000 and moved into rented premises. The factory had been purchased in April 1988 for £100,000. The company purchased fixed plant in December 1997 costing £180,000 and elected to 'hold-over' any gain on the sale of the building against the cost of the plant.

You are required:

(i)   to calculate the chargeable gain on the sale of the factory and the effect of the 'hold-over' claim on the chargeable gain; and **(2 marks)**

(ii)   to state the earliest time the 'hold-over' would cease to be effective. **(3 marks)**
(Total: 13 marks)
(ACCA Dec 93)

16   UNBELIEVABLE UPSHOTS LTD

Unbelievable Upshots Ltd is a UK resident company which manufactures industrial springs. It has no associated companies. It commenced trading in 1989 in a factory which it purchased that year for £40,000. The cost of administration offices included in the original purchase price of £40,000 was £5,000.

The company's results for the year ended 28 February 1999 are summarised below:

	£
Adjusted trading profit before capital allowances	283,000
Dividends received from UK companies (June 1998)	33,000
Bank interest receivable	3,000
Loan interest receivable from UK companies (gross amount)	10,000
Chargeable gains	50,000

Included in the adjusted trading profit is a deduction for debenture interest of £2,000 (gross amount). The debentures were for trading purposes.

An extension to the original factory was built in 1990 and cost £70,000 of which £25,000 was for administration offices.

In 1992 a premium of £22,500 was paid to the local authority for the long lease of a new factory costing £50,000, erected on a nearby industrial estate. The local authority had made the appropriate joint election with Unbelievable Upshots Ltd. Neither factory was situated in an Enterprise Zone but both were in use for qualifying purposes at 28 February 1999.

In the year ended 28 February 1999 the amounts of interest paid and received are the same as the amounts accrued.

On 1 March 1998 the tax written-down values of plant and machinery were:

	£
Pool	75,000
Expensive car	7,000
Car pool	27,000
Short life asset (spring end grinding machine)	17,500

The short-life asset was purchased in August 1993 and sold on 19 November 1998 for £5,000.

On 1 January 1999 the expensive car was traded in for £6,000 against a new car costing £14,000.

There were no other purchases or sales during the year.

Notes:

(1)   The company had no trading losses to carry forward on 1 March 1998.

(2)   There were capital losses brought forward at 1 March 1998 of £60,000.

(3)   The company had always made up accounts to the end of February.

You are required to calculate the corporation tax payable for the year ended 28 February 1999.

(26 marks)
(ACCA Dec 92)

17   UNIMAGINABLE UTILITIES LTD

Unimaginable Utilities Ltd is a United Kingdom resident trading company which manufactures motor vehicle components. It has been trading since 1986 and has no associated companies.

The company's results for the year ended 31 January 1999 are summarised as follows:

	£
Trading profits (as adjusted for taxation but before capital allowances)	311,000
Dividend from UK company	7,500
Loan interest received (gross)	4,760
Bank interest received	1,250

Included in the adjusted trading profit is a deduction for debenture interest of £4,000 (gross amount). The debentures were for trading purposes.

In the year ended 31 January 1999 the amounts of interest paid and received are the same as the amounts shown in the accounts on an accruals basis.

Capital acquisitions and disposals during the year were:

	£
Acquisitions	
'Expensive' motor car (10 June 1998)	16,000
Two other cars (£7,500 each and to be used by the company's salesmen - 18 August 1998)	15,000
Plant (9 May 1998)	24,000
Disposals	
Plant (sold for less than cost)	24,000
'Expensive' motor car (the one owned at 1 February 1998)	8,000
Two cars (both costing less than £8,000)	4,000

Written down tax values at 1 February 1998 were:

	£
Main pool	25,000
'Expensive' motor car	11,000
Car pool	7,500

The company has operated from two factories, neither of which is in an Enterprise Zone. Factory 1 was acquired in 1989 when new, and cost £250,000 including land £50,000 and integral administration offices £40,000. Factory 2 was purchased second-hand on 1 February 1993 for £120,000, when the residue of expenditure after sale was £100,000 and the building was five years old.

Factory 2 was sold on 1 July 1998 for £169,520 and not replaced. There has not been any non-qualifying use of either factory.

Notes:

(1)   The dates in brackets are those upon which the transactions occurred.
(2) · Income tax has been deducted from the loan interest received and the debenture interest paid.
(3)   The company has no losses to carry forward on 1 February 1998.

You are required to calculate the corporation tax payable for the year ended 31 January 1999.

(26 marks)
(ACCA Dec 90)

RPI for July 1998 is to be taken at 162.6

18   CASH ACCOUNTING

You are asked to prepare a draft memorandum to send to all your firm's clients on the subject of cash accounting for VAT.

The memorandum should explain how the cash accounting scheme works and the conditions which must be met to satisfy Customs and Excise. You should also mention any advantages or disadvantages of the scheme.

(11 marks)
(Pilot paper)

8 ANSWERS TO PRACTICE QUESTIONS

1 GENERAL AND SPECIAL COMMISSIONERS

(a)   Both the General and Special Commissioners act as the first appellate body to hear appeals against decisions of the Inland Revenue disputed by the taxpayer. Both bodies possess equal powers to 'determine' appeals and in most cases the taxpayer can choose whether he wishes the appeal to be heard by the General or Special Commissioners, although there are instances where cases must be heard by one body of Commissioners.

The General Commissioners are local people giving their part-time services voluntarily, as do magistrates. They are not required to be qualified in taxation and are advised by the Clerk to the General Commissioners, who is normally a lawyer, on matters of procedure and law. Normally at least two Commissioners hear appeals.

The General Commissioners are appointed by the Lord Chancellor.

The Special Commissioners are full-time civil servants who are legally qualified experts. Normally at least two Commissioners hear appeals, although in certain cases they can sit alone. The Clerk to the Special Commissioners is solely an administrator. The Special Commissioners are appointed by the Lord Chancellor.

(b)   Further appeal to a higher court against a decision of the General Commissioners is by the 'case stated' procedure and can be made only on questions of law. The appellant must request the case to be stated within 30 days of the decision being given by the General Commissioners. Decisions by the Special Commissioners are automatically accompanied by a statement of the facts of the case and the reasons for the Special Commissioners' decision.

Appeals from the General and Special Commissioners lie to the Chancery Division of the High Court and thence to the Court of Appeal and, with leave, to the House of Lords.

2 ARTHUR

Calculation of property income assessable for 1998/99

(a)   Furnished house in holiday resort

	Days
Actual commercial letting in 1998/99	
April	7
May	14
June	7
July	31
September	14
	73

As this satisfies the minimum requirement of 70 days actual commercial letting and the house is available for at least 140 days a year, the net income can be calculated as if the activity was a trade.

	£	£
Rent received		1,900
Less: General expenses		
Insurance	250	
Repairs	308	
Water rates	160	
Cleaning	480	
Interest	608	
	1,806	
$^{11}\!/_{12}$ thereof		(1,655)
Letting expenses		
Accountancy	60	
Advertising	200	
Wear and tear $10\% \times £(1,900 - 160 \times {}^{11}\!/_{12})$	175	
		(435)
Loss		190

The loss can be relieved against Arthur's other income under S380 as it arises from the letting of qualifying furnished holiday accommodation.

(b)   Letting of shops – Schedule A 1998/99

	Shop 1 £	Shop 2 £
Rents accrued $^{3}\!/_{12} \times £3,000 + {}^{6}\!/_{12} \times 4,000$	2,750	
$£6,000 \times {}^{6}\!/_{12}$		3,000
Premium $£2,000 - 2\% \, (7 - 1) \times £2,000$		1,760
	£2,750	£4,760
Less: Insurance	190	300
Ground rent	10	40
Repairs and decorating	3,900	2,000
Accountancy	50	50
Advertising for tenant	100	100
	4,250	2,490
	(1,500)	2,270
		(1,500)
Profit assessable under Schedule A in 1998/99		770

Profits and losses from letting property are pooled without regard to repairing provisions in the leases.

(Tutorial note: repairs in a void period which is preceded by a lease at full rent are allowable (Shop 1).

Repairs relating to conditions present when the building is purchased are not generally allowable (dry rot in Shop 2).*)*

3	ALEXANDER AND SONIA

(a)   The Schedule E assessment is based on the emoluments received in the year of assessment irrespective of when the emoluments were earned.

Emoluments are treated as being received on the earliest of the following events:

(i)   when payment is made of, or on account of, the emoluments;

(ii)   when a person becomes entitled to payment of, or on account of the emoluments;

(iii)   in the case of company directors:

(1)   when sums on account of the emoluments are credited in the company's accounts or records;

(2)   when the amount of the emoluments for a period is determined before the period ends;

(3)   when the amount of the emoluments for a period is not known and determined until after the period has ended, the date when it is so determined.

(b)   The measure of the benefit for employees earning less then £8,500 pa is the second-hand value of the benefit, unless otherwise provided by statute, eg season tickets, assuming that the benefit is convertible into money. Benefits which cannot be converted into moneys worth are not generally taxable.

The measure of the benefit for employees earning £8,500 pa and over is normally equivalent to the cost incurred by the employer in providing the benefit, eg season tickets, or in accordance with a prescribed scale, eg fuel benefits. Where in-house benefits are provided to employees (for example free or discounted school places provided to children of teachers at fee-paying schools) the benefit is the marginal cost of the benefit (**Pepper v Hart**).

(c)   (i)   Maintenance payments are paid gross.

(ii)   Sonia is not chargeable to tax on the payments.

(iii)   Alexander will obtain 15% rate income tax relief on payments to Sonia up to the amount of the married couple's allowance as a 15% tax credit but will not obtain relief on any payments made to Nicholas.

(iv)   Nicholas is not chargeable to tax on the payments.

4	MICHAEL

Schedule D Case I assessable amounts for 1995/96 to 2002/03

		£	£
1995/96	Actual (1.3.96 - 5.4.96) $(^{36}/_{426} \times 15,000)$		1,268
1996/97	Actual (6.4.96 - 5.4.97) $(^{365}/_{426} \times 15,000)$		12,852
1997/98	'CYB' (1.5.96 - 30.4.97) $(^{365}/_{426} \times 15,000)$		12,852

(overlap relief 1.5.96 - 5.4.97 $^{340}/_{426} \times 15,000$ £11,972)

1998/99	CYB (year to 30.4.98)			17,000
1999/00	CYB (year to 30.4.99)			12,000
2000/01	CYB (year to 30.4.00)			14,000
2001/02	CYB (year to 30.4.01)			18,000
2002/03	(1.5.01 - 31.10.02)			
	Year to 30.4.02		13,000	
	Period to 31.10.02		3,000	
			16,000	
	Less overlap relief		(11,972)	4,028

| Check: Total profits assessed | | £92,000 |
| Total profits (as adjusted) earned | | £92,000 |

(Tutorial note: for a business commencing on or after 6 April 1994 when the first period of account exceeds 12 months, and ends in the third tax year, as is the case with Michael, the bases of assessment for the first five years are as follows:

Tax year	Basis period	
1	Actual	1.3.96 - 5.4.96
2	Actual	6.4.96 - 5.4.97
3	12 months ending on the accounting date	1.5.96 - 30.4.97
4	Current year basis	1.5.97 - 30.4.98
5	Current year basis	1.5.98 - 30.4.99*)*

5   ROGER RIVIERE

(a)

Roger Riviere
Profit adjustment statement year ended 30 June 1998

			+ £	− £
	Net profit per accounts		36,000	
(1)	Sales - Goods for own use $\left(500 \times {}^{400}\!/_{240}\right){}^{\text{(Sales)}}_{\text{(Re-stated cost of sales)}}$ −500		333	
(2)	Stock (difference increased by 50%)			8,000
(3)	Wages - Roger's drawings		2,600	
	- Roger's NIC		320	
(4)	Repairs and renewals			
	Capital cost of fitting covers		3,000	
(5)	Miscellaneous			
	Political donation		100	
	Taxation		15,590	
(6)	Bad debts			
	Loan to former employee		250	
	Reduction in general provision			150
(7)	Legal expenses			
	Cost in connection with lease of new and larger premises		250	
	Cost in connection with tax appeal		200	
	Defending Roger in connection with speeding offence		190	
	Depreciation		570	

(8)   Lease rental on car $8,400 - 8,400 \times \dfrac{12,000 + \frac{1}{2}(30,000 - 12,000)}{30,000}$ 2,520

Private use element on lease rental (11) $8,400 - 2,520 = 5,880 \times \frac{1}{3}$ 1,960

Loss on sale of office furniture   60

(9)   Deeds of covenant - Local children's hospital   50

Oxfam   30

(10)   Interest

Interest on overdue tax   130

NSB interest   160

(11)   Motor car running expenses

Fine   65

$\frac{1}{3}$ of remaining expenses   645

(12)   Premium on lease   6,000   900

Lease premium assessable on landlord is $[6,000 - 2\% (6 - 1)] = 5,400$

5,400 allowable to over six years ie, 900 pa

(13)   Re-location expenditure   2,400

73,263	9,210
(9,210)	

Less: Capital allowances   (480)

1998/99 Adjusted Case I profit   63,573

(b)
Roger Riviere
National insurance contributions Class 4

£25,220 − £7,310 = £17,910 at 6% = £1,075

(c)
Roger Riviere
Computation of income tax liability 1998/99

	Total £	Non-savings £	Savings £
Adjusted Case I profit	63,573	63,573	-
Personal pension contributions ($17\frac{1}{2}\% \times 63,573$)	(11,125)	(11,125)	-
	52,448	52,448	-
Case III interest (180 − 70)	110		110
	52,558		
Deeds of covenant	(80)	(80)	-
	52,478	52,368	110
Personal allowance	(4,195)	(4,195)	
Taxable income	48,283	48,173	110

Income tax
£   £

On non-savings income

4,300 at 20%	860
22,800 at 23%	5,244
21,073 at 40%	8,429
	14,533

On savings income
110 at 40%   44
                                                _____
                                                  14,533

Less: Tax credit on MCA (1,900 × 15%)   (285)
Income tax on deeds of covenant   18
                                                _____
Income tax liability   14,310
                                                _____

Relief at 10% will have been given under the MIRAS arrangements on interest on the first £30,000 of the loan. Interest payments made through MIRAS income tax computation have no effect on the income tax computation.

The income tax payable is payable in two equal instalments on 31 January 1999 and 31 July 1999 (based on the 1997/98 liability), with a balancing payment due on 31 January 2000 when the self assessment return is submitted.

(Tutorial notes:

(1)   Savings income is treated as the top slice of income and is taxed at 20% if it falls in the lower or basic rate band, otherwise at 40%.

(2)   In this example the savings income is all clearly taxable at 40%, so there is no need to analyse income between 'savings' and 'non-savings'. The suggested answer does so to illustrate the technique.*)*

6   CHANGE OF ACCOUNTING DATE

(a)   Conditions to be met

-      The change of accounting date must be notified to the Inland Revenue on or before 31 January following the tax year in which the change is to be made.

-      The first accounts to the new accounting date must not exceed 18 months in length.

       If the period between the old accounting date and the proposed new accounting date is longer than 18 months, then two sets of accounts will have to be prepared.

-      There must not have been another change of accounting date during the previous five tax years.

       This condition may be ignored if the Inland Revenue accept that the present change is made for genuine commercial reasons.

(b)   If the conditions are not met, the old accounting date will continue to apply.

(c)   Schedule D I assessments

                                                                            £

(i)   1998/99   Year to 30.6.98   48,000
                      Three months to 30.9.98   15,000
                                                                      _____
                                                                        63,000

         Less: three months of overlap relief
                ³⁄₉ × 12,000   (4,000)
                                                                      _____
                                                                        59,000
                                                                      _____

         1999/00   Year to 30.9.99   60,000
                                                                      _____

(Overlap relief to carry forward: 6 months; £8,000)

			£
(ii)	1998/99	Year to 30.6.98	48,000
	1999/00	15 month period to 30.9.99	75,000
		less overlap profits 12,000 × $\frac{3}{9}$	(4,000)
			71,000

The 1999/00 profits for 15 months are assessed. The normal basis of assessment is 12 months. 3 months of the overlap profits that arose on commencement may be offset.

7   DOMINIC AND JUSTIN

		Total	Dominic	Justin	Simon
		£	£	£	£
A/cs to 30/6/97		10,000	5,000	5,000	-
A/cs to 30/6/98	$^{184}/_{365}$	6,805	3,402	3,403	-
	$^{181}/_{365}$	6,695	2,232	2,231	2,232
		13,500	5,634	5,634	2,232
A/cs to 30/6/99		18,000	6,000	6,000	6,000

Dominic and Justin will both be assessed on the following figures

		£
1996/97	£5,000 × $^{279}/_{365}$	3,822
1997/98	A/cs to 30/6/97	5,000
1998/99	A/cs to 30/6/98	5,634
1999/00	A/cs to 30/6/99	6,000

They will both be entitled to overlap relief of £3,822.

Simon will be assessed as follows:

		£
1997/98	£2,232 × $^{95}/_{181}$	1,171
1998/99	£2,232 + (£6,000 × $^{184}/_{365}$)	5,257
1999/00	A/cs to 30/6/99	6,000

Simon will be entitled to overlap relief of £4,196, which is made up as follows:

	£
1/1/98 to 5/4/98	1,171
1/7/98 to 31/12/98	3,025
	4,196

(*Tutorial note:* The profits must be allocated between the partners. Remember that as Simon joins the partnership part of the way through the accounting year ended 30 June 1998, the profits for that year will need to be time-apportioned prior to allocation. Once the profits have been allocated between the partners, each partner is then treated as if he is carrying on a business alone. Simon is treated as commencing trading on 1 January 1998. Simon's

1998/99 assessment is based on the profits of the first 12 months of trading as his share of the accounts to 30/6/98 does not cover a full 12 months.)

8   HECTOR, ZAZA AND KIKI

Allocation of profits for the year ended 31 December 1998.

	Total £	Hector £	Zaza £	Kiki £
Interest on capital	3,600	1,200	1,080	1,320
Salaries	18,000	8,000	10,000	-
Balance	10,000	5,000	3,000	2,000
	31,600	14,200	14,080	3,320

Tax liability for 1998/99

	Hector £	Zaza £	Kiki £
Schedule E	-	-	30,000
Share of trading profit	14,200	14,080	3,320
Charitable covenant	(2,500)	(1,500)	(1,000)
	11,700	12,580	32,320
Personal allowance	(4,195)	(4,195)	(4,195)
Taxable income	7,505	8,385	28,125
£4,300 at 20%	860	860	860
£3,205/4,085/22,800 at 23%	737	940	5,244
£1,025 at 40%	-	-	410
	1,597	1,800	6,514
Retained on charges	575	345	230
	2,172	2,145	6,744

(Tutorial note: When computing the partners' 1998/99 liabilities, note that the charges relieved are those paid in 1998/99 as opposed to those paid during the accounts year ended 31 December 1998.*)*

9   BERT AND HAROLD

(a)   **Time apportionment of 1998/99 Schedule DI income**

The profits assessable in 1998/99 will be those for the accounts to 30 September 1998. The profit-sharing arrangement was changed on 1 July 1998 which is nine months into the accounting period. The profits will therefore be time-apportioned as follows:

Old arrangement	£16,500 × $273/365$ = £12,341
New arrangement	£16,500 × $92/365$ = £4,159

(b)   **Allocation of 1998/99 Schedule DI income**

	Total £	Bert £	Harold £
1/10/97 to 30/6/98			
Salaries ($273/365$)	3,740	2,244	1,496
Balance (3:2)	8,601	5,161	3,440
	12,341	7,405	4,936
1/7/98 to 30/9/98			
Salaries ($92/365$)	2,520	1,512	1,008
Balance (2:1)	1,639	1,093	546
	4,159	2,605	1,554
Total allocation	16,500	10,010	6,490

(c)   **Allocation of partnership loan interest**

The loan interest assessable in 1998/99 will be that received in the accounts year ended 30 September 1998. As before, the income will be allocated according to the profit-sharing arrangement in force during the year ended 30 September 1998:

	Total £	Bert £	Harold £
£900 × $273/365$ (3:2)	673	404	269
£900 × $92/365$ (2:1)	227	151	76
	900	555	345

This investment income will also be assessable on the partners individually.

(Tutorial note: All partnership income received gross is assessable using the case I basis period rules irrespective of its source. This means that any partnership investment income received gross is assessable on an accounts year basis rather than a tax year basis.*)*

10   KEVIN WINTERBURN

(a)   (i)   **Kevin**

Income tax liability - 1998/99

	£
Schedule D Case I	15,000
Bank interest ($990 \times {}^{100}\!/_{80}$)	1,238
STI	16,238
Loss (S380)	(16,238)
Taxable income	-
Income tax on	Nil
Tax repayment	
Bank interest £1,238 × 20%	£248

Loss remaining: 20,000 − 16,238 = £3,762. This is available for relief in 1999/2000 under S380 against total income or in future years under S385 against future profits from the same trade.

Capital gains liability - 1998/99	£
Agreed gain	7,100
Annual exemption	(6,800)
	300 at 20% = £60

(Tutorial notes:

(1)   The unused personal allowance is not available to use against the assessable capital gains.

(2)   Under S380, a loss may be relieved against the STI of the fiscal year in which the loss arises and/or the preceding year. Thus the loss of the year ended 31.12.99 may be set against the STI of 1998/99.

(3)   A claim under S72 FA91 has not been considered because although it would save tax of £60 it will result in wasting the CGT exemption.)

(ii)   **Susan**

Income tax liability - 1998/99

	£	Total £	Non-savings £	Savings £
Salary		25,000	25,000	–
Benefits-in-kind				
Car (W)	1,225			
Fuel (W)	505	1,730	1,730	
		26,730	26,730	
House (Note 1)	exempt			
House services	1,500			
	1,500			

(no restriction on house services
- less than 10% of 26,730) (Note 2)   1,500   1,500

	28,230	28,230	
Bank interest ($10 \times {}^{100}/_{80}$)	12		12
	28,242	28,230	12
Personal allowance	(4,195)	(4,195)	–
Taxable income	24,047	24,035	12

Non-savings
4,300 at 20%   860
19,735 at 23%   4,539
Savings 12 at 20%   2

                                                             5,401
Less: Tax credit on MCA
       (transfer from Kevin) 1,900 × 15%   (285)
Income tax on bank interest   (2)

Income tax liability   5,114

Capital gains tax liability - 1998/99
       Agreed gain   3,000
       Annual exemption   3,000

                                              -

WORKING

		£	£
Car			
35% × £7,000		2,450	
Available for six months			1,225 ${}^{6}/_{12}$
Fuel			
Under 1400 cc (petrol)		1,010	
Available for six months			505 ${}^{6}/_{12}$

(Tutorial notes:

(1)   As the occupation of the house is 'job-related' there is no charge.

(2)   Where there is no charge for 'job-related' accommodation any charge for ancillary services is restricted to 10% of the other net emoluments (excluding the charge for ancillary services).*)*

Elections to be made:

(1)   Under S380 for Kevin's loss arising in 1999/2000 to be set against his income for 1998/99.

(2)   Kevin should transfer the married couple's allowance to Susan since his own tax liability in 1998/99 is insufficient to utilise the tax credit.

(3)   Since Susan pays income tax at a higher rate than Kevin, it will probably be beneficial for Kevin to be assessed on most of the joint income, say 99 : 1. They must, therefore, make a joint declaration of their actual beneficial interests in the asset and the income from it on a Revenue form to that effect. Such a declaration will be binding for all future tax years.

(b)   A share in the land owned by Kevin might have been transferred to Susan before the sale, thereby utilising the unused balance of her annual exemption and reducing Kevin's liability.

---

11   DAWN WARR

(Tutorial note: this question requires an income tax computation covering trading income for part of the tax year followed by permanent cessation of trade and income from employment, including car benefits, for the remainder of the year, together with other sources of income and charges on income and pension contributions with calculations of capital gains tax payable on net gains for the same tax year.*)*

(a)   **Income from business**

(i)   **Capital allowances computation**

	Plant and machinery	Dawn car (1) (Business Use 25%)	Dawn car (2) (Business Use 25%)	Car pool	Total
	£	£	£	£	£
Y/e 30.4.97					
Additions	3,200	5,600		4,000	
WDA 25%	(800)	(1,400) × 25%		(1,000)	2,150
	———	———		———	
	2,400	4,200		3,000	
Y/e 30.4.98					
Additions	1,000		7,800		
Sale	–	(3,000)			
	———	———			
	3,400	1,200			
Balancing allowance		(1,200) × 25%			300
WDA 25%	(850)		(1,950) × 25%	(750)	2,088
	———	———	———	———	———
	2,550	–	5,850	2,250	2,388
P/e 30.9.99					
Additions	500				
Sales	(2,500)		(6,000)	(2,000)	
	———		———	———	
	550		(150)	250	
Balancing charge			150 × 25%		(37)
Balancing allowance	(550)			(250)	800
	———		———	———	———
	-		-	-	763

(ii)   **Adjusted profit**

	£
Year ended 30 April 1997	
(15,000 – 2,150)	12,850
Year ended 30 April 1998	
(12,000 - 2,388)	9,612
Period ended 30 September 1998	
(9,000 – 763)	8,237

(iii)   **Case I assessments**

	£	£
1996/97 (1.5.96 - 5.4.97)		
12,850 × $^{340}/_{365}$		11,970
1997/98 (y/e 30.4.97)		12,850
1998/99 (1.5.97 - 30.9.98)		
9,612 + 8,237	17,849	
Less: overlap relief (1.5.96 - 5.4.97)	(11,970)	
		5,879

(b)   **Income tax computation 1998/99**

	£	£	Total £	Non savings £	Savings £
Earned income					
Schedule D Case I (net)		5,879			
Schedule E $^{6}/_{12}$ × 24,000	12,000				
Benefits-in-kind					
Car (W)	569				
Fuel (W)	640				
	13,209				
17.5% PPC	(2,312)				
		10,897			
			16,776	16,776	-
Unearned income					
Barlloyd Bank					
£491 × 100/80	614				
NSB ordinary account					
Actual basis					
(199 – 70)	129				
			743	-	743
			17,519	16,776	743
Charges on income					
Deed of covenant			(100)	(100)	
Total income			17,419	16,676	743
Personal allowance			(4,195)	(4,195)	
Taxable income			13,224	12,481	743
Income tax on					
non savings income					
4,300 @ 20%			860		
8,181 @ 23%			1,882		
12,481			2,742		
Income tax on					
savings income					
743 @ 20%			149		
			2,891		

Basic rate relief retained
  Deed of covenant
    100 @ 23%   23
  Personal pension plan
    2,312 @ 23%   532

		555
Income tax liability		3,446

WORKING

Car	£	£
35% × £9,750	3,412	
Mileage reduction	(2,275) ⅔	
	1,137	
Available for six months		569 6/12
Fuel		
1401 cc to 2000 cc (petrol)	1,280	
Available for six months		640 6/12

Tax on chargeable gains 1998/99

		£
Agreed gain		22,000
Annual exemption		(6,800)
Assessable gain		15,200

Chargeable @ 23% 27,100 – 13,224	13,876	3,191
@ 40%	1,324	530
	15,200	3,721

---

12   JOSHUA WREKIN

(a)

Profit adjustment statement 1 May 1998 to 30 April 1999

	£
Net profit per accounts	7,250
Add: Reference books (Munby v Furlong)	300
Depreciation - car	1,600
- furniture and equipment	250
Car expenses (4,510 – 1,600) × 1/11	265
Lease premium	2,500
	12,165
Less: Lease premium (W)	(205)
Adjusted profit	11,960

WORKING

Lease premium

	£
Premium	2,500
Less: $2\% \times (10 - 1)$	(450)
Assessable on landlord	2,050

Allowable to Joshua at the rate of £205 ($2,050 \div 10$) for each of the 10 years of the lease. Not restricted in the first year as commenced at the start of the year.

Basis of assessment

1998/99	1.5.98 - 5.4.99
1999/2000	y/e 30.4.99
2000/01	y/e 30.4.2000

(Tutorial note: In the opening years, the basis of assessment for businesses starting on or after 6.4.94 is as follows:

Year 1	Actual profits from commencement to 5 April
Year 2	Either:
	(i) 12 months ending with the accounting date in the year; or
	(ii) 12 months from commencement date **unless** no accounting period ends in the year, in which case the fiscal year basis applies.
Year 3	12 months ending with the accounting date in the year.*)

Capital allowances computation

	Pool £	Car ($^{10}\!/_{11}$ business use) £	Total £
Y/e 30.4.99			
Additions			
Car		6,500	
Reference books	300		
Furniture	1,000		
Computer	1,500		
Photocopier	920		
	3,720	6,500	
FYA @ 50%/WDA @ 25%	(1,860)	(1,625)$^{10}\!/_{11}$	3,337
	1,860	4,875	
Y/e 30.4.2000			
WDA @ 25%	(465)	(1,219)$^{10}\!/_{11}$	1,573
Addition qualifying for FYA			
Telephone and fax	1,088		
FYA @ 40%	(435)		435
	2,048	3,656	2,008

(Tutorial note: Capital allowances are a deduction in computing trading profits, and are therefore tied to a period of account. The 25% WDA is scaled down (or up) according to the length of the period of account.*)*

Schedule D Case II

Year ended 30 April 1999

	£
Adjusted profit	11,960
Less: Capital allowances	(3,337)
	8,623

Year ended 30 April 2000

	£
Adjusted profit	10,000
Less: Capital allowances	(2,008)
	7,992

Schedule D Case II assessments

		£
1998/99	(1.5.98 - 5.4.99)	
	$^{340}/_{365} \times 8,623$	8,032
1999/2000	(y/e 30.4.99)	8,623
2000/01	(y/e 30.4.2000)	7,992

(b)

Joshua Wrekin
Income tax computation 1998/99

Wenlock Engineers Ltd	£	£
Salary		2,775
Ex-gratia - cash	27,250	
- car	6,500	
	33,750	
- exemption	30,000	
		3,750
Benefits-in-kind		
- car (W1)	360	
- fuel charge (W1)	157	
- BUPA	42	
		559
Retirement pension		4,082
Own business - Net assessment		8,032
STI		19,198
Allowances: Personal (W2)		(4,195)
Taxable income		15,003
Income tax liability:		
£4,300 at 20% =		860
£10,703 at 23% =		2,462
Less: Tax credit on MCA (W3) (3,021 × 15%)		(453)
Income tax liability		2,869

WORKINGS

(W1)   Benefits-in-kind

	£	£
Car		
35% × £18,500	6,475	
Age reduction		
(Over 4 years by 5 April 1999)	(2,158) ⅓	
	4,317	
Available for one month		360 (¹⁄₁₂)
Fuel		
2001cc and above (petrol)	1,890	
Available for one month		(157) (¹⁄₁₂)

(W2)   Personal allowance

	£
Total income	19,198
Age allowance income limit	(16,200)
Excess	2,998
Personal allowance	5,410
Less ½ of excess	(1,499)
	3,911

As this reduction takes the level of personal allowance below £4,195 it will be restricted to an amount (£1,215) to leave the allowance at £4,195 the basic personal allowance.

(W3)   Married couple's allowance

The reduction of £1,215 in the personal allowance will be taken into consideration.

	£	£
Married couple's allowance		3,305
Less: ½ of excess	1,499	
Reduction in personal allowance	(1,215)	
		(284)
		3,021

(c)

Brenda Wrekin
Income tax computation 1998/99

	Total	*Tax suffered*
	£	£
Wages from husband (£350 × 11)	3,850	
Income element of annuity	600	120
Building society interest	2,190	438
	6,640	558
Charges on income - Deed of covenant payment	(1,200)	
Total income	5,440	
Personal allowance (no restriction)	(5,410)	
Taxable income	30	

	£
Income tax liability:	
30 at 20%	6
Retained on payment of charges on income	
1,200 at 23%	276
	282
Income tax suffered	
2,790 at 20%	(558)
Income tax repayment	276

(Tutorial notes:

(1)   Joshua's car was over four years old at 5.4.99: the benefit is therefore reduced by $\frac{1}{3}$ for 1998/99.

(2)   A personal age allowance is reduced when total income is in excess of £16,200 for 1998/99. Where the reduction would take the age allowance below the normal personal allowance value, it is restricted to leave the allowance at the same level as the normal personal allowance (£4,195 for 1998/99). When calculating the age related married couple's allowance, the reduction due to the level of income is restricted by the same amount less any part of the restriction applied against the personal allowance.

(3)   When an individual purchases a life annuity, the money received from the annuity is split into a capital and an income element. The income element, received net of lower rate tax, is taxable.)

13   MAURICE THISTLETHWAITE

Income tax computations for 1998/99

Maurice

	£	*Total* £	*Non-savings* £	*Savings* £
Salary		23,500	23,500	-
Less: Pension scheme 5%		(1,175)	(1,175)	-
		22,325	22,325	-

Health insurance	375	375	-
Car benefit (W)	1,692	1,692	-
Fuel benefit (W)	533	533	-
	24,925	24,925	-
Less: Professional fees	(81)	(81)	-
	24,844	24,844	-

Schedule D Case I	1,973			
Less: PPC maximum 30%	(592)			
		1,381	1,381	-
Joint bank interest 50% $\times$ 3,000 $\times \frac{100}{80}$		1,875	-	1,875
Joint BSI 50% $\times$ 4,000 $\times \frac{100}{80}$		2,500	-	2,500
UK dividends (joint) 50% $\times$ 3,733 $\times \frac{100}{80}$		2,333	-	2,333
		32,933	26,225	6,708
Deed to church 250 $\times \frac{100}{77}$		(325)	(325)	-
STI		32,608	25,900	6,708
Less: PA		(4,195)	(4,195)	-
Taxable income		28,413	21,705	6,708

Income tax payable

	£
On non savings income	
4,300 @ 20%	860
17,405 @ 23%	4,003
On savings income	
5,395 @ 20%	1,079
1,313 @ 40%	525
	6,467
Less: Tax credit on MCA (1,900 $\times$ 15%)	(284)
Add: Tax retained on charge (325 $\times$ 23%)	75
Income tax liability	6,257

WORKING

	£	£
Car		
35% $\times$ £11,600	4,060	
Available for five months		1,692
Fuel		
1401cc to 2000 cc (petrol)	1,280	
Available for five months		533

Marjorie

	Total £	Non-savings £	Savings £
Salary	17,000	17,000	-
Less: Pension scheme 6%	(1,020)	(1,020)	-
Free-standing AVC $(900 \times {}^{100}\!/_{77})$	(1,169)	(1,169)	-
	14,811	14,811	-
Less: Professional fees	(50)	(50)	-
Cost of gown	(75)	(75)	-
	14,686	14,686	-
Joint bank interest 50% $\times$ 3,000 $\times {}^{100}\!/_{80}$	1,875	-	1,875
Joint BSI 50% $\times$ 4,000 $\times {}^{100}\!/_{80}$	2,500	-	2,500
UK dividends (joint) 50% $\times$ 3,733 $\times {}^{100}\!/_{80}$	2,333	-	2,333
STI	21,394	14,686	6,708
Less: PA	(4,195)	(4,195)	-
	17,199	10,491	6,708

Income tax liability

	£
On non savings income	
4,300 @ 20%	860
6,191 @ 23%	1,424
On savings income	
6,708 @ 20%	1,342
	3,626
Add: Tax retained on AVC (1,169 × 23%)	269
Income tax liability	3,895

Capital gains

	£	£
Joint gains	6,850	6,850
Less Nil exemptions	(6,800)	(6,800)
	50	50
Tax on chargeable gains @ 40%/23%	£20	£11

*(**Tutorial note:** savings income is taxed as the top slice of an individual's income. It is taxed at 20% to the extent that it falls below £27,100 and 40% above £27,100.)*

14   ANGELA

(a)

Angela
Capital gains tax computation 1998/99

(1)   Scott Stockings Ltd is a 'personal' company since Angela has at least 5% of the voting rights.

(2)   'Chargeable business assets' are:

	£'000
Land and buildings	2,000
Plant and machinery	1,000
Goodwill	500
	3,500

(3)   There are no 'chargeable non-business assets'.

(4)   The assessable capital gain is:

		£
Chargeable gain as calculated		290,000
Less: Retirement relief:		
(i) basic relief (60% × 250,000) *(note 1)*	150,000	
(ii) 50% × (290,000 – 150,000) *(note 2)*	70,000	(220,000)
		70,000
Gain tapered to 92.5%		64,750
Annual exemption		(6,800)
		57,950

Notes:

(1)   Lower of 60% (time as full-time working officer) and 80% (time shares owned).

(2)   Maximum gain eligible for relief is £600,000 (£1,000,000 × 60%).

(b)

Victor
Capital gains tax computation 1998/99

(i)   FA 1985 pool (6.4.82 to 6.4.98)

	Shares	Unindexed cost	Indexed cost
1.4.87 Bought	1,000	11,000	11,000
Indexation to September 1989			
$\dfrac{116.6 - 101.8}{101.8} \times £11,000$	-		1,599
			12,599
1.9.89 1 for 2 rights	500	3,000	3,000
	1,500	14,000	15,599

Indexation to April 1998

$$\frac{161.2-116.6}{116.6} \times £15,599$$

	-	5,967
1,500	14,000	21,566

Disposal

(1,500)	(14,000)	(21,566)
-	-	-

Sale proceeds

$$\frac{1,500}{2,100} \times £45,150$$

	32,250

Less: Unindexed cost (14,000)

Unindexed gain 18,250

Less: Indexation allowance 21,566 − 14,000 (7,566)

  10,684

(ii) FA 1982 pool (6.4.65 - 5.4.82)

	Cost		*Market value at 31.3.82*	
	£	£	£	£

Sale proceeds $\dfrac{600}{2,100} \times 45,150$ 12,900   12,900

Original shares (1.8.78)
400 shares
$$\frac{400}{600} \times 7,200$$
4,800

Rights issue (1.9.89)
200 shares at £6 1,200 (6,000)

Original shares (31.3.82)
400 at £8   3,200

Rights issue (1.9.89)
200 at £6   1,200 (4,400)

Unindexed gains 6,900   8,500

Indexation allowance to April 1998
Original shares

$$\frac{161.2-79.44}{79.44}(1.029)$$

on 4,800 (cost greater than
31.3.82 value) 4,939   4,939

Rights issue

$$\frac{161.2-116.6}{116.6}(.383)$$

on 1,200 460 (5,399) 460 (5,399)

    1,501   3,101

Take the lower index and gain

Summary

	£
FA 1985 pool	10,684
FA 1982 pool	1,501
Gain, before annual exemption	12,185

(Tutorial notes:

(1)   Shares are matched firstly with shares acquired since 6 April 1998 (if any), then with shares from the FA 1985 pool, and then with shares from the FA 1982 pool.

(2)   When a rights issue takes place, the shares purchased at different times are increased by the rights issue. Expenditure on a rights issue can only be indexed from the date of the issue, not the date of acquisition of the original holding.*)

---

15   KATHLEEN

(a)   (i)

	Cost £	31.3.82 value £
Deemed proceeds	1,050,000	1,050,000
Cost	250,000	
MV at 31 March 1982		200,000
Unindexed gain	800,000	850,000
Indexation allowance $\dfrac{161.2 - 79.44}{79.44}$ (1.029) (on £250,000)	257,250	257,250
	542,750	592,750

Lower gain is £542,750.

Retirement relief.

Qualifying period is the lower of:

- ownership of shares (maximum)   - 10 years
- full-time working directorship,   - 5 years
  ie, 5 years

	£
First tranche (£250,000 × 50%)	125,000
Second tranche 50% (£500,000* − £125,000)	187,500
	312,500

* Upper limit of second tranche relief for Kathleen is 50% × £1,000,000 = £500,000.

	£
Indexed gain	542,750
Retirement relief	312,500
Capital gain (before taper relief)	230,250
Gain tapered is 92.5% (before annual exemption)	212,981

(Tutorial note:

In order to get full retirement relief Kathleen must have had a personal company (ie. owned 5% of the shares) **and** been a working officer or employee of the company for ten years.*)*

(ii)   If an election for gift relief is made the capital gain (before taper relief) which would otherwise be assessable on Kathleen is deducted from the deemed cost of acquisition of the shares by Corinne and Stephen (ie, open market value), eg:

	£
Base cost	1,050,000
Capital gain	230,250
Reduced base cost	819,750

divided equally between Corinne and Stephen.

On a subsequent disposal by one of Kathleen's children the sale proceeds received by them would be compared with the reduced base cost for capital gains tax purposes. Taper relief would be available from October 1998 (ie, only on the donee's period of ownership).

The effect of the election is to defer the tax charge until disposal of the original shares by the donee. The permanent loss of taper relief on the held over gain results in more gain being chargeable overall, until the children have held the shares long enough to build up their own taper relief.

(b)   (i)   **Ranek Innovators Ltd**

	£
Proceeds	200,000
Cost	100,000
Unindexed gain	100,000
Indexation allowance $\dfrac{163.9 - 105.8}{105.8}$ (0.549)	54,900
	45,100
'Held-over' gain	25,100
Chargeable	20,000

ie, amount not re-invested (200,000 − 180,000)

(ii)   The gain 'held-over' against the purchase of the plant is simply a deferral of the gain until the earliest of:

–   disposal of the plant;
–   December 2007 (ie, 10 years after acquisition of the plant); or
–   the date the plant ceased to be used in the trade of Ranek Innovators Ltd.

(Tutorial notes:

(1)   With replacement of business asset relief, the amount of proceeds not reinvested is taxable now.

(2)   When the asset is replaced with a depreciating asset (one with an expected life of less than 60 years) the gain is simply deferred, not rolled over against the base cost.*)*

16   UNBELIEVABLE UPSHOTS LTD

Corporation tax computation - year ended 28 February 1999

	£	£
Adjusted trading profit		283,000
Capital allowances:		
Industrial buildings (W1)		(4,100)
Plant and machinery (W2)		(32,625)
Schedule D Case I profit		246,275
Schedule D Case III (3,000 + 10,000)		13,000
Chargeable gain	50,000	
Losses brought forward	(50,000)	-
(Balance of capital losses £10,000 carried forward)		
PCTCT		259,275
£259,275 × 31%		80,375
Less: Marginal relief		
$\frac{1}{40}$ (1,500,000 − 300,525) $\frac{259,275}{300,525}$		(25,871)
		54,504
Less: Income tax (W4)		(1,600)
Corporation tax payable		52,904

WORKINGS

(W1)   **Industrial Buildings Allowances**

Administration offices - 25% test.

The total cost of the original factory and extension is £110,000 and the total cost of the administration offices is £30,000. As this is more than 25% the cost of the administration offices must be excluded from the claims.

			£
(1)	Original factory and extension 4% × £80,000		3,200
(2)	Lease on new factory 4% × £22,500		900
			4,100

(W2)   **Plant and machinery allowances**

	Pool	Expensive car (1)	Expensive car (2)	Car pool	Short-life asset	Total
	25%	25%	25%	25%	25%	
	£	£	£	£	£	£
WDV b/f	75,000	7,000		27,000	17,500	
Transfer	17,500				(17,500)	
	92,500				-	
Disposals	(5,000)	(6,000)				
Additions			14,000			
	87,500	1,000				
Claim						
Balancing allowance		(1,000)				1,000
Writing-down allowances	(21,875)		(3,000)	(6,750)		31,625
WDV c/f	65,625	-	11,000	20,250	-	32,625

(Tutorial notes:

(1)   The short life asset is transferred to main pool on 28 February 1998 as the asset was not sold within four years of end of AP in which purchased.

(2)   The maximum allowance on an expensive car is £3,000.)

(W3)   PCTCT   =   £259,275

      'Profits'   =   £259,275 + £33,000 × $\frac{100}{80}$

                =   £300,525.

As 'profits' are above the lower limit (£300,000) marginal relief applies.

(W4)   **Income tax on unfranked investment income**

	£
Income tax suffered on unfranked investment income (10,000 at 20%)	2,000
(a) Set-off against income tax on debenture interest paid (2,000 at 20%)	400
(b) Set-off against corporation tax payable	1,600
	2,000

17   UNIMAGINABLE UTILITIES LTD

Calculation of corporation tax for the year to 31 January 1999

	£	£
Trading profit before capital allowances		311,000
Add: Balancing charge on Factory 2 (W2)		25,000
		336,000
Less Capital allowances on		
Plant (W1)	22,875	
Industrial buildings (W2)	8,000	
		(30,875)
Sch D Case I		305,125

Sch D Case III (1,250 + 4,760)	6,010
Capital gain (W3)	29,000
Profits chargeable to corporation tax	340,135

CT liability (W4)

£340,135 × 31%   105,442

Less: $\frac{1}{40} \times (1,500,000 - 349,510) \times \dfrac{340,135}{349,510}$ (27,991)

                                                    77,451

Less Income tax on surplus UFII £(4,760 – 4,000) × 20%   (152)

Corporation tax payable   77,299

WORKINGS

(1) **Capital allowances on plant**

	Main pool £	Inexpensive car pool £	Expensive car 1 £	Expensive car 2 £	CA summary £
CAP year to 31.1.99					
Tax WDV b/f	25,000	7,500	11,000	–	
Additions without FYA	-	15,000		16,000	
	25,000	22,500			
Disposals	(24,000)	(4,000)	(8,000)		
Balancing allowance			£3,000		3,000
	1,000	18,500			
WDA @ 25% (expensive car restricted)	(250)	(4,625)		(3,000)	7,875
Additions with FYA	24,000				
FYA 50%	(12,000)				12,000
Total allowances					22,875
Tax WDV c/f	12,750	13,875		13,000	

(2) **Industrial buildings allowances**

    (i)   **Factory 1**

Qualifying cost (offices less than 25%)	£200,000
WDA @ 4%	£8,000

    (ii)   **Factory 2**

$$\text{WDA per annum} = \frac{£100,000}{20} = £5,000$$

As the factory is sold above cost all the IBAs claimed will be clawed back as a balancing charge.

Balancing charge £5,000 × 5 =	£25,000

(3)   **Capital gain on Factory 2**

		£
Sale proceeds (1 July 1998)		169,520
Less Cost (1 February 1993)		(120,000)
		49,520
Less Indexation allowance £120,000 $\times \left(\dfrac{162.6 - 138.8}{138.8} \right)$, ie 0.171		(20,520)
Capital gain		29,000

(4)   **Rate of tax**

	£
PCTCT	340,135
Add FII (£7,500 × 100/80)	9,375
Profits	349,510

The profits lie between the upper limit and lower limit and so marginal relief applies. Apportionment is not necessary as the limits are the same for both FY97 and FY98.

---

18   CASH ACCOUNTING

Memorandum

To: All clients
From: An accountant
Subject: Cash accounting for VAT
Date:

(1)   The cash accounting scheme enables you to account for tax on the basis of cash paid and received, rather than invoices issued and received. The date of payment or receipt determines the VAT return in which the transaction is included.

(2)   The scheme can only be used if your expected annual taxable turnover (excluding VAT) does not exceed £350,000.

(3)   To be accepted on the scheme, all VAT returns and payments must be up to date (or no more than £5,000 VAT is outstanding and arrangements have been made to pay it).

(4)   Once you have joined the scheme, you must stay with it for at least two years. However, if the value of taxable supplies has exceeded £437,500 in any 12 month period to the end of a VAT accounting period, and the value is expected to exceed £350,000 in the next 12 months, you must leave the scheme.

Main advantages:

•   automatic bad debt relief, as you only account for VAT once you have been paid

•   VAT return can be prepared straight from the cash book.

Disadvantage:

•   VAT on your purchases can only be reclaimed once you have paid for them, rather than when you are invoiced.

9 NEW SYLLABUS EXAMINATIONS

19 (Question 1 of examination)

Unpretentious Undercurrents Ltd (UUL) is a United Kingdom resident trading company which manufactures swimwear.

It has no associated companies.

The company's results for the year ended 31 December 1998 are summarised as follows:

	£
Trading profits (as adjusted for taxation but before capital allowances)	700,000
Dividends received from UK companies	60,000
Bank interest receivable	1,700
Building society interest receivable	2,700
Chargeable gains	20,000

Capital acquisitions and disposal of plant and machinery during 1998 were:

			£
Acquisitions:	1	Machinery (not to be treated as a short-life asset) purchased on 1.5.98	32,500
	2	Managing director's car (20% private use) purchased on 1.8.98	21,000
	3	Four cars (costing £9,000 each) purchased on 1.8.98	36,000
Disposals:	1	Machinery (disposal proceeds less than original cost)	5,000
	2	Managing director's previous car (cost £13,000)	4,000
	3	Four cars (from car pool at less than original costs)	9,000

The written-down values at 1 January 1998 were:

	£
Main pool	80,000
Managing director's car	7,500
Car pool	12,000

The company purchased the factory, which it had previously rented, on 1 January 1998 for £350,000. The factory had cost £250,000 when new and was brought into use on 1 January 1993 by the first owner, whose accounting date was 31 December. The building had always been in industrial use and was not situated in an Enterprise Zone.

The following additional information is available:

(1) The company had no losses to carry forward on 1 January 1998.
(2) There were capital losses brought forward of £25,000 on 1 January 1998.

You are required to calculate the corporation tax payable for the year ended 31 December 1998.

(25 marks)

20   (Question 2 of examination)

Clayton Delaney commenced trading as an electrician on 6 April 1996. His business was centred on a shop from which he sold electrical goods to the public and to the electrical trade. He also carried out electrical work himself for his customers.

His adjusted profits for tax purposes for the year ended 5 April 1997 (before deduction of capital allowances) were £25,000 and for the year ended 5 April 1998, £26,000.

Because of deteriorating health his wife could no longer look after the shop in Clayton's absence and she retired on 20 June 1998. She had no source of income thereafter. Clayton decided to permanently cease trading on 30 June 1998 and on 1 July 1998 commenced working for a firm of electrical contractors.

His summarised accounts for the period ended 30 June 1998 are as follows:

Profit and loss account period ended 30 June 1998

	£		£
Telephone (1)	240	Gross profit on sales	2,645
Repairs (2)	1,180	Bank interest received (note 4 of	
Depreciation	1,350	other relevant information)	200
Buildings insurance (3)	600	Profit on sale of shop fittings	120
Lighting and heating (3)	420	Work done for customers	13,500
Car expenses (4)	1,750		
Bad debts (5)	950		
Rates (6)	1,850		
Wages and National Insurance			
contributions – Mrs Delaney (7)	2,500		
Wages and National Insurance			
contributions – Mr Delaney	2,850		
Bank interest paid (8)	630		
General expenses (9)	1,995		
Net profit	150		
	16,465		16,465

Figures in brackets refers to notes in accounts.

Notes to accounts:

(1)   Telephone: included in the figure of £240 is the rental of £80 which is treated as business expenditure, one-fifth of the charge for calls is treated as private.

(2)   Repairs (see also note 3):

	£
Roof repairs	650
Re-decorating bedroom	230
Replacing floor tiles in shop	300
	1,180

(3)   Clayton and his wife live on the shop premises. Two-thirds of the household expenditure is in respect of the living accommodation.

(4)   Car expenses: The total mileage in the period was 5,000 of which one-half was private. This was the same fraction as in earlier years.

(5) Bad debts:

	£		£
Trade debts written off	300	Specific debt provision b/f	300
Loan to customer written off	500	Recovery of trade debt previously	
Specific debt provision c/f	800	written off	350
		Profit and loss account	950
	1,600		1,600

(6) Rates:

	£
Business rates	1,200
Council tax	650
	1,850

(7) Mrs Delaney's wages: Mrs Delaney looked after the shop in Mr Delaney's absence and ran the clerical side of the business.

(8) Bank interest paid: The interest was paid on the business account overdraft.

(9) General expenses:

	£
Accountancy	600
Legal costs in defending claim for allegedly faulty work	200
Printing, stationery and postage	220
Gifts to trade customers - one food hamper each, costing £30	900
Donation of prize in local carnival (a free advertisement was	
provided in the programme)	50
Donation to a national charity	25
	1,995

In addition Clayton had taken stock from the shop for personal use. The cost price of these items was £600 and the average gross profit percentage was 20%. No payment had been made for the goods by Clayton.

Clayton brought the following assets to the business on 6 April 1996:

	£
Car (market value)	5,700
Plant	190

On 31 January 1997 Clayton traded in his car for £4,500 and purchased a new one costing £9,000. He purchased an electronic till for the shop on 8 April 1997 for £300.

On 30 June 1998 the items in the pool were sold for £400 (all less than original cost) and the car had a market value of £3,500.

Other relevant information is:

(1) Clayton earned £1,350 gross per month, payable on the last day of the month in arrears. Because he was expected to travel around in his employment he was provided with a company car by his employer.

(2) The car had an engine with a capacity of 1300cc and cost £10,000 when new on 1 August 1994. Clayton's mileage in the car between 1 July 1998 and 5 April 1999 was 21,000 of which one-third was private. Clayton's employer agreed to provide fuel for the first 5,000 miles of his private motoring during 1998/99.

(3) Clayton decided to rent out the shop from 1 July 1998. The rent received was:

Until 31 December 1998 at the rate of £1,500 per annum payable quarterly in arrears on 30 September and 31 December 1998.

From 1 January 1999 at the rate of £2,000 per annum payable quarterly in arrears on 31 March 1999.

Outgoings were:

	£
Estate agents' fees for finding tenant	350
Legal fees for drawing up tenancy agreement	150
	500

(4)   Clayton had opened an ordinary account with the National Savings Bank in May 1996. Interest had been credited as follows:

	£
31 December 1996	190
31 December 1997	220
31 December 1998	200

(5)   Clayton had purchased a life annuity and received a monthly gross amount of £100 on the first of each month commencing 1 September 1998. The capital element of the payment was agreed by the Revenue to be £50 per month. The income element of the annuity was received net of lower rate tax.

You are required:

(a)   to calculate the amount of the final assessments for the years 1996/97, 1997/98 and 1998/99;   **(19 marks)**

(b)   to calculate the amount of Clayton's income tax liability for 1998/99.   **(8 marks)**

(Total: 27 marks)

---

21   (Question 3 of examination)

(a)   On 31 July 1998, his 56th birthday, Oskar Barnack retired as sales manager of European Traders Ltd and sold his 10% ordinary shareholding in the company. He had been a full-time manager of the company for 12 years. The sale of the shares on 31 July 1998 realised £550,000. Oskar inherited the shares on 1 August 1991 at a valuation of £125,000.

The market values of the assets of the company at 31 July 1998 were:

	£
Land and buildings	700,000
Goodwill	300,000
Shares held as an investment	200,000
Stock	160,000
Bank and cash balances	25,000
Government securities	220,000

You are required to calculate Oskar's chargeable gain for 1998/99, before annual exemption.

(6 marks)

(b)   Walter purchased his business premises in October 1973 for £10,000. In May 1983 he gave them to his son Darren when the value was £50,000. The appropriate joint election for gift relief was made. The value of the premises on 31 March 1982 was £40,000. On 12 April 1998 Darren sold the premises for £200,000. The disposal did not qualify for the business rate of taper relief.

You are required to calculate the capital gain assessable on Darren for 1998/99, before annual exemption.

(5 marks)

(c)   **You are required** to calculate the capital gains assessable for 1998/99 and any losses carried forward in each of the following situations:

(i)   Marlene had capital gains for the year 1998/99 of £12,000 and capital losses for the year 1998/99 of £8,000;

(ii)   Moira had capital gains for the year 1998/99 of £12,000 and capital losses brought forward of £7,700;

(iii)   Marina had capital gains for the year 1998/99 of £3,000 and capital losses brought forward of £8,000; and

(iv)   Melissa had capital gains for the year 1998/99 of £12,000, capital losses for the year 1998/99 of £8,000 and capital losses brought forward of £4,000.   **(4 marks)**

   (Total: 15 marks)

You should assume in each case that the gains qualify for the business rate of taper relief and the assets had been held on 17 March 1998.

---

22   (Question 4 of examination)

You are required to state:

(a)   who should register for value added tax;

(b)   within what time limit and from when should such a person register for value added tax;

(c)   the consequences of late registration for value added tax;

(d)   the details shown on the certificate of registration;

(e)   why a person with a turnover below the statutory limit should wish to voluntarily register for value added tax.

   (11 marks)

---

23   (Question 5 of examination)

(a)   Brandleswulf has been farming at Holme Farm since May 1995.

His recent results, adjusted for tax, were:

			£
Year ended 31 March 1997	–	profit	30,000
Year ended 31 March 1998	–	profit	10,000
Year ended 31 March 1999	–	loss	(8,000)

You are required to state the claims which Brandleswulf can make to minimise his taxation liabilities and to advise him how he could best utilise those claims.   **(6 marks)**

(b)   Bill, who started trading in May 1995 and makes up accounts to 31 March, erected a poultry house on 31 December 1996 at a cost of £30,000, when initial allowances were not available.

On 31 December 1998 he sold the poultry house and the land on which it stood to Ben, whose accounting date is 30 June. The poultry house was sold for £20,000.

You are required to show the allowances which Bill and Ben can claim for all relevant years:

(i)   assuming Bill and Ben make an election on the sale; and
(ii)   assuming no election is made.   **(5 marks)**

   (Total: 11 marks)

---

24   (Question 6 of examination)

(a)   The basic married couple's allowance may be allocated by one of four methods.

You are required to state, for each method, how the allowance is allocated and by whom and by when the necessary action must be taken.   **(4 marks)**

(b)   Abel and Zoe were married on 17 May 1997 when they were both 20. On 21 March 1998 Zoe gave birth to twins, Brendan and Yvonne. On 7 June 1998 Abel and Zoe separated in circumstances likely to be permanent, Brendan staying with his father and Yvonne staying with her mother. On 7 December 1998 Abel and Zoe were divorced. From 6 July 1998 Abel was required by a court order to pay maintenance of £45 per week to Zoe.

These amounts were to be increased on 1 January 2000 to £55 per week by court order.

Neither Abel nor Zoe plan to re-marry nor live with a new partner. Abel was in full-time employment. Zoe did not work and had no income from State benefits after 7 June 1998.

You are required to state the amount of the allowances to which Abel and Zoe are entitled for the tax years 1997/98, 1998/99 and 1999/2000. (You may assume the amounts of available allowances for all years are the same as for 1998/99.)

(7 marks)

(Total: 11 marks)

---

25   (Question 7 of examination)

(a)   **You are required** to state the normal due dates of payment of the following taxes:

(i)   capital gains tax;
(ii)   mainstream corporation tax;
(iii)   payments on account of income tax;
(iv)   income tax not collected at source nor paid in the payments on account.   **(4 marks)**

(b)   Not reproduced as no longer examinable.

---

26   (Question 8 of examination)

(a)   Hilda who is 53 years old and unmarried is a part-time employee with a firm of estate agents. Her employers did not have an employee's pension scheme and Hilda took out a personal pension policy with an insurance company. In 1998/99 Hilda's earnings were £6,840 from which the correct amount of PAYE tax, £529, had been deducted. She paid the maximum amount into her personal pension plan during the tax year.

You are required to calculate Hilda's tax liability for 1998/99, compare this liability with the tax paid and explain to Hilda the reason for any over- or underpayment of income tax for the year.   **(4 marks)**

(b)   Sarah, who was born on 2 April 1955, is a self-employed computer consultant. Her agreed taxable profits were as follows:

	£
1999/2000	50,000
1998/99	30,000
1997/98	10,000
1996/97	9,000
1995/96	8,000
1994/95	7,000
1993/94	6,000
1992/93	5,000
1991/92	4,000

She tells you, her accountant, on 1 June 1999 that she has never paid any personal pension premiums and that in view of her recent high profits she now wishes to make premium payments sufficient to utilise as much of the previous years' unused relief as possible.

You are required to calculate the amount of the premiums which Sarah should pay and explain how the premiums should be applied.

(7 marks)

(Total: 11 marks)

JUNE 1994 EXAMINER'S COMMENTS

Overall the Tax Framework paper should have presented few problems to the well prepared student.

Question 1: A straightforward mainstream corporation tax computation for a 12-month chargeable accounting period. The question included capital allowances for a second hand industrial building and for plant and machinery.

Question 2: An extremely long income tax computation which required a methodical approach in order to successfully complete the question in the allotted time.

Question 3: A standard capital gains tax question with retirement relief and gift relief which should not have presented any problems to the well prepared student.

Question 4: A basic question on VAT, which most students would have attempted.

Question 5: An unexpected question on a fringe area - farmers averaging and agricultural building allowances.

Question 6: I would expect this question to be a popular choice with students due to the changes introduced recently on the married couples allowance.

Question 7: Not reproduced in full, as no longer examinable.

Question 8: A basic question on pensions, probably a popular question with most students.

JUNE 1994 ANSWERS

19   (Answer 1 of examination)

A corporation tax computation testing:

(1)   Calculation of liability to corporation tax where accounting period straddles 31 March.

(2)   Capital allowances computations covering both plant and machinery and industrial buildings.

Unpretentious Undercurrents Ltd
Corporation tax computation chargeable accounting period ended 31 December 1998

	£
Adjusted trading profit	700,000
Capital allowances – Plant and machinery (W1)	(51,250)
– Industrial buildings (W2)	(12,500)
Schedule D Case I profit	636,250
Bank interest	1,700
Building society interest	2,700
Chargeable gains (W3)	Nil
Chargeable profits	640,650
Corporation tax payable (W4)	181,047

WORKINGS

(W1)   Capital allowances – Plant and machinery

	Main pool £	Expensive cars (1) £	(2) £	Car pool £	Claim £
WDV b/f 1.1.98	80,000	7,500		12,000	
Acquisitions without FYA	-		21,000	36,000	
Disposals	(5,000)	(4,000)		(9,000)	
	75,000	3,500	21,000	39,000	
Balancing allowance		3,500			3,500
WDA 25%	(18,750)	–	(3,000)	(max)(9,750)	31,500
Additions with FYA	32,500				
FYA (50%)	(16,250)				16,250
WDV c/f 31.12.98	72,500		18,000	29,250	51,250

(W2)   Capital allowances – Industrial buildings

WDA of £10,000 per annum (4%) will have been claimed for five years, (31 December 1993 to 31 December 1997 inclusive).

	£
Original cost	250,000
5 × 4%	50,000
Residue before sale	200,000
Sale proceeds (restricted to original cost)	250,000
Balancing charge	50,000

Residue after sale
   Residue before sale   200,000
   Balancing charge   50,000

Residue after sale   250,000

Annual allowance £250,000 ÷ 20 (25 − 5) = £12,500

(W3)   Chargeable gains

	£
Chargeable gains	20,000
Losses brought forward	25,000
Losses carried forward	5,000

(W4)   Corporation tax payable

'Chargeable profits' = £640,650
'Profits' = £640,650 + FII £75,000 = £715,650

As there is no change in the upper and lower limits or rates of corporation tax during the chargeable accounting period there is no requirement to apportion the 'profits' to and from 31 March 1998. 'Profits' lie between the upper and lower limits.

	£
640,650 × 31%	198,601
Less: Marginal relief	
$\frac{1}{40} \times (1,500,000 - 715,650) \times \frac{640,650}{715,650}$	(17,554)
	181,047

(Tutorial notes:

(1)   Capital allowances: each expensive car must be dealt with in a separate column. The private use by the director is irrelevant: this is taxed on the director as a benefit in kind.

(2)   Industrial buildings allowances: if the building is second hand, the allowance is:

$$\frac{\text{residue after sale}}{\text{remaining life of the building}})$$

20   (Answer 2 of examination)

An income tax question requiring a profit adjustment statement with capital allowances and assessments on permanent cessation, from a profit and loss account, together with an income tax computation including other sources of income, namely Schedule E, with benefits-in-kind, Schedule A, annuity and untaxed investment income.

(a)   (i)
Clayton Delaney
Profit adjustment statement period ended 30 June 1998

	+ £	– £
Net profit as per accounts	150	
Telephone $\frac{1}{5} \times (240 - 80)$	32	
Repairs – $\frac{2}{3} \times 650$ (roof repairs)	433	
– bedroom	230	
Depreciation	1,350	
Insurance – $\frac{2}{3} \times 600$	400	
Lighting and heating ($\frac{2}{3} \times 420$)	280	
Car expenses ($\frac{1}{2} \times 1,750$)	875	
Bad debts – loan to customer	500	
Rates – council tax	650	
Mr Delaney's wages	2,850	
General expenses – gifts	900	
– national charity	25	
Goods for own use – $600 \times \frac{5}{4}$	750	
Interest received		200
Profit on sale of shop fittings		120
	9,425	320
	320	
Adjusted profit before capital allowances	9,105	

(ii)   **Capital allowances**

	Pool £	Car (pte ½) £	Car (pte ½) £	Claim £
y/e 5.4.97				
Additions	190	5,700		
Sales		(4,500)		
Balancing allowance		1,200 (½)		600
Addition			9,000	
WDA – 25%	(48)		(2,250)(½)	1,173
	142		6,750	1,773
y/e 5.4.98				
Addition	300			
	442			
WDA – 25%	(111)		(1,688)(½)	955
	331		5,062	
p/e 30.6.98				
Sales/valuation	(400)		(3,500)	
Balancing charge	69		–	(69)
Balancing allowance	–		1,562 (½)	781
				712

(iii)   **Adjusted profit**

	£
y/e 5 April 1997 (25,000 – 1,773)	23,227
y/e 5 April 1998 (26,000 – 955)	25,045
p/e 30 June 1998 (9,105 – 712)	8,393

(iv)   **Assessments**

	£
1996/97 (6.4.96 – 5.4.97)	23,227
1997/98 (y/e 5.4.98)	25,045
1998/99 (6.4.98 to 30.6.98)	8,393

(b)

Clayton Delaney
Income tax liability 1998/99

	£	Total £	Non-savings £	Savings £
Earned income				
Schedule D – Case I		8,393	8,393	–
Schedule E – wages (9 × £1,350)	12,150			
– car benefit				
($\frac{9}{12}$ × £10,000 × 35% × $\frac{1}{3}$ × $\frac{2}{3}$)	583			
– fuel benefit ($\frac{9}{12}$ × £1,010)	757			
		13,490	13,490	–
		21,883	21,883	–
Investment income				
Schedule A – rent (£750 + £500)	1,250			
– outgoings (£350 + £150)	(500)	750	750	–
– National Savings Bank (£200 – £70)		130	–	130
– purchased life annuity (8 × £50)		400	–	400
Total income		23,163	22,633	530
Personal allowance		(4,195)	(4,195)	–
Taxable income		18,968	18,438	530
On non-savings income				
4,300 at 20%		860		
14,138 at 23%		3,252		
On savings income				
530 at 20%		106		
		4,218		
Less: Tax credit on MCA (£1,900 × 15%)		(285)		
Income tax liability		3,933		

(Tutorial notes:

(1)   This question originally dealt with the cessation of a pre 6 April 1994 business; as this is no longer examinable the question has been changed so that the business is a post 5 April 1994 one.

(2)   Mr Delaney's wages are not allowable; they are drawings, not a business expense. Mrs Delaney's wages are allowable as she is an employee.

(3)   When a trader takes goods for his own use the selling price of these items must be added back, not the cost.

(4)   When a car is provided for private use to an employee an assessable benefit arises.

The amount of the benefit is: 35% × list price when new

This is reduced by:

$\frac{2}{3}$ as the annual business mileage is at least 18,000 (business mileage is 21,000 × $\frac{2}{3}$ over a 9 month period which is equivalent to 18,667 a year); and then

$\frac{1}{3}$ as the car is at least four years old at the end of the tax year.

(5)   When a life annuity is purchased, the amount received is split into a capital and income element. The income element is taxable and is received net of lower rate tax.*)*

---

21   (Answer 3 of examination)

A three-part capital gains tax question:

(a)   sale of shares in a 'personal' trading company by a taxpayer qualifying for retirement relief;

(b)   sale of an asset after 5 April 1988 which was acquired under the gift relief provisions after 31 March 1982 but before April 1988 and therefore restricting the base cost by one-half of the held-over gain;

(c)   treatment of losses brought forward and current losses in the case of personal taxpayers.

(a)

Oskar Barnack
Capital gain computation 1998/99

			£	£
July 1998	Sale proceeds			550,000
August 1990	Acquisition 'cost'			125,000
	Unindexed gain			425,000
	Indexation allowance			
	$\dfrac{161.2 - 134.1}{134.1} \times 125,000$			25,261
	Indexed gain			399,739
	Retirement relief			
	First tranche (70% × 250,000)		175,000	
	Second tranche $\dfrac{333,116 - 175,000}{2}$		79,058	
				254,058
Chargeable gain				145,681
Tapered to 92.5%				134,755

$$399,739 \times \frac{1,000,000 \,(\text{Chargeable business assets})}{1,200,000 \,(\text{Chargeable assets})} = £333,116$$

Note: maximum second tranche relief is:

£525,000 [70% × (1,000,000 − 250,000 = £750,000)]

Total chargeable assets:

	£
Land and buildings	700,000
Goodwill	300,000
Investment shares*	200,000
	1,200,000

* Non-business assets.

(Tutorial notes:

(1) When shares in a personal company are disposed of, the gain qualifying for relief is:

$$\text{Gain on shares} \times \frac{\text{chargeable business assets}}{\text{chargeable assets}}$$

(2) The first £250,000 gains are exempt and 50% of the gains between £250,000 and £1,000,000. The limits are proportionately reduced if the shares have been owned for less than 10 years (seven years in this case).*)

(b) **Walter – 1983/84 (first disposal)**

	£
Value of premises	50,000
Cost	10,000
Unindexed gain	40,000
Indexation allowance * $\dfrac{84.64 - 79.44}{79.44} = 0.065 \times £10,000 \text{ (MV)}$	650
Indexed gain	39,350
Hold-over relief	39,350
Assessable 1983/84	–

* For pre 6.4.85 disposals indexation allowance was based on cost (not March 1982 MV)

Darren – 1998/99 (second disposal)

	£
Sale proceeds	200,000
Base cost $\left(50{,}000 - \text{held-over gain} \dfrac{39{,}350}{2}\right)$	30,325
	169,675
Indexation allowance $\dfrac{161.2 - 84.64}{84.64} = 0.905 \times £30{,}325$	27,444
Assessable gain	142,231

(Tutorial notes:

(1) When an asset which was acquired under the gift relief provisions is sold the deemed acquisition cost is reduced by the heldover gain.

(2) When the disposal of the asset is after 5 April 1988 and it was acquired by way of a gift between 1 April 1982 and 5 April 1988 (having been acquired by the donor before 1 April 1982), the acquisition cost is reduced by only 50% of the held over gain.

(3)   The premises would have been a business asset for taper relief purposes if it had been used since 6 April 1998 in a trade either conducted by Darren himself or by a partnership of which he was a partner or by a company which is a qualifying company in relation to Darren.)

(c)   (i)   **Marlene**

	£
Gains – 1998/99	12,000
Losses – 1998/99	8,000
	4,000
Annual exemption	4,000
Assessable	–
Losses c/f	Nil

(ii)   **Moira**

	£
Gains – 1998/99	12,000
Losses b/f	5,200
	6,800
Annual exemption	6,800
Assessable	–
Losses c/f	2,500

(iii)   **Marina**

	£
Gains – 1998/99	3,000
Annual exemption	3,000
Assessable	–
Losses c/f	8,000

(iv)   **Melissa**

	£
Gains - 1998/99	12,000
Losses – 1998/99	8,000
	4,000
Annual exemption	4,000
Assessable	–
Losses c/f	4,000

(*Tutorial notes:*

(1)   Gain and losses in the same year must be netted off, even if the annual exemption is wasted.

(2)   The set-off of losses brought forward may be restricted to avoid wasting the annual exemption.

(3)   Taper relief is only given a gains remaining chargeable before deducting the annual exemption. Obviously, if there is only £6,800 or less remaining at this stage these is no purpose in reducing it by taper relief as it is already covered by the annual exemption).

22   (Answer 4 of examination)

(a)   A 'person' making or intending to make 'taxable supplies' of goods or services in the course or furtherance of a business in the UK is required to be registered if taxable turnover, or prospective turnover, exceeds or is expected to exceed, certain prescribed limits.

(b)   (i)   The Customs and Excise should be notified within 30 days of the end of the month in which the annual threshold is exceeded and registration is then from the beginning of the next month; or

         (ii)   if taxable supplies in the next 30 days (eg, new business) are expected to exceed the annual threshold the Customs and Excise should be notified within 30 days from that date and registration is then from the beginning of that 30 day period.

(c)   Unless there is 'reasonable excuse' for late registration the registration will be back-dated and penalties will be charged. The practical effect of the back-dating will be that value added tax will have to be accounted for from the correct date whether or not it has been charged. As it may prove impossible to recover this from customers a considerable loss of revenue may ensue.

(d)   The details shown on the certificate of registration are:

         (i)   VAT registration number;

         (ii)   date of registration;

         (iii)   the date on which the first VAT accounting period ends;

         (iv)   the length of future accounting periods which will normally be three months but may be monthly where there will normally be regular repayments.

(e)   The principal reason for voluntary registration is that it will be possible to reclaim input tax. Because of the addition of value added tax the impression may be given of substantial business activity and tax invoices can be provided for registered customers. If the customer is registered for VAT the imposition of VAT will not cost them any more as they can set the input tax against their own taxable supplies.

23   (Answer 5 of examination)

(a)   **Brandleswulf**

         (i)   The claims which Brandleswulf could make are farmer's averaging and loss relief claims under S380.

         (ii)   A farmer's averaging claim should be made for 1996/97 and 1997/98 as follows:

	Original £	Amended £
1996/97 y/e 31.3.97	30,000	20,000
1997/98 y/e 31.3.98	10,000	20,000
	40,000	40,000

         There are two advantages in making this claim:

         (1)   1996/97 higher rate tax is avoided.

         (2)   The 1997/98 assessment is increased to £20,000, thereby allowing a S380 claim for 1997/98 to be made, at the earliest time, against the amended 1997/98 assessment without any loss of personal allowances.

There would be nothing to be gained by doing a second averaging claim as follows:

		Original £	*Amended* £
1997/98 y/e 31.3.98		20,000	10,000
1998/99 y/e 31.3.99		Nil	10,000
		20,000	20,000

As S380 claim for either of these two years would result in a loss of personal allowances.

(b)   (i)   **Agricultural buildings allowances**

		£	£
Bill:			30,000
y/e 31.3.97	WDA @ 4%	1,200	
y/e 31.3.98	WDA @ 4%	1,200	
		2,400	
			27,600
y/e 31.3.99	Balancing allowance		7,600
Sale proceeds 31 December 1998			20,000

Ben:

WDA of £870 (£20,000 ÷ 23) per annum from year ended 30 June 1999

(ii)   **Bill:**

		£
y/e 31.3.97	WDA @ 4%	1,200
y/e 31.3.98	WDA @ 4%	1,200
y/e 31.3.99	(1.4.98 – 31.12.98) WDA @ 4% $\times \frac{275}{365}$	904
		3,304

Ben:

		£
y/e 30.6.99	WDA (1.1.99 – 30.6.99) $\frac{181}{365} \times £1,200$	595
	WDA of £1,200 per annum	24,000
	WDA in final accounting period	2,101
		26,696

(Tutorial notes:

(1)   When an election is made, agricultural buildings allowances operate in a similar way to industrial buildings allowances.

(2)   If no election is made, an allowance is available for the accounting periods up to, and including, the one in which the sale takes place.*)*

---

24   (Answer 6 of examination)

(a)   (1)   The allowance is allocated to the husband. This is done automatically by the Revenue in the absence of any action under paragraphs 2–4 below.

(2)   50% of the allowance may be allocated to the wife. This will be done on receipt by the Revenue of a claim by the wife before the beginning of the tax year, except in year of marriage.

(3)   All the allowance may be allocated to the wife. This will be done on receipt by the Revenue of a joint claim by husband and wife before the beginning of the tax year.

(4)   If one spouse has insufficient tax liability to absorb their allowance that spouse may notify the Revenue that the unused amount be transferred to the other spouse. The notification must be made within five years of 31 January following the end of the tax year involved.

(b)   (1)   Both Abel and Zoe will receive the personal allowance of £4,195 for all three years.

(2)   Abel will receive the married couple's allowance for 1997/98. This will be £1,900 – ($\frac{1}{12}$ × 1,900) = £1,742.

(3)   For 1998/99, the year of separation, additional personal allowance of £1,900 may be claimed by both Abel and Zoe.

This allowance will be reduced by the amount of married couple's allowance which either spouse is claiming for 1998/99.

(4)   For 1998/99 Abel will be entitled to a tax credit at 15% on £1,755 (39 × £45) for his maintenance payments to Zoe.

(5)   For 1999/2000 both Abel and Zoe will be entitled to additional personal allowance of £1,900 each.

(6)   For 1999/2000 Abel will be paying maintenance of £2,470 (39 × £45 = £1,755) + (13 × £55 = £715). The maximum allowance he is allowed for these payments is £1,900.

(Tutorial notes:

(1)   In the year of marriage the MCA is reduced by $\frac{1}{12}$ × 1,900 for each complete tax month that the couple remain unmarried. This reduction only applies in the year of marriage, there is no equivalent reduction in the year of separation, or death.

(2)   Each parent may claim an APA as they each have a qualifying child living with them for at least part of the year.

(3)   In the year of separation, if APA is being claimed, it is reduced if MCA is claimed in addition, such that the total of the two allowances cannot exceed £1,900 per claimant.*)

25   (Answer 7 of examination)

(a)   (i)   31 January following the tax year.
        (ii)   9 months after the end of the accounting period.
        (iii)   31 January in and 31 July following the tax year.
        (iv)   31 January following the tax year.

(b)   Not reproduced as no longer examinable.

26   (Answer 8 of examination)

(a)   **Hilda – Income tax liability 1998/99**

	£	£
Salary		6,840
Personal pension premium (30%)	2,052	
Personal allowance	4,195	
		6,247
Taxable income		593

593 at 20%   119
Basic rate tax retained on payment of premium (2,052 at 23%)   472
                                                                                                  ————
                                                                                                   591
PAYE tax deducted from salary   529
                                                                                                  ————
Underpayment   62
                                                                                                  ————

Reconciliation

Whereas basic rate relief was given on payment of the premium, there was £3,707 of the lower rate band (4,300 – 593) which was unused and £2,052 of this amount charged at the difference in the rates, (23% – 20%) 3%, is £62, the amount of the underpayment. The tax deducted from the premium payment is not, however, clawed back where the taxpayer is liable only at the lower rate of income tax or indeed has no income tax liability.

(b)   The applicable percentage for all the tax years in question is 20% and the unused relief is therefore:

                                                                                                     £

1999/2000   10,000
1998/99   6,000
1997/98   2,000
1996/97   1,800
1995/96   1,600
1994/95   1,400
1993/94   1,200
1992/93   1,000
1991/92   800

(i)   Sarah can pay a premium for 1999/2000 in 1999/2000 of £10,000.

(ii)   She can also pay a premium in 1999/2000 for 1998/99 of £6,000 and elect before 31 January 2001 to carry this amount back to 1998/99.

(iii)   Having paid the maximum for 1998/99 Sarah can then utilise unused relief for the preceding six years, ie, 1992/93 to 1997/98 inclusive, which is £9,000. This should also be paid in 1999/2000 and an election made before 31 January 2001 to carry premiums back to 1998/99 of £9,000. The premiums which should be paid in 1999/2000 amount to £25,000.

DECEMBER 1994 QUESTIONS

27 (Question 1 of examination)

Unknown Underlings Ltd (UUL) is a United Kingdom resident manufacturing company which has been trading since 1953. It has no associated companies. The company's results for the year ended 30 September 1998 are summarised as follows:

	£
Trading profits (as adjusted for taxation but before capital allowances and debenture interest paid)	300,000
Dividends received from UK companies	22,000
Bank interest received (note 1)	2,900
Loan interest received (note 2)	28,000
Debenture interest paid (note 3)	18,000

Notes:

(1)   Bank interest received

The amounts of interest received from Lloyds Bank were:

	£
31 December 1997	1,700
30 June 1998	1,200
	2,900

The accrued amount shown in the accounts as receivable for the year ended 30 September 1998 was £3,000.

(2)   Loan interest received

The gross amounts received from which income tax has been deducted were:

	£
31 October 1997	8,000
30 April 1998	4,000
31 August 1998	16,000
	28,000

The amount receivable on an accruals basis for the year ended 30 September 1998 was £29,600.

(3)   Debenture interest paid

The gross amounts paid from which income tax has been deducted were:

	£
1 December 1997	5,000
1 June 1998	9,000
1 July 1998	4,000
	18,000

The amount payable on an accruals basis for the year ended 30 September 1998 was £22,000. The debenture monies were applied for a trading purpose.

(4)   A new factory had been purchased in 1961 for £82,500 which was still in use on 30 September 1998. No initial allowance had been claimed. The factory had always been used for qualifying activities.

(5)   The company had no losses to carry forward at 30 September 1997.

You are required:

(a)   to prepare entries relating to income tax as they would appear on forms CT 61 to be submitted to the Collector of Taxes for the periods to 30 September 1998; and

(13 marks)

(b)   to calculate the corporation tax payable for the year ended 30 September 1998.

(15 marks)
(Total: 28 marks)

28	**(Question 2 of examination)**

(a)   Joseph Kent commenced in business on 1 October 1996 as a joiner making conservatories. His tax-adjusted profits were as follows:

	£
Period to 31 December 1997	35,000
Year ended 31 December 1998	24,000
Year ended 31 December 1999	42,000

Capital additions and disposals were as follows:

			£
Additions:	1 October 1996	car[1] (at valuation)	12,200
	1 October 1996	trailer	2,000
	1 October 1996	plant and machinery	8,000
	1 December 1998	car[2]	13,000
	1 December 1999	plant and machinery	6,000
Disposals:	1 December 1998	car[1]	7,000
	1 January 1999	plant and machinery (at less than cost)	2,000

Private use of cars[1] and [2] has been agreed with the Revenue at 20%. No claim is made to treat any of the assets as short-life assets.

Joseph manufactured the conservatories in rented premises until 1 January 1997 when he purchased a new factory unit for £20,000 on an industrial estate (not an enterprise zone). All assets were brought into use immediately on acquisition.

You are required to calculate the assessable amounts of his business profits for the years 1996/97 to 1999/00 inclusive and the amount of any overlap profits.

(18 marks)

(b)   His wife Sephora was a solicitor employed by a practising firm at a salary of £30,000 per annum. The following additional information is provided for 1998/99.

(1)   A new 2500cc petrol-engine car was provided for Sephora's use in August 1997. The list price at that time was £25,000. Of this amount £4,000 was contributed by Sephora so that a better car could be provided. She was required to pay £25 per month towards the private use of the car but not towards the private fuel, all of which was provided by her employers. The business mileage in 1998/99 is 10,000.

(2)   Sephora has received a loan of £60,000 on the matrimonial home from her employers on which she pays interest at 3%. The interest is paid gross.

(3)   Sephora made a 'qualifying donation' to the Oxfam charity on 1 July 1998 of £385 under the gift aid scheme.

(4)   Sephora had made the appropriate election to have one-half of the married couple's allowance set-off against her tax liability for 1998/99. Both Joseph and Sephora are under 65 years old.

You are required to calculate Sephora's income tax liability for 1998/99.

Assume that the official rate of interest is 10%.

(7 marks)
(Total: 25 marks)

| 29 | **(Question 3 of examination)** |

(a) Doris had the following dealings in the shares of Palace Varieties Ltd, an unquoted company with an issued share capital of 50,000 £1 ordinary shares.

	Date	No. of shares	£
Purchases	12.4.75	400	1,600
	12.7.79	200	1,000
	12.10.84	600	3,600
	12.8.92	800	6,400
Sale	12.10.98	1,700	27,200

The value of the remaining unsold shares on 12 October 1998 was £3,000. The 31 March 1982 value was £3.50 per share. No election had been made to 're-base' the cost of all assets held by her on 31 March 1982 at their value on 31 March 1982.

You are required to calculate Doris' capital gain for 1998/99 before the annual exemption.   **(9 marks)**

(b) Boris had acquired a 30 year lease on 30 September 1981 for £15,000. It was assigned on 30 June 1998 for £25,000. The value at 31 March 1982 was £17,500. Boris has made an election to 're-base' the cost of all assets held by him on 31 March 1982 at their value on 31 March 1982.

You are required to calculate Boris' capital gain for 1998/99 before the annual exemption.

(5 marks)
(Total: 14 marks)

| 30 | **(Question 4 of examination)** |

You are required to answer the following questions in connection with value added tax.

(a) When is de-registration for value added tax compulsory?   **(2 marks)**

(b) When can voluntary de-registration be applied for?   **(1 mark)**

(c) What are the consequences of a trader de-registering for value added tax?   **(2 marks)**

(d) Under what circumstances can traders not on the cash accounting scheme claim bad debt relief and thereby repayment of value added tax?   **(2 marks)**

(e) For whom is cash accounting advantageous and who is eligible to use the scheme?   **(4 marks)**
(Total: 11 marks)

| 31 | **(Question 5 of examination)** |

Reginald owns four houses which he lets unfurnished with the exception of number 4 which is let furnished. All rents are receivable quarterly in advance on the usual quarter days, 25 March, 24 June, 29 September and 25 December. The properties are all let on landlord's repairing leases with the exception of number 3 which is let on a tenant's repairing lease.

House number 1

A lease at an annual rental of £4,000 ended on 23 June 1998. The house was then occupied by Reginald until 24 December 1998. Between these dates it was re-decorated internally at a cost of £2,000. It was re-let from 25 December 1998 on an annual tenancy of £5,000 per annum.

House number 2

This property was purchased by Reginald on 1 June 1998. Immediate repair work costing £3,000 was carried out on the leaking roof. The property was let on 29 September 1998 on a seven year lease at an annual rental of £4,000. The incoming tenant was charged a premium of £2,000.

House number 3

A lease at an annual rental of £3,000 expired on 28 September 1998. Internal and external painting and decorating was carried out at a cost of £2,500. The property was re-let on 25 March 1999, again on a tenant's repairing lease, at an annual rental of £4,000. The property remained empty between 29 September 1998 and 24 March 1999.

House number 4

Although this house is let furnished, it is not a holiday letting. The annual rent is £6,000. Total allowable expenditure is £7,000 including water rates, £200, council tax, £600 and loan interest of £2,000 on a loan taken out to purchase the property. The loan interest was paid gross. It had been agreed with the Inland Revenue that a 10% wear and tear allowance be given instead of capital allowances. This wear and tear allowance is not included in the £7,000.

You are required to calculate the amounts assessable on Reginald for 1998/99 in respect of the above properties. You should show how any losses have been dealt with.   **(11 marks)**

---

32   (Question 6 of examination)

Jacqueline retired from her 'Do-it-yourself' shop on 28 February 2000 after trading for several years.

Her adjusted profits/loss had been agreed with the Inland Revenue as follows:

	£
Year ended 31 July 1997	13,000 profit
Year ended 31 July 1998	8,000 profit
Year ended 31 July 1999	3,000 loss
Period to 28 February 2000	4,500 loss

There are overlap profits of £2,500.

The tax written-down value of the 'pool' after the capital allowances claim for the year ended 31 July 1996 was £1,200. There were no further additions. The items in the 'pool' were sold for £75 on 28 February 2000.

You are required:

(a)   to quantify the assessable amounts after the capital allowances for the final three years of assessment before terminal loss relief;   **(6 mark)**

(b)   to calculate the amount of the 'terminal loss'; and   **(4 marks)**

(c)   to state how the 'terminal loss' is to be relieved.   **(1 mark)**
                                                                    (Total: 11 marks)

---

33   (Question 7 of examination)

You are required to contrast the income tax and National Insurance consequences of a taxpayer being held to be:

(a)   employed;
(b)   self-employed,

by both the Inland Revenue and the Department of Social Security.   **(11 marks)**

34 (Question 8 of examination)

As a certified accountant in public practice you have been approached by your local district society to deliver a short address to members of the students' society on the PAYE (pay as you earn) system whereby income tax is deducted at source on income liable to tax under Schedule E.

You are required to write your proposed speech outlining the operation of the PAYE system, including the procedure adopted when an employee changes jobs and the procedure to be followed at the end of the income tax year.

(11 marks)

DECEMBER 1994 EXAMINER'S COMMENTS

Question 1: Part (a) required the preparation of entries in relation to income tax as they would appear on forms CT 61 for the year ended 30 September 1998.

In general, the performance of candidates on this question was disappointing. In many cases candidates demonstrated a lack of knowledge of the basic corporation tax rules and layout. Specifically:

(a)   The CT 61 computation appeared to discriminate between the stronger and weaker candidates with marks correspondingly polarising. The most common errors involved the distinction between gross and net figures. Errors of form included not following the CT 61 format. Errors of substance included grossing up interest figures that were already given in gross terms in the question. Bank interest was also re-grossed for inclusion in the corporation tax question and also in many cases included on the CT 61.

(b)   Furthermore the CT 61 was poorly done with candidates failing to realise that income tax cannot be reclaimed until after it has been paid.

(c)   As in previous papers the industrial buildings allowances computations were weak in the majority of cases. This was despite the computation being very straightforward.

Question 2: Part (a) required the calculation of assessable profits net of capital allowances for the first four years of assessment.

Part (b) required the calculation of the income tax liability of a taxpayer with car and fuel benefits and a beneficial loan, who is entitled to married couple's allowance and loan interest relief as a tax reducer.

The question was generally well answered and the candidates' overall performance showed a definite improvement in the light of comments made in previous examiner's reports.

In part (a) the computation of the income tax assessable amounts was generally well done except for the apportionment of profits, when many candidates used the wrong fraction in computing the assessable amount for the first year.

There was plenty of evidence of problems experienced in dealing with the restriction for private use, and the treatment of 'expensive' cars for capital allowances. Scant attention was paid to basis periods when computing industrial buildings allowance and several candidates used 2% writing down allowance instead of 4%. Some candidates, when summarising the assessable profits after capital allowances went on, unnecessarily, to compute taxable income and income tax liability for all years.

In part (b) many candidates restricted the car and fuel benefits on a time basis by wrongly assuming the car was purchased in August 1998 when it was purchased in August 1997. In the intended absence of any data on car benefits on the paper several candidates chose to ignore any taxable car benefits.

There were many errors in the treatment of the £4,000 capital contribution. Many candidates also applied the private use contribution to both the car and fuel benefit. It was also disappointing to note that despite comments on several occasions in the previous examiners' reports there were numerous errors relating to the grossing up of charges on income (gift aid in this case). The calculation of the loan benefit was very well done but only a few calculations of the £300 'tax reducer' were in evidence. Otherwise the calculation of the liability including the treatment of the married couple's allowance and the related tax reduction were generally well handled.

Question 3: Part (a) required the calculation of a capital gain arising on the sale of part of a holding of unquoted shares, some of which had been acquired prior to 31 March 1982, where no re-basing election had been made in respect of all assets held on 31 March 1982.

Part (b) required the calculation of a capital gain arising on the assignment of a short lease acquired prior to 31 March 1982 where a re-basing election had been made in respect of all assets held on 31 March 1982.

Part (a): Many candidates seemed unaware of the FA 1985 pool and the FA 1982 frozen pool rules and hence were unable to identify the shares sold. An additional common mistake was to assume the FA 1985 pool commenced in April 1985, resulting in the October 1984 share acquisition being excluded from both pools and treated separately as an afterthought.

Part (b): The answers to this part of the question were generally poor. Most candidates ignored the short leaseholds depreciation table provided and others could not use it properly. A common mistake was to ignore the fact that a 're-basing' election had been made.

Question 4: tested candidates' knowledge of VAT registration and de-registration, bad debt relief and cash accounting.

This was the best answered question on the paper with the majority of candidates providing meaningful answers to most of the sections. The most common mistake was in part (e) where many candidates assumed that cash accounting would be advantageous for traders who sold items for cash. There was also confusion between the answers provided for parts (a) and (b).

Question 5: tested candidates' knowledge of property income with loss relief.

As with previous Schedule A questions most candidates were unable to correctly calculate the rent accruing. The calculations of deductions for repairs and wear and tear allowances were only marginally better done.

Question 6: required a calculation of terminal loss.

Only a few candidates displayed any knowledge of the constituent elements of the terminal loss and in part (c) many answers stated that the terminal loss be carried forward against future trading income.

Question 7: required candidates to contrast the tax and national insurance consequences of a taxpayer being held to be employed or self-employed.

As in previous papers any mention of both Schedule D and Schedule E in the same question encourages candidates to launch into a discussion on the badges of trade. This question was no exception even though it required a contrast of the consequences of a decision having been made. Candidates tended to concentrate on national insurance contribution differences. Many candidates simply stated that expenses were more difficult to obtain for employees than for the self-employed without any reference to the conditions. Very few candidates gave adequate answers for pension arrangements.

Question 8: required to prepare a speech on the PAYE system for delivery to their local students' society.

Instead of concentrating on specific points many answers were too general and statements that were made were incorrect.

DECEMBER 1994 ANSWERS

27   (Answer 1 of examination)

A two-part corporation tax question testing:

(a)   the preparation of entries in relation to income tax as they would appear on forms CT 61 for the year ended 30 September 1998; and

(b)   the calculation of the corporation tax liability for the year ended 30 September 1998.

(a)   **CT 61 forms**

Income tax (20%)

CT 61 period	Tax deducted on payment £	Tax suffered on receipt £	IT payable (re-payable) £
1.10.97 - 31.12.97	1,000	1,600	–
1.4.98 - 30.6.98	1,800	800	
	2,800	2,400	400
1.7.98 - 30.9.98	800	3,200	
	3,600	5,600	(400)*

        * Restricted to amount paid.

The balance of the excess of the income tax suffered over the income tax deducted (£2,000) will be set-off against the mainstream corporation tax.

(b)   **Unknown Underlings Ltd**

Corporation tax computation
Chargeable accounting period ended 30 September 1998

	£
Trading profit	300,000
Debenture interest payable	(22,000)
Capital allowances (W1)	(1,650)
Schedule D Case I profit	276,350
Bank interest receivable	3,000
Loan interest receivable	29,600
Chargeable profits	308,950
Corporation tax payable (W2)	69,063
Income tax suffered (see part (a)(ii) of answer)	(2,000)
Final corporation tax payable	67,063

WORKINGS

(W1)   Industrial building allowance

            2% × 82,500 = £1,650

(W2)   Corporation tax payable

			£
I	=	chargeable profits	308,950
P	=	chargeable profits	308,950
	+	franked investment income 22,000 × $^{100}/_{80}$	27,500
			336,450

Financial years 1997/1998

The limits are:

Upper £1,500,000
Lower £300,000

As P is between the upper and lower limits the marginal rate applies.

	£
Corporation tax payable:	
308,950 × 31%	95,774
Marginal relief $(1,500,000 - 336,450) \times \dfrac{308,950}{336,450} \times \frac{1}{40}$	(26,711)
	69,063

---

28   (Answer 2 of examination)

Income tax question testing;

(1)   the calculation of profits net of capital allowances assessable for the first four years of assessment; and

(2)   the calculation of the income tax liability of a taxpayer with car and fuel benefits and a beneficial loan, who is entitled to married couple's allowance and loan interest relief as a tax reducer.

(Tutorial note:

Part (a) originally dealt with the opening years of a pre 6 April 1994 business. This question has been rewritten to reflect the current year basis.*)*

(a)   **Income tax assessable amounts**

			£
1996/97	Actual 1.10.96 - 5.4.97	£27,863 (W3) × $^{187}/_{457}$	11,401
1997/98	Year ended 31.12.97	£27,863 × $^{365}/_{457}$	22,254
1998/99	Year ended 31.12.98		17,928
1999/00	Year ended 31.12.99		36,912

Overlap profits 1.1.97 - 5.4.97: 27,863 × $^{95}/_{457}$ = £5,792.

WORKINGS

(W1)   Capital allowances computation

	Pool £	Car$^{(1)}$ £	20% pte £	Car$^{(2)}$ £	20% pte £	Total £
1.10.96 - 31.12.97						
Additions						
Car		12,200				
Trailer	2,000					
P and M	8,000					
	10,000					
WDA 25% × $^{457}/_{365}$	3,130	3,756	(751)			6,135
	6,870	8,444				
1.1.98 - 31.12.98						
Addition - Car$^{(2)}$				13,000		
Sale - Car$^{(1)}$		(7,000)				
		1,444				
Balancing allowance		1,444	(289)			1,155
		—				
WDA 25%	1,717			3,000	(600)	4,117
	5,153			10,000		5,272
1.1.99 - 31.12.99						
Addition						
P and M	6,000					
Sale	(2,000)					
	9,153					
WDA 25%	2,288			2,500	(500)	4,288
WDV c/f	6,865			7,500		

(W2)   Industrial building allowance

Factory unit

		£	£
Cost		20,000	
Period ended 31.12.97	IBA 4% × $^{457}/_{365}$	1,002	1,002
		18,998	
Year ended 31.12.98	IBA 4%	800	800
		18,198	
Year ended 31.12.99	IBA 4%	800	800
Carry forward		17,398	

(W3)   Summary

	Adjusted profit £	CA £	IBA £	Total £
15 months to 31.12.97	35,000	6,135	1,002	27,863
Year ended 31.12.98	24,000	5,272	800	17,928
Year ended 31.12.99	42,000	4,288	800	36,912

(b)   **Sephora Kent**

Income tax liability 1998/99

	£	£
Salary		30,000
Car benefit		
Cost	25,000	
Contribution	4,000	
21,000 × 35% =	7,350	
Mileage reduction $(\frac{1}{3})$	2,450	
	4,900	
Contribution	(300)	
		4,600
Fuel benefit		1,890
Beneficial loan 60,000 × (10% − 3%)		4,200
		40,690
Charge on income - gift aid		(500)
Total income		40,190
Personal allowance		(4,195)
Taxable income		35,995

Income tax liability		
4,300 at 20%		860
22,800 at 23%		5,244
8,895 at 40%		3,558
35,995		9,662

Married couple's allowance - £950 at 15%	142	
Loan interest - (£30,000 at 10%)		
£3,000 at 10%	300	(442)
		9,220
Add back tax retained on charge		115
		9,335

(Tutorial notes:

(1)   When working out the car benefit, the price is reduced by any capital contribution, up to a maximum of £5,000.

(2)   When an employee is given a beneficial loan the benefit is the interest on the loan at the official rate less interest actually paid.

(3)   The relief for mortgage interest is given as a tax credit on interest paid on amounts up to £30,000. Here, relief is given at the official rate of interest.*)

---

29   **(Answer 3 of examination)**

A capital gains tax question testing:

(a)   the calculation of a capital gain arising on the sale of part of a holding of unquoted shares, some of which were acquired prior to 31 March 1982, where no re-basing election has been made in respect of all assets held on 31 March 1982; and

(b) the calculation of a capital gain arising on the assignment of short lease acquired prior to 31 March 1982 where a re-basing election has been made in respect of all assets held on 31 March 1982.

(a) **Doris**

(i) **FA 1985 pool**

	Shares	Unindexed cost £	Indexed cost £
October 1984	600	3,600	3,600
Indexation to April 1985			
$\dfrac{94.78 - 90.67}{90.67} = 0.045 \times 3,600$	–	–	162
	600	3,600	3,762
Indexation to August 1992			
$\dfrac{138.9 - 94.78}{94.78} \times 3,762$	–	–	1,751
	600	3,600	5,513
August 1992 purchase	800	6,400	6,400
	1,400	10,000	11,913
Indexation to April 1998			
$\dfrac{161.2 - 138.9}{138.9} \times 11,913$	–	–	1,913
	1,400	10,000	13,826
October 1998 - sale	1,400	10,000	13,826
	–	–	–

	£
Disposal proceeds - $\dfrac{1,400}{1,700} \times 27,200$	22,400
Less: Cost	(10,000)
Indexation allowance	(3,826)
Indexed gain on FA 1985 pool	8,574

(ii) **1982 holding**

	Shares	Cost £
April 1975	400	1,600
July 1979	200	1,000
	600	2,600
Allocated cost $2,600 \times \left(\dfrac{4,800}{4,800 + 3,000}\right)$	300	1,600
Carried forward	300	1,000

Calculation of gain

	Cost £	31 March 1982 value £
Disposal proceeds $\frac{300}{1,700} \times £27,000$	4,800	4,800
Cost	1,600	–
31 March 1982 value (300 at £3.50)	–	1,050
Unindexed gain	3,200	3,750
Indexation allowance $\frac{161.2 - 79.44}{79.44} = 1.029 \times 1,600$	1,646	1,646
	1,554	2,104

Lower gain is £1,554.

Summary

	£
FA 1985 pool	8,574
1982 holding	1,554
	10,128

(*Tutorial notes:*

(1)   Note that the pooling provisions apply to unquoted shares as well as quoted shares.

(2)   As the value of the unsold shares are given in the question, the cost to be taken out of the 1982 holding is computed using the part disposal formula, $\frac{A}{A+B}$ where A is the proceeds and B is the value of the remainder.

(3)   Even if Doris had worked full time for the company, the business rate of taper relief could not apply as her holding did not amount to 5% of the company's shares.)

(b)   **Boris**

	£
Disposal proceeds	25,000
31 March 1982 value = 17,500	
Proportion allowed is $\frac{13.25 \text{ years}}{29.5 \text{ years}} = \frac{56.868}{86.778} \times 17,500$	11,468
Unindexed gain	13,532
Indexation allowance $\frac{161.2 - 79.44}{79.44} = 1.029 \times 11,468$	11,801
Indexed gain	1,731

---

30   (Answer 4 of examination)

(a)   De-registration is compulsory where:

(i)   registration was wrongly obtained;
(ii)   taxable supplies have, or will, cease; or
(iii)   there is a change in the legal status of the registered business (eg. incorporation).

(b)   A trader can apply to be de-registered if the tax-exclusive value of supplies in the following 12 months is not expected to exceed the annual de-registration limit, at present £48,000.

(c)   Consequences of de-registration

(i)   Value added tax must no longer be charged on supplies, and input tax can no longer be reclaimed on goods and services provided to the trader.

(ii)   There is a deemed supply of assets and trading stock held on de-registration which is valued at cost plus value added tax.

(d)   Bad debt relief can be claimed:

(i)   when the debt has been written off in the trader's books of account;

(ii)   the payment was due at least six months earlier; and

(iii)   the output tax in respect of the supply of the goods has been properly accounted for.

(e)   (i)   Cash accounting is advantageous:

–   for traders who give extended periods of credit to customers; and
–   for traders with high levels of bad debts, thereby providing immediate relief for bad debts.

(ii)   The following traders are eligible to use the scheme:

–   those with a clean value added tax record*; and
–   those with an annual value added tax exclusive turnover of less than £350,000.

* A clean value added tax record means:

(1)   having made arrangements with Customs and Excise to clear the total amount of VAT payable (including surcharges and penalties);

(2)   not having been convicted of any VAT offence in the last year;

(3)   not having been assessed to penalties for VAT evasion involving dishonest conduct in the last year; and

(4)   not having accepted an offer to compound proceedings in connection with a VAT offence in the last year.

31	**(Answer 5 of examination)**

	House 1 £	House 2 £	House 3 £	House 4 £
Rent accruing	2,250	2,000	1,500	6,000
Premium assessable	–	1,760	–	–
Repairs	(2,000)	–	(2,500)	–
Expenses	–	–	–	(7,000)
W and T allowance	–	–	–	(520)
	250	3,760	(1,000)	(1,520)

The assessable amount for 1998/99 under Schedule A will be:

$(250 + 3,760 - 1,000 - 1,520) = £1,490$

Notes:

(1) House number 1

    (a) Rent from expired lease: £4,000 × $\frac{3}{12}$ = £1,000

    (b) Rent from new tenancy: £5,000 × $\frac{3}{12}$ = £1,250

    (c) Re-decoration costs may not be allowed in full as it was owner-occupied. However we assume that Reginald can argue that the expense was wholly and exclusively for the Schedule A business.

(2) House number 2

		£
(a) Premium		2,000
Discount $(7 - 1) \times 2\%$		(240)
		1,760

    (b) Roof repairs not allowable as they were making good a deficiency on purchase.

(3) House number 3

    (a) Rent from expired lease: £3,000 × $\frac{6}{12}$ = £1,500

    (b) Rent from new lease: Nil

    (c) Re-decoration costs allowed as clearly wholly and exclusively incurred for the letting business.

(4) House number 4

    (a) Wear and tear allowance on: $(6,000 - 200 - 600) = 5,200 \times 10\% = £520$

    (b) £2,000 loan interest allowable as an expense of the letting business.

---

32   (Answer 6 of examination)

(Tutorial note:

This question originally dealt with the closing years of a pre 6 April 1994 business which is now no longer in the syllabus. It has been rewritten to reflect the current year basis.*)*

(a) **Assessable amounts**

	Allowances
	£
Capital allowances	
Brought forward	1,200
y/e 31.7.97 WDA × 25%	(300)
	900
y/e 31.7.98 WDA × 25%	(225)
	675
y/e 31.7.99 WDA × 25%	(169)
	506
Sale proceeds in period to 28.2.2000	(75)
	431
Balancing allowance	(431)
	–

Adjusted profit

	£
Year ended 31 July 1997 (13,000 − 300)	12,700
Year ended 31 July 1998 (8,000 − 225)	7,775
Year ended 31 July 1999 (3,000 + 169)	(3,169)
Period to 28 February 2000 (Loss 4,500 + 431)	(4,931)

Assessable amounts

	£	£
1997/98		
y/e 31.7.97		12,700
1998/99		
y/e 31.7.98		7,775
1999/00		
1.8.98 − 28.2.2000		
3,169 + 4,931	8,100	
Add: Overlap relief	2,500	
	10,600	Nil

(b) **Calculation of terminal loss**

			£	£
(1)	6.4.99 - 31.7.99	($^{117}/_{365}$ × 3,169)	(1,016)	
	1.8.99 - 28.2.00		(4,931)	
			5,947 Loss	5,947
(2)	1.3.99 - 5.4.99	($^{36}/_{365}$ × 3,169)	313 Loss	313
	Add: Overlap relief			2,500
				8,760

(c) **Allowance of terminal loss**

	1998/99 £	1997/98 £
Case I	7,775	12,700
Terminal loss	(7,775)	(985)
Net assessable amount	–	11,715

The unrelieved balance of the loss of the year to 31 July 1999 £2,856 (3,169 − 313) would be allowed in 1998/99 and/or 1999/00 under S380 ie, against STI.

(Tutorial note:

A terminal loss may be relieved against assessable trading profit of the year of assessment in which the discontinuance occurs, and the three years preceding it.*)*

33   (Answer 7 of examination)

(1)   **Basis of assessment**

    (a)   The taxpayer will be assessable on the actual amounts received in the tax year.

    (b)   The taxpayer will be assessed on the current year basis, with special rules applying to opening and closing years.

(2)   **Income tax payment dates**

    (a)   Income tax will be deducted periodically, weekly or monthly, from the emoluments under PAYE system.

    (b)   Income tax will be payable in two equal payments on account on 31 January in the year of assessment and on 31 July following the year of assessment, with a balancing payment due on the following 31 January.

(3)   **National Insurance contributions**

    (a)   Class 1 National Insurance contributions will be payable by both employer and employee on a weekly or monthly basis.

    (b)   Class 2 National Insurance contributions will be payable by monthly direct debit or by a quarterly cheque payment. Class 4 National Insurance contributions will also be payable on profits between lower and upper annual limits at the same time as income tax payments (2(b) above).

(4)   **Deductibility of expenses**

    (a)   Expenses will only be allowed where incurred wholly, exclusively and necessarily in the performance of the duties of the employment.

    (b)   Only expenditure incurred wholly and exclusively for business purposes will be deductible.

(5)   **Pension contributions**

    (a)   An employee may be eligible to join the employer's pension scheme and also to 'top-up' total tax-deductible pension contributions to 15% of total emoluments. Where the employer does not have a pension scheme an employee may take out a personal pension plan and pay tax-deductible premiums by reference to age-determined percentages on net relevant earnings.

    (b)   A personal pension plan may be taken out and tax-deductible premiums paid by reference to age-determined percentages.

(6)   **Social Security benefits**

    Employed taxpayers are entitled to jobseeker's allowance which is not available to self-employed taxpayers who cease to be self-employed.

34   (Answer 8 of examination)

Employers are required to apply PAYE when the emoluments of an employee exceed the weekly or monthly equivalent of the personal allowance.

A code number is calculated for each employee by reference to the allowances and expenses claimed on the income tax return. In arriving at the code number deductions are made for small amounts of untaxed income, benefits-in-kind and under-payments of tax from earlier years. $\frac{1}{12}$ (for monthly paid employees) or $\frac{1}{52}$ (for weekly paid employees) of the net allowances reflected in the code number is given against the earnings on each pay day in the tax year. The balance of the earnings not covered by the allowances is charged to income tax at the appropriate rates, 20%, 23% or 40%. The

PAYE tax deducted from the employee's earnings, together with National Insurance contributions, is to be forwarded to the Collector of Taxes, by the 19th day of each month.

When an employee leaves an employment a form P45 showing details of cumulative pay and tax, code number and date of leaving is prepared. Part 1 of the form is forwarded to the tax district and parts 2 and 3 are handed to the employee. Upon commencing a new employment parts 2 and 3 are handed to the new employer. Part 2 is kept by the new employer as a permanent record of the information contained therein. Part 3 is forwarded to the new employer's tax district who in turn forward it to the previous tax district. The details on the part 3 are checked with the original details on the part 1 and the employee's tax file is forwarded to the new tax district dealing with the new employer. The employee receives a copy of part 1 (part 1A) to retain for his own records.

At the end of the tax year, 5 April, each employee is provided with a form P60 which is a record of earnings, tax, pension contributions and National Insurance contributions. A form P11D is forwarded to the tax office giving details of non-cash benefits provided for employees earnings over £8,500 per annum.

A summary of the tax deductions during the year is sent to the Collector on a form P35. After checking these details are forwarded to the Inspector prompting him to send the taxpayer a tax return thereby generating a self-assessment.

JUNE 1995 QUESTIONS

35   (Question 1 of examination)

Unseen Ultrasonics Ltd (UUL) is a United Kingdom resident company which manufactures accessories for telecommunication systems. It has no associated companies.

The company's results for the year ended 31 December 1998 were as follows:

	£
Trading profits (as adjusted for taxation but before capital allowances) (note 1)	2,300,000
Dividends received from UK companies (note 2)	60,000
Bank interest receivable	1,500
Chargeable gains	25,000
Debenture interest received (gross amount) (note 5)	80,000
Payment under deed of covenant to a national charity (gross amount)	5,000

The debenture interest received is the same as the amounts credited in the accounts on an accruals basis.

The company has traded in a purpose built unit since 1 January 1992. The total cost of the unit was made up as follows:

	£
Freehold land	50,000
Manufacturing area	240,000
Canteen	30,000
Design office	90,000
General office	70,000
	480,000

The unit was not situated in an Enterprise Zone.

On 1 July 1998 an extension to the general office was completed costing £60,000.

On 1 January 1998 the tax written-down values of plant and machinery were:

	£
Pool	160,000
Car pool (five vehicles)	30,000
Short-life asset	4,000

The short-life asset was purchased on 1 December 1993 and sold on 31 July 1998 for £10,000.

On 1 August 1998 a new car costing £18,000 was purchased for the managing director. The car previously used by him had cost £10,000 in April 1996 and was sold for £8,000. A new precision engineering machine was purchased on 1 May 1998 for £90,000: it was expected that the machine would be obsolete within three years and the appropriate election was made for de-pooling.

Notes:

(1)   In arriving at the adjusted trading profit an adjustment had been made for small capital additions acquired in January and February 1998 totalling £39,000 which the company had written off as repairs but which the Inspector of Taxes had insisted were added-back.

(2)   The company had received the following dividend:

28 February 1998   £60,000

(3)   On 1 January 1998 the company had capital losses brought forward of £30,000.

(4)   On 1 January 1998 the company had trading losses brought forward of £567,750.

(5)   Income tax has been deducted from the debenture interest received.

(6)   The deed of covenant payment was made in July 1998.

You are required to calculate the mainstream corporation tax payable for the year ended 31 December 1998. You should also state how any unrelieved amounts are to be dealt with.

(17 marks)

---

36   (Question 2 of examination)

Michael and Rose were married on 14 February 1999. Michael had been a widower for several years and Rose's previous husband had died in October 1997. Michael was born on 5 November 1936 and Rose on 5 April 1936.

Their respective incomes for 1998/99 were:

Michael	£
Gross earnings as salesman (PAYE paid £6,052)	25,720
Dividends (amount received)	5,000
Building society interest (net amount received)	400

Michael is provided with a company car by his employers. Until 31 July 1998 the car was a petrol-engined 1100cc Rover which had cost £7,500 when new on 1 August 1994. On 1 August 1998 the car was exchanged for a new diesel-engined 1900cc Rover which cost £12,500. Michael was required to pay to his employers £20 per month towards private usage of the cars and £10 per month towards the cost of fuel for private motoring. The cost of all fuel, business and private, was met by the employer. Michael's total mileage in the tax year 1998/99 was 20,000 of which 10,000 was private. The mileage was done evenly throughout the year.

Rose	£
Gross pension from late husband's employer (PAYE paid £706)	9,000
National Savings Bank ordinary account	
The account had been opened in May 1996 and recent interest credited as follows:	
31 December 1997	150
31 December 1998	140

Rose owned a cottage which she had furnished and rented out with rent receivable in advance on the usual quarter days. These are 25 March, 25 June, 29 September and 25 December.

The previous three-year lease, under which the annual rent was £5,000 ended on 29 September 1998 and was replaced by a similar lease under which the annual rent was £6,000. It had been agreed with the Inland Revenue to claim a 10% wear and tear allowance instead of capital allowances. Expenditure incurred during 1998/99 was:

	£
Water rates	250
Council tax	700
Repairs	800
Insurance	600

Rose sold the cottage on 24 March 1999 for £78,000. The cottage had been purchased by Rose's late husband in May 1993 for £50,000 and left to Rose in his will. Value at death was agreed at £60,000 with the Inland Revenue.

You are required:

(a)   to calculate the tax liabilities of Michael and Rose for 1998/99; and   **(25 marks)**

(b)   to show how Michael's liability would be collected.   **(2 marks)**

(Total: 27 marks)

37	**(Question 3 of examination)**

(a) Ashley sold his house for £196,500 on 31 January 1999. The house had been purchased in 1978 for £71,200. In 1981 a conservatory was added to the house costing £7,000.

Ashley lived in the house until 31 August 1992 when he let it for residential purposes and moved into a nearby flat.

The value of the house on 31 March 1982 was £72,000.

You are required to calculate the capital gain for 1998/99. No election has been made to 're-base' the cost of all assets held on 31 March 1982 at their value on that date. **(7 marks)**

(b) Gillian purchased 10,000 ordinary shares in Downtown plc in January 1990 for £20,000. In October 1998 Upmarket plc acquired the whole of the share capital of Downtown plc following a take-over bid. The terms of the take-over offer were:

> One ordinary share in Upmarket plc
> Two preference shares in Upmarket plc and £3 cash

for every five shares held in Downtown plc.

The share prices of Upmarket plc immediately after the take-over were:

> ordinary shares £10 each; and
> preference shares £3 each.

You are required to calculate the capital gain for 1998/99. **(6 marks)**

(c) Jeffrey bought 3,000 shares in Metropolitan plc in May 1979 for £6,000. In April 1992 there was a 2 for 3 rights issue which Jeffrey took up for £1.50 per share. In March 1999 he sold 2,500 shares for £15,000.

The value per share on 31 March 1982 was £3.50.

You are required to calculate the capital gain for 1998/99. No election has been made to 're-base' the cost of all assets held on 31 March 1982 at their value on that date. **(4 marks)**
(Total: 17 marks)

38	**(Question 4 of examination)**

(a) You are provided with the following information relating to Octavius for the quarter ended 31 May 1999:

(1) The VAT-exclusive management accounts:

	£	£
Sales		16,500
Sales returns		(1,100)
		15,400
Purchases	9,600	
Purchases returns	(300)	
	9,300	
Bad debts written off	1,500	
Other expenses	2,400	
		13,200
Profit		2,200

(2) The sales and other expenses are all standard-rated for VAT.

(3)   The purchases are all deductible for VAT.

(4)   The sales and purchases returns are all evidenced by credit notes issued and received.

(5)   The bad debts were written off in May 1999. Payment for the original sales was due by February 1999.

(6)   A sales invoice for £3,000 excluding VAT had been omitted in error from the VAT return for the quarter to 28 February 1999.

(7)   Included in the expenses figure is the cost of both business and private petrol for Octavius' car which had an engine capacity of 1800cc. The quarterly car fuel charge (VAT exclusive) of a car with cubic capacity 1401–2000 is 228.

Required:

(i)   You are required to complete the VAT account for the three month period ended 31 May 1999, showing how much VAT is payable to Customs and Excise. The 'cash accounting' scheme is not being used.   **(7 marks)**

(ii)   When is the tax shown by (a)(i) above payable?   **(1 mark)**

(b)   (i)   What course of action is open to a taxpayer who disagrees with a decision by Customs and Excise on the application of VAT before lodging a formal appeal to a VAT tribunal?   **(1 mark)**

(ii)   What are the consequences of any action taken by the taxpayer in (b)(i) above?

(2 marks)
(Total: 11 marks)

---

39   (Question 5 of examination)

Chatru commenced trading on 1 November 1995. His first accounts were made up to 30 April 1997 and thereafter to 30 April annually. He ceased trading on 31 March 2000.

His trading results, adjusted for income tax purposes were:

	£
1.11.95 – 30.4.97	40,500
Year ended 30.4.98	12,000
Year ended 30.4.99	24,000
Period to 31.3.00	36,000

You are required:

(a)   To calculate the assessable income for all years in question, and   **(8 marks)**

(b)   To calculate whether there would have been any income tax benefit in Chatru continuing to trade one extra month and making up final accounts to his normal accounting date, on the assumption that his tax-adjusted profit for April 2000 was £4,200.   **(3 marks)**
(Total: 11 marks)

---

40   (Question 6 of examination)

The following items are charged against profit in the accounts of Uranus Ltd, a trading company, for the year ended 31 March 1999:

(1)   Running expenses (including depreciation of £6,000) of the managing director's BMW totalling £10,000. His total mileage in the year was 12,000 of which 6,000 was private. The car was owned by Uranus Ltd.

(2)   Entertainment expenditure totalling £25,000 of which £10,000 was incurred on overseas customers, £11,000 on UK customers and £4,000 on the annual company dinner for 200 employees.

(3)   £2,500 being the costs of registering a patent to protect a process developed by the company.

(4)   Lease rental of £6,000 on sales director's car costing £20,000.

(5)   A payment of £616 to the Royal National Lifeboat Institution under a four-year deed of covenant.

(6)   A payment for £30,000 for the granting of a six year lease on a factory.

(7)   Debenture interest of £27,000 of which £3,000 was a closing accrual.

(8)   A provision of £8,000 against a trade debt of the company, being 80% of the debt. The liquidator of the debtor company had advised Uranus Ltd of this figure but in the event £5,000 of the debt was paid in May 1999.

(9)   Repairs to a ship purchased on 1 April 1998 totalling £160,000 to make it seaworthy. The annual maintenance cost of the ship was £40,000.

(10)   Canteen subsidy costs of £100,000. This figure included the cost of providing subsidised meals to directors of £7,500. The meals of all other employees were subsidised at 50% of the cost of a director's meal.

(11)   Permanent repairs to the roof of a warehouse which was purchased on 1 August 1998 for £25,000. The warehouse, which was used to store raw materials, had a leaking roof when purchased but pending the permanent repairs this was covered by plastic sheeting to enable it to be used from the date of purchase.

You are required to state how you would deal with each of the above items when preparing the company's taxation computations for the year ended 31 March 1999.

(11 marks)
(ie, 1 mark per item)

---

41   (Question 7 of examination)

You are required to state the criteria which will be applied by the Inland Revenue and the Department of Social Security in deciding whether a taxpayer is 'employed' or 'self-employed'.

(11 marks)

---

42   (Question 8 of examination)

Charlie, Juliette and Mike are interior design consultants and have been in partnership since 1 October 1994 trading as CJM Designs. They prepare annual accounts to 30 September. Details of their profit-sharing arrangements, which were changed on 31 March 1998 are:

	to 31 March 1998	from 1 April 1998
Interest on fixed capital	5%	4%
Partner's annual salary	Charlie £6,000	none
Profit-sharing ratio	Charlie 1/5	Charlie 1/3
	Juliette 2/5	Juliette 1/3
	Mike 2/5	Mike 1/3

Fixed capital accounts have remained unchanged since 1994 and are:

	£
Charlie	12,000
Juliette	16,000
Mike	18,000

In the year ended 30 September 1998 the partnership sustained its first ever trading loss, as adjusted for income tax, of £20,000. All partners have sufficient other income to absorb any trading losses and wish to utilise their share of the loss in this manner rather than carry it forward.

(a)   **You are required** to calculate the amount of each partner's share of the trading loss sustained in the year to 30 September 1998 on the basis of a set-off against other income.

(10 marks)

(b)   Had the partners had no other income, and wished therefore to carry forward the loss, how would the loss have been allocated?

(*Note:* Calculations are not required for part (b).

(1 mark)

(11 marks)

JUNE 1995 ANSWERS

35   (Answer 1 of examination)

(Examiner's comments and marking guide)

A question testing the calculation of a corporation tax liability with trading and capital losses brought forward, Industrial Buildings Allowances and plant and machinery allowances with short life assets, and calculation of set-off of tax suffered on unfranked investment income after set-off of Income Tax retained on payment of charges on income.

The performance of the majority of candidates on this question was disappointing. In many cases candidates demonstrated a lack of knowledge of anything more than the very basic principles of corporation tax. Specific areas of weakness were:

(a)   IBA computations (as they have been at previous sittings).

(b)   In the capital allowance computation few candidates correctly transferred the short life asset to the main pool or included the small capital additions in the main pool. On the positive side, most candidates correctly restricted the allowance on the expensive car and there was some improvement in the layout of the capital allowance computation over previous sittings.

(c)   Many candidates failed to demonstrate sufficiently clearly the treatment of losses brought forward and, as a result, lost marks. In particular, the trading losses were not specifically set-off against trading profit (in many cases being set-off against the total profit or some interim figure).

While the answer in this particular question would have been the same, such candidates did not display sufficient knowledge of the relevant principle.

(d)   Many candidates ignored the income tax set-off arising from UFII and charges.

(e)   Frequently, the bank interest received was grossed up.

The above is clearly not an exhaustive list of errors but many of these areas are core to the syllabus and should be considered as aspects of corporation tax over which the average candidate has a firm grasp. Regrettably, many of these comments have been made in previous sittings yet continue to occur.

				Marks
Computation	-	Trading losses against Sch DI income		1
	-	Bank interest not grossed-up		1
	-	Chargeable profits		1
W1 IBA	-	25% tests	2	
	-	calculation	1	
			—	3
W2 P and M	-	switch of short-life asset	1	
	-	disposal in correct columns	1	
	-	£39,000 addition	1	
	-	other additions in correct columns	1	
	-	WDA calculation including £3,000 restriction	1	
			—	5
W3 Chargeable gains				1
W4 Rate of corporation tax - 31%				2
W5 Income tax				
Tax on debenture interest			1	
Tax on covenant			1	
Set-off			1	
			—	3
Total				17

The marking scheme has been modified to reflect changes in legislation and exclusions from the syllabus since the question was set.

(**Step by step answer plan**)

Overview

Question 1 always requires a CT computation for all or most of the marks and is a vital element in passing the paper. You know that your answer will consist of a PCTCT layout followed by a standard CT layout. On your first reading of the question you should try to spot the complications the examiner has built-in. For example, your answer will clearly need P&M CA and IBA workings.

You might like to make the question more manageable by high lighting key words such as 'trading losses b/f *(Note 4)* or bracketing text in the margin. For example, it is fairly obvious which bit of text concerns IBAs and the following piece of text, to the end of Note 1, will generate the CA figure for P&M. You are thereby actively reading - ie, not being passive - and envisaging where the information will be needed in your answer.

Step 1   Head up the PCTCT layout and fill in the labels leaving plenty of room for items you might not yet have recognised - eg. there is a capital gain awaiting you.

Step 2   Work down through the question producing working notes for the two categories of CAs and the for the net capital gain.

Step 3   Generate the Schedule D I figure on your main layout by deducting the two CA amounts.

Step 4   You know there is a trading loss b/f so deduct that next.

Step 5   Clear out all the other PCTCT items from the text of the question by looking down the 'results' paragraph and referring to 'notes' as appropriate.

Step 6   Just check through the question and your workings once more to ensure that anything impacting on PCTCT has been dealt with in your answer so far. For example, it is good practice to show the gains figure in the PCTCT layout even though your working shows them as nil.

Step 7   Next compute CT. Clearly the £1,500,000 limit has been exceeded even before adding in FII. It is good exam practice, however, to show you have considered the point. Even without marginal relief or without the complication of a FY "straddle" as we have here, the examiner clearly prefers to see the CT calculated in a working note.

Step 8   The final working concerns income tax still recoverable after the process of the quarterly accounting system.

Step 9   Make sure all workings are cross referenced to the main layout or, where appropriate, to other workings.

Step 10   Finally re-read the "requirements". It is so easy to waste marks by overlooking the extra requirements. You have already calculated the excess capital loss. All you have to do is write it out clearly and describe briefly how it will be dealt with. Oddly it is not clear from the marking guide how the marks will be given but it is shown clearly in the examiner's answer so it must have attracted marks in the actual marking process.

The examiner's answer

Corporation tax computation
Chargeable accounting period ended 31 December 1998

			£
Trading profit			2,300,000
Capital allowances	–	IBA (W1)	(14,400)
	–	P and M (W2)	(111,500)
Schedule D Case I profit			2,174,100
Trading losses brought forward			(567,750)
			1,606,350
Bank interest receivable			1,500
Chargeable gains (W3)			Nil
Debenture interest receivable			80,000
			1,687,850
Charges on income – Deed of covenant			(5,000)
Chargeable profits			1,682,850

	£
Corporation tax payable (W4) @ 31%	521,683
Income tax suffered (W5)	(14,850)
Mainstream corporation tax payable	506,833

Capital losses carried forward against future capital gains:

30,000 – 25,000 (W3)	5,000

WORKINGS

(W1)   Industrial Buildings Allowance

	£
Manufacturing area	240,000
Canteen	30,000
Design office	90,000
General office (Note 1)	70,000
	430,000
General office (Note 2) extension	60,000
	490,000

Notes:

(1)   The cost of the general office is less than 25% of the cost of the unit (70,000/430,000 = 16.3%); but

(2)   the combined cost of the general office and general office extension is now more than 25% of the cost of the unit (130,000/490,000 = 26.5%).

Writing-down allowance for CAP to 31 December 1998 is, therefore, only due on £360,000 (240,000 + 30,000 + 90,000) at 4% = £14,400.

(W2)   Capital allowances on plant and machinery

	Main pool £	Car pool £	Expensive car £	Short-life asset £	Short-life asset £	Total £
WDV b/f 1.1.98	160,000	30,000		4,000		
	4,000			(4,000)*		
	164,000			–		
Disposals	(10,000)	(8,000)				
Additions without FYA	–	–	18,000			
	154,000	22,000	18,000			
WDA 25%	(38,500)	(5,500)	(3,000) (max)	–		47,000
Additions without FYA	39,000**				90,000	
FYA @ 50%	(19,500)				(45,000)	64,500
WDV c/f 31.12.98	135,000	16,500	15,000	–	45,000	111,500

* Transferred to main pool on 1 January 1998 as asset not sold within four years of the end of the accounting period in which purchased.

** Transferred from 'repairs'

(W3)   Chargeable gains

	£
Chargeable for year	25,000
Losses brought forward and utilised	25,000
Assessable in year	–

(W4)   As 'I' and therefore 'P' is clearly over the £1,500,000 upper limit (FYs 1997 and 1998) the full rate of corporation tax (ie, 31%) will apply.

(W5)   Income tax

	£
Tax suffered on debenture interest received £80,000 at 20%	16,000
Tax deducted on deed of covenant £5,000 at 23%	1,150
Set-off against corporation tax	14,850

Tutorial notes:

1   IBAs are available on expenditure for a general office if it represents less than 25% of the qualifying expenditure (including the general office). Thus, when the unit was built in 1992, allowances would have been available on the general office. However, when the extension was built in 1998 the total cost of the general office (original cost and cost of extension) is now greater than 25% of the total cost, and so allowances for year ended 31 December 1998 will only be available on qualifying expenditure, ie, excluding all expenditure on the general office.

2   Assets may be depooled for capital allowance purposes, which has the effect of accelerating allowances if the asset is sold at a loss. Note however, that if the asset is not sold within four years of the accounting period in which it was bought, the asset can no longer be dealt with separately; the tax written down value in transferred to the general pool.

3   When calculating the corporation tax liability, do not forget to consider the income tax position, which is as follows:

   •   If tax suffered on taxed income exceeds tax which has been retained on payments, the excess is given as a credit, or repayment if appropriate.

> • If tax suffered on taxed income is less than tax which has been retained on payments, no adjustment is necessary, as the payment will have been made via the quarterly returns.)
>
> 4   Note that bank and building society interest is always received gross by a company. The examiner actually allocated a mark for not making the common heinous error of grossing up the bank interest.

36   (Answer 2 of examination)

(Examiner's comments and marking guide)

A personal tax question including the rules for charging dividends to income tax; personal reliefs, married couple's allowance in year of marriage and widow's bereavement allowance: the rules for taxing company cars and fuel provided for private use: the rules for granting the '£1,900' allowances; summary of collection methods of a taxpayer's liability; furnished lettings; National Savings Bank interest and capital gains on property transferred on death of spouse.

Part (a) of the question was generally well answered. The calculation of the car benefit and the fuel benefit was reasonably well done. However numerous errors were made in treating Michael's contribution towards the provision of car and fuel, many deducting the contribution towards the car before the mileage, age and availability reductions, and others forgetting that the fuel benefit is based on an 'all or nothing basis' and that the contribution towards fuel should have been ignored. The fractions for mileage, age and availability reductions were also incorrectly applied in many cases and some candidates completely ignored the 35% basic charge or used an incorrect percentage.

(b)   Many candidates were unable to distinguish between the treatment of savings and non-saving income when computing the Income Tax liability. This part of the answer was messy and only a few candidates were able to correctly compute the reduction for the married couple's allowance.

(c)   Calculation of the wear and tear allowance was poorly handled, many omitting the adjustment for Council Tax.

(d)   Widows' bereavement allowance was well handled, although some candidates restricted the allowance, unnecessarily.

(e)   In calculating the Capital Gains Tax liability many candidates whilst correctly using the probate value as the base cost, based the indexation allowance, incorrectly, on the date of purchase. Many candidates produced two computations, one based on cost (unnecessary) and the other based on probate value, although some of these did later arrive at the correct conclusion as the latter computation produced a lower gain.

Part (b) however was poorly done, most candidates mentioning instalments and dates etc, and, a few simply stating that the tax will be collected through direct assessment. Very few candidates appeared to understand this part of the question, although some did answer part of it by producing an extended answer to (a) in computing the tax payable.

(Tutorial note: the examiner's comments on part (b) concern the collection rules applying before 'self-assessment'.*)*

				Marks
(a)	(i)	Dividends		1
		Building society interest		1
		Benefits-in-kind - Cars -	35%	1
			- Mileage reduction	1
			- Age reduction	1
			- Availability 4 months/8 months	1
			- Contribution	1
			- Fuel benefits - petrol and diesel	2
			- Fuel contributions ignored	1
		Income tax payable -	20%	1
		-	23%	1
		-	20% (savings)	1
		-	40% (savings)	1
		Married couple's allowance		1
				— 15

(ii)	Furnished lettings	-	Rent	1		
		-	W and T	1		
		-	Deductions	1		
				—	3	
	NSB interest				2	
	Capital gains	-	Probate value	1		
		-	Indexation	1		
		-	Annual exemption	1		
		-	Charged at 23%	1		
				—	4	
	Widow's bereavement allowance				1	
					—	10
(b)	Method of tax collection	-	at source		1	
		-	under self-assessment		1	
					—	2
Total						27

Guide has been modified for new legislation.

Step by step answer plan

Overview

Question 2 is always on personal tax and usually, as here, concerns mainly income tax but with a small capital gains tax part. This is clearly a 'husband and wife year of marriage' exercise. Ages can be deduced from the d.o.b.s given but neither spouse is over 65 by 5 April 1999 so age relief is not in point. The other age related tax topic occurs in pension contributions but this point does not seem to arise in the question. Nevertheless these thoughts should cross your mind when age is mentioned. The other "overview" point on H & W questions is whether there is interaction. For example will there be surplus MCA to transfer? It does not appear to be the case here but keep it in mind. There is mercifully very little H & W interaction so part (a) is virtually two separate questions - one for H and one for W.

Step 1 Head up Michael's Taxable income/IT Comp and fill in the figures which can be lifted straight from the question, albeit grossing up as appropriate.

Step 2 Produce separate workings for the benefits taking care to make the adjustments accurately and to provide enough labels to show you understand the points of principle.

Step 3 Compute the tax separately first on the non-savings then on the savings income: then deduct the tax reducer for MCA (restricted for year of marriage) and any tax credits.

Step 4 Conduct a similar exercise for Rose's income tax liability with a separate working for her furnished lettings and not forgetting the WBA.

Step 5 Compute Rose's capital gain and CGT liability.

Step 6 Make sure you do not overlook part (b) of the question. It may only be for 2 marks but it would be foolish to waste them. Even if Michael's income tax is not correctly computed in part (a) (i) of your answer you should receive credit for commenting on the collection mechanism.

Step 7 Finally re-read the question to ensure that all the relevant points have been dealt with in your answer. For example, you probably spotted in the first paragraph that WBA was available. Did you high light this or write "WBA" in the margin? And if so, have you ticked it off as actioned in your answer?

(**The examiner's answer**)

(a)   (i)   **Michael – 1998/99 income tax liability**

			£		£
Salary					25,720
Dividends (5,000 × $^{100}/_{80}$)					6,250
Building society interest (400 × $^{100}/_{80}$)					500
Benefits-in-kind (see W1)	Cars		2,094		
	Fuel		1,190		3,284
					35,754
Personal allowance					4,195
					31,559

Taxable income
(Savings: 6,250 + 500 = 6,750; non-savings 31,559 – 6,750 = 24,809)

Income tax payable

		£		£
Non-savings income:				
4,300 × 20%				860
20,509 × 23%				4,717
24,809				
Savings income:(TN 1)				
2,291 × 20%				458
4,459 × 40%				1,784
6,750				7,819
Less: MCA 1,900 × $^{2}/_{12}$ = 317 × 15%				(48)
				7,771
Less: PAYE		6,052		
Tax on savings income 6,750 × 20%		1,350		7,402
				369

(ii)   **Rose – 1998/99 income tax liability**

		Non-savings income	Savings income
	£	£	£
Pension	9,000	9,000	
Furnished letting (see W2)	2,695	2,695	
National Savings Bank (140 – 70)	70	–	70
	11,765	11,695	70
Personal allowance	4,195	4,195	–
	7,570	7,500	70

Income tax payable

	£
On non-savings income	
Lower rate – 4,300 at 20%	860
Basic rate – 3,200 at 23%	736
On savings income	
Lower rate - 70 at 20%	14
	1,610
Less: Widow's bereavement allowance £1,900 at 15% (TN 2)	(285)
	1,325
Less: PAYE	(706)
	619

Rose – Capital gains liability 1998/99

	£	£
Sales proceeds		78,000
Probate value – deemed cost (TN 3)	60,000	
Indexation $\dfrac{161.2 - 159.5}{159.5}$ (0.011)	660	
		(60,660)
		17,340
Annual exemption		(6,800)
		10,540
	at 23%	2,424

WORKINGS

(W1) Benefits-in-kind

	£	£
Car 1		
35% × £7,500	2,625	
Mileage reduction (equivalent of between 2,500 and 17,999)	(875) ⅓	
	1,750	
Age reduction (over four years old at 5.4.98)	(583) ⅓	
	1,167	
Available for four months		389 (⁴⁄₁₂)
Car 2		
35% × £12,500	4,375	
Mileage reduction (equivalent of between 2,500 and 17,999)	(1,458) ⅓	
	2,917	
Available for eight months		1,945 (⁸⁄₁₂)
		2,334
Contribution		(240)
		2,094

	£	£
Fuel Car 1		
Under 1400cc (petrol)	1,010	
Available for four months		337 $(\frac{4}{12})$
Fuel Car 2		
1401cc to 2000cc (diesel)	1,280	
Available for eight months		853 $(\frac{8}{12})$
		1,190

Contribution ignored as it clearly does not cover the whole of the private fuel used. (TN4)

(W2)   Furnished letting ('accruals basis')

		£	£
Rent	$-\ \frac{6}{12} \times 5,000$		2,500
	$-\ \frac{6}{12} \times 6,000$		3,000
			5,500
Wear and tear*		455	
Water rates		250	
Council tax		700	
Repairs		800	
Insurance		600	
			(2,805)
			2,695

* Wear and tear $10\% \times (5,500 - 250 - 700)$

Did you answer the question?

You are not required to discuss whether taper relief would be available.

(b)

Michael – collection of income tax liability 1998/99

		£
(1)	Operation of PAYE	6,052
(2)	Tax payable on self-assessment pay days:	
	Savings income at 20% (40% – 20%) 4,459 × 20%	892
	Over payment under PAYE	(523)
(3)	Tax paid on income	
	(a) Income tax on building society interest £500 at 20%	100
	(b) Tax credits on dividend income £6,250 at 20%	1,250
		7,771

Tutorial note:

1   Only part of all the savings income falls into the higher rate band so it is necessary to calculate tax on savings and non-savings income in separate steps.

It would be neater to schedule out the income between savings and non-savings income as shown in the layout for Rose (a). When the question was originally set, the savings treatment only applied to dividends, not interest, so a columnar layout was not shown in the examiner's answer. We therefore show the alternative layout techniques as a legitimate update modification - non columnar is probably quicker to produce but columnar may be easier to follow.

2	Rose is entitled to the widow's bereavement allowance in the year of her husband's death, and the following year, providing that she hasn't remarried at the start of it (ie, by 6 April 1998).
3	Assets are transferred during lifetime on a no gain, no loss basis between husband and wife. However, when an asset is transferred on death, the base cost for the recipient is market value, and it will be indexed from the date of death.
4	A contribution towards the private use of a car is deductible from the benefit. However, a contribution towards private fuel is only deductible if it covers the total cost of fuel used for private purposes.

37   (Answer 3 of examination)

Examiner's comments and marking guide

This was a three part Capital Gains Tax question testing: the calculation of a gain where there is a principal private residence letting; calculation of a gain resulting from a takeover where part of the offer is in the form of cash and the calculation of a gain on the disposal of quoted shares acquired prior to 5 April 1982 and followed by a rights issue after 5 April 1982.

Overall this question was poorly done. In (a) most candidates successfully calculated the indexed gain although several included both the enhancement expenditure and the 31.3.82 market value in the 31.3.82 market value column. The majority of candidates were aware of principal private residence exemption in one form or another but letting relief was largely ignored.

In (b) most candidates stated correctly that the cash element of the takeover consideration was chargeable and that the new shares took over the base cost of the old shares. The correct apportionment of the original cost and hence a correct computation were achieved by only a few.

In (c) many candidates put the rights issue shares in a FA 1985 pool instead of relating them back to the original holding. Most candidates who originally correctly allocated the rights issue shares then indexed the cost of the rights issue from 31.3.82 instead of the date of payment for the rights issue.

			Marks
(a)	Indexation allowance on cost and on enhancement expenditure	1	
	Two columns (or explanation) and lower gain taken	1	
	161 months	1	
	202 months	1	
	Letting relief - lower of: gain	1	
	£40,000 and	1	
	PPR exemption	1	
			7
(b)	Calculation of new shareholding	1	
	Recognition of capital gains tax charge	1	
	Apportionment of original cost	3	
	Calculation of gain	1	
			6
(c)	Identification of shares sold	1	
	Unindexed gain	1	
	Indexation allowance on original shares	1	
	Indexation allowance on rights issue	1	
			4
Total			17

Step by step answer plan

Overview

Question 3 always consists of 2 or 3 quite separate CGT questions. Part (a) is clearly on PPR; Part (b) requires a knowledge of how to treat shares and securities exchanged on a company take-over; and part (c) tests a situation in which shares are disposed from a 1982 holding on which there had been a rights issue. If this was a choice question you would have to decide if you were confident to cope with each of these three topics. As it is a compulsory question you just have to attempt it to the best of your ability. As we'll see it is not so daunting.

Step 1   Compute the gains on the house in part (a) based on cost and on March 1982 value. Remember that the 1981 enhancement must be excluded from the March 1982 gain calculation. As it happens, there are two marks for this relatively easy exercise.

Step 2   Analyse the period from March 1982 to the date of sale between periods of 'occupation' and periods of 'non-occupation'.

Step 3   Deduct PPR relief for the 'occupation' portion of the gain.

Step 4   Deduct letting exemption showing clearly the three limiting figures.

Step 5   In part (b) list out the value received on the take-over.

Step 6   Show that only the cash element will be immediately chargeable and identify the amount of the original cost apportioned to the cash element.

Step 7   Compute the gain in the normal way - ie, proceeds less cost less IA.

Step 8   In part (c) construct a normal 'two-gain' layout treating the rights issue as an element of enhancement.

Step 9   High light the lower gain as chargeable.

The examiner's answer

(a)   **Ashley**

	On cost £	On 31 March 1982 value £
Sale proceeds	196,500	196,500
Cost	(71,200)	
Enhancement expenditure	(7,000)	
31 March 1982 value		(72,000)
Unindexed gain	118,300	124,500
Indexation allowance (TN1):		
on cost $\dfrac{162.2 - 79.44}{79.44}$ (1.029) × 71,200	(73,265)	(73,265)
on enhancement expenditure		
$\dfrac{161.2 - 79.44}{79.44}$ (1.029) × 7,000	(7,203)	(7,203)
	37,832	44,032

	£
Lower gain is	37,832
Less: Principal private residence exemption	
$\dfrac{161}{202}$ (April 1982 - August 1992 + final 36 months) (April 1982 - January 1999)	30,153
	7,679
Letting relief – lowest of:	
(a) gain on letting £7,679	
(b) £40,000	
(c) principal private residence exemption £30,153	7,679
Chargeable gain	Nil

(Tutorial note:

1   The indexation allowance is on the higher of cost and 31 March 1982 value. In this situation, cost is £78,200 (71,200 + 7,000) as the enhancement expenditure was incurred before 31 March 1982.)

(b)   **Gillian**

As a result of the take-over Gillian will receive the following:

	£
2,000 ordinary shares in Upmarket plc at £10	20,000
4,000 preference shares in Upmarket plc at £3 each	12,000
and £6,000 cash	6,000
	38,000

The cash element of £6,000 is greater than 5% of £38,000 (£1,900) (and greater than £3,000) and will, therefore, become liable to capital gains tax immediately.

Apportionment of original cost:

	£
2,000 ordinary shares in Upmarket plc - $20,000 \times \dfrac{20,000}{38,000}$	10,526
4,000 preference shares in Upmarket plc - $20,000 \times \dfrac{12,000}{38,000}$	6,316
Cash - $20,000 \times \dfrac{6,000}{38,000}$	3,158
	20,000

	£
Capital gain - Cash received	6,000
- Attributable cost	3,158
	2,842
Indexation allowance $\dfrac{161.2-119.5}{119.5} \times 3,158$	1,102
Indexed gain	1,740

(c) **Jeffrey**

	On cost £	On 31 March 1982 value £
Sale proceeds	15,000	15,000
Original shares (1,500 × £2)	(3,000)	
Rights issue (1,000 × £1.50)	(1,500)	
Original shares (1,500 × £3.50)		(5,250)
Rights issue (1,000 × £1.50)		(1,500)
Unindexed gain	10,500	8,250

Indexation allowance (TN2)

- original shares $\dfrac{161.2 - 79.44}{79.44}$ (1.029) (5,402) (5,402)

On 31 March 1982 value (5,250)

  - rights issue $\dfrac{161.2 - 138.8}{138.8}$ (0.161) on £1,500 (241) (241)

	4,857	2,607

Lower gain is £2,607.

(Tutorial note:

2   A rights issue is deemed to have been acquired at the same time as the original shares. However, the indexation allowance must be calculated separately as the rights issue can only be indexed from the date of the expenditure on the rights.*)*

38 (Answer 4 of examination)

Examiner's comments and marking guide

This was a VAT question requiring candidates to prepare a VAT account from data provided and to explain certain aspects of the VAT appeals procedure.

Most candidates made a reasonable attempt at part (a) of the question although several candidates assumed the figures provided were VAT inclusive. Many candidates erroneously claimed bad debt relief. Many candidates did not know the date the tax was due for payment.

There were few correct answers to part (b).

				Marks
(a)	(i)	Input tax on purchases and expenses	1	
		Input tax on returns from suppliers	1	
		Output tax on sales	1	
		Output tax on omitted invoice	1	
		Car fuel charge	1	
		Output tax on returns from customers	1	
		No relief on bad debts	1	
			—	7
	(ii)			1
(b)	(i)			1
	(ii)	Confirm	1	
		Revise	1	
			—	2
Total				11

(**Step by step answer plan**)

Overview

Question 4 is always on VAT. Part (a) requiring a quarterly VAT account is relatively simple. Part (a) is mainly therefore an exercise in basic bookkeeping. Part (b) however requires you to know the time limit rules on VAT appeals initially before progressing to a VAT tribunal - something you either know or have to guess.

[Step 1]   For part (a) draw up and label a T account.

[Step 2]   Work through the 7 notes in the question deciding what credits and debits are needed in the account to represent respectively the amounts owing to and by Customs.

[Step 3]   Balance the account.

[Step 4]   Don't forget to claim the easy mark for part (a) (ii)

[Step 5]   If you know the answer to part (b) make sure you answer it in the two parts as required in the question.

(**The examiner's answer**)

(a)   (i)

VAT account

	£		£
Input tax on purchases		Output tax on sales	
9,600 at 17.5%	1,680	16,500 at 17.5%	2,887
Input tax on expenses		Understatement of Output	
2,400 at 17.5%	420	tax on previous return	
	———	3,000 at 17.5%	525
	2,100	Car fuel charge 228 at 17.5%	40
Input tax on returns to		(TN2)	———
suppliers 300 at 17.5%	(52)		3,452
	———	Output tax on returns from	
	2,048	customers 1,100 at 17.5%	(192)
VAT payable	1,212		———
	———		3,260
	3,260		
	———		

(ii)   The VAT is payable within one month of the end of the quarter, ie, by 30 June 1999.

(b)   (i)   A taxpayer who disagrees with a decision by Customs and Excise on the application of VAT may apply within 30 days to the local VAT office asking them to re-consider their decision.

(ii)   After re-considering their decision the Customs and Excise will do one of two things:

(1)   Confirm their original decision. The taxpayer then has 21 days to submit an appeal to a VAT tribunal; or

(2)   Revise their original decision. The taxpayer then has 30 days to submit an appeal to a VAT tribunal, if appropriate.

(Tutorial notes:

(1)   The VAT on a bad debt can only be reclaimed when the payment date of the debt is 6 months old.

(2)   If input tax is reclaimed on petrol (business and private) then Octavius must account for output VAT on the car fuel charge.*)

---

39   (Answer 5 of examination)

Examiner's comments and marking guide

The question originally dealt with the opening years of a pre 6 April 1994 business. This question has been re-written to reflect the current year basis and the examiner's comments have been omitted as being no longer relevant.

			Marks	
(a)	(i)	1995/96	1	
		1996/97	1	
		1997/98	1	
		Overlap relief to c/fwd	1	
			—	4
	(ii)	1998/99	1	
		1999/00	1	
		Application of overlap relief	1	
		Check of total	1	
			—	4
(b)		1999/00	1	
		2000/01	1	
		Discussion of difference	1	
			—	3
Total				11

The guide has been modified to reflect introduction of the current year basis

Step by step answer plan

Overview

Part (a) is clearly a simple exercise in applying the opening and closing rules for Schedule D I. Part (b) then requires you to modify your answer to part (a) and consider some elementary tax planning on choice of closure date.

Step 1   For part (a) determine the assessable amounts year by year remembering to use daily apportionment and applying overlap relief in the final year.

Step 2   Part (b) requires a rerun of part (a) except that the assessment for 1999/00 will be now be different as it is no longer the final year and there will now be an assessment for 2000/01 - the new final year.

Step 3   Part (b) is not complete until you have commented on the contrast of your answer to part (a) and part (b).

The examiner's answer

(a)   Assessable amounts

	£	£
1995/96		
(1.11.95 – 5.4.96)		
$^{156}/_{546} \times 40{,}500$		11,571
1996/97		
(6.4.96 – 5.4.97)		
$^{365}/_{546} \times 40{,}500$		27,074
1997/98		
(12 months ended 30.4.97)		
$^{365}/_{546} \times 40{,}500$		27,074
1998/99		
(y/e 30.4.98)		12,000
1999/00		
1.5.98 to 31.3.00		
(24,000 + 36,000)	60,000	
Less: Overlap profit		
(1.5.96 – 5.4.97)		
$^{340}/_{546} \times 40{,}500$	(25,219)	
		34,781
Total amount assessable		**112,500**
Check:		
Total profits		
(40,500 + 12,000 + 24,000 + 36,000)		112,500

(b)   Assessments (cessation 30.4.00)

	£	£
1995/96		
(as above)		11,571
1996/97		
(as above)		27,074
1997/98		
(as above)		27,074
1998/99		
(as above)		12,000
1999/00		
(y/e 30.4.99)		24,000
2000/01		
(1.5.99 – 30.4.00)		
(36,000 + 4,200)	40,200	
Less: Overlap profit		
(1.5.96 – 5.4.97)		
$^{340}/_{546} \times 40{,}500$	(25,219)	
		14,981
		116,700
Check:		
Total profits (112,500 + 4,200)		116,700

Did you answer the question?

Strictly there is no need to provide a proof in parts (a) and (b) that total profits earned equals total profits assessed but it is good practice and will uncover any arithmetic mistakes for you to go back and correct.

Assessments under the current year basis ensure that all profits earned are assessed (TN 1). If Chatru continues to trade for one extra month, earning an additional £4,200 his total assessments will increase by £4,200. However, by trading for one extra month, the amount assessed in 1999/00 is reduced from £34,781 to £24,000. This may be an income tax benefit if Chatru has little or no other income, as profits are now covered by the basic rate band.

Tutorial notes

1   Under CYB there is the opportunity to alter the timing of assessments over the final years and this should be considered in this form of question.

---

40   (Answer 6 of examination)

Examiner's comments and marking guide

This question listed a series of items appearing as charges against profits in a set of company accounts and candidates had to state how each item would be dealt with.

There was sufficient material in the question for most candidates to score reasonably well. Many candidates gave hazy answers and did not state for example that a charge on income had to be added back in the Case I computation and deducted in arriving at the profit figure chargeable to Corporation Tax.

Perhaps the most surprising item was number 7 which most candidates treated as a credit to the accounts.

	Marks
1 mark per item	11

Step by step answer plan

Overview

This is a series of 11 separate questions on profit adjustment for a mark each.

Step 1   Make sure you have read the requirements carefully before starting. Note that it is not just a question of adjusting profit. The question asks for the effect on the tax computations so, for example, in (5) the charge on income aspect must be mentioned.

Step 2   You are expected to deal with each part in the order presented. Leave a gap for any item you cannot answer in case you want to return to it later.

The examiner's answer

(1)   Add back depreciation of £6,000. No further adjustment necessary as dealt with under benefit-in-kind legislation.

(2)   Add back £21,000 as all entertaining expenditure other than for staff is disallowable. Allow £4,000 for company dinner. (By concession, no benefit arises for the employees, £20 per head being a 'reasonable' amount.)

(3)   Allow £2,500 (by statute).

(4)   .   The allowable element of the charge is calculated as follows:

$$£6,000 \times \frac{12,000 + 4,000}{20,000} = 4,800$$

£1,200 will therefore be added back.

(5)   This is treated as being a payment after deduction of basic rate tax and relief given as a charge on income. The £616 will be added back and £800 allowed as a charge on income.

(6)   The £30,000 will be added-back. The amount assessable on the lessor will be:

	£
	30,000
Less: 2% (6 – 1)	3,000
	27,000

This amount will be relieved to Uranus Ltd over the duration of the lease in equal instalments of £4,500 per annum for six years restricted for any AP where the lease does not run throughout (ie, first and last AP).

(7)   Allow interest calculated on accruals basis as a trading expense provided loan was for a trading purpose.

(8)   Allow the specific provision of £8,000 which was the best estimate at the balance sheet date.

(9)   Add back £120,000 as capital expenditure being the excess over the normal maintenance expenditure on a newly acquired asset. The annual maintenance cost equivalent will be allowed.

(10)   Allow the total cost as the subsidy is part of the cost of employing staff.

(11)   Allow the total cost as the warehouse could be used for its intended purpose from the date of purchase.

Did you answer the question?

The question does not ask for reasons although the examiner does give brief reasons in his answer in several places. It seems likely that with only one mark per point a correct answer would be sufficient without giving a reason.

Tutorial notes:

1   The allowable amount of lease rentals for expensive cars is:

$$\text{Hire charge} \times \frac{£12,000 + \frac{1}{2}(\text{retail price} - £12,000)}{\text{retail price}}$$

2   Accounts are prepared on the accruals and prepayments basis; however charges on income are the amounts actually paid.)

---

41   (Answer 7 of examination)

(**Examiner's comments and marking guide**)

This question required candidates to state the criteria which is applied in deciding whether a taxpayer is to be treated as 'employed' or 'self-employed'.

Answers were generally superficial - few criteria being given and these often repeated in two sections eg, an employer supplies his own tools, and later, an employee is supplied with tools.

Others answers were vague, describing the areas but failing to point out the deciding factor eg, specified hours (without mentioning the employee) or the supply of tools (without mentioning the employer).

Stronger candidates described the consequences of determining the position of an individual and described in full detail the various tax schedules and pension and National Insurance contributions as well as badges of trade.

	Marks
Contract for services and contract of service	1
Points 1 to 9	9
Combination of factors	1
	—
Total	11
	—

Step by step answer plan

Overview

This is a standard question on the tests developed primarily by case law to decide whether an individual is employed or self-employed.

Step 1 Plan out your answer carefully. At the very least jot down in rough all the tests you can remember before starting your formal answer. This is the time when you can concentrate best on recalling most of the tests.

Step 2 Start by stating the main difference - ie, the form of contractual relationship between the parties.

Step 3 List out all the tests you can remember - hopefully from your answer plan - writing a few words of explanation against each one.

The examiner's answer

The generally accepted main difference between employed (Schedule E) and being self-employed (Schedule D) is the difference between a contract of service and a contract for services. A contract of service is freely entered into between employer and employee where an employer offers employment and the employee agrees to work for him. A contract for services is an agreement between two persons relating to the provision of specific services, payment being made against an invoice.

The Inland Revenue and Department of Social Security, however, will specifically look at the following areas to assist them to determine whether a person is in the employed or self-employed category.

(1) **Work performance**. Employees must do work designated to them themselves. Self-employed persons can hire other people to do the work for them.

(2) **Control**. Employees work is controlled by the employer who will also stipulate hours of work. Self-employed persons decide when and how the work is done.

(3) **Payment and financial risk**. Employees are normally paid for a week's or a month's work and incur no personal financial risk. They may also receive overtime pay, holiday pay and sick pay. Self-employed persons are not normally paid time-related fixed amounts and bear the full financial risk of their business.

(4) **Place of work**. Employees will be told where to work, be it either at the employer's place of business or the employer's clients/customers. Self-employed persons will normally be free to choose whether to work at home or at the client's/customer's premises.

(5) **Equipment**. An employer will normally provide equipment for his employee's use. Self-employed persons will normally have to provide their own.

(6) **Work correction**. Employees will normally correct work during normal working hours and will not, as a result, suffer any financial loss. Self-employed persons may not be paid for unsatisfactory work which may have to be corrected in their own time.

(7) **Engagement and dismissal**. Employers have powers to take on and dismiss employees. Self-employed persons and their clients/customers will agree the terms surrounding the beginning and end of a contract.

(8) **Insurance**. Employers normally provide insurance cover for the actions of their employees. Self-employed persons will have to provide for their own insurance needs.

(9) **Exclusivity**. Employees normally work for only one employer. Self-employed persons may work for a number of clients/customers.

The final decision in any one case will probably depend upon a combination of the above factors and may ultimately have to be decided by the courts.

Did you answer the question?

It would be very easy to wander off the point and discuss the different tax or NIC treatment resulting from being assessable as an employee rather than self-employed This was not asked for and it would therefore not gain any marks!

Tutorial notes

1   As the answer asks for 'criteria' (ie, tests) - and there are in practice well over 10 - you can be fairly sure that you will earn more marks by listing down 9 or 10 tests with a brief comment on each than you could by listing 3 or 4 tests and describing them in detail

---

42   (Answer 8 of examination)

Examiner's comments and marking guide

This question required candidates to calculate each partner's share of a trading loss on the basis of (a) a set-off against their other income and (b) a carry forward against future trading income.

Many candidates obtained good marks on this question.   Of those carrying through their efforts many failed to apportion the accounts into 2 six-month periods.   Candidates who scored well in part (a) tended to receive the additional mark in part (b).

			Marks
(a)	Year to 30.9.98		2
	1.10.97 - 31.3.98		
	Interest on capital	1	
	Salary	1	
	Balance in psr	1	
	Cs notional profit	2	
		—	5
	1.4.98 - 30.9.98		
	Interest on capital	1	
	Balance in psr	1	
		—	2
	Total for year		1
(b)	Same basis of allocation		1
			—
Total			11
			—

Step by step answer plan

Overview

This is a standard loss apportionment question for a partnership with a change in the apportionment arrangements part way through the accounting period.

Step 1   For part (a) start by heading up an apportionment layout with a column for each partner and a total column.

Step 2   Take the first 182 days worth of the loss and apply the apportionment arrangements for the period up to 31 March 1998.

Step 3   As this results in a notional profit for one partner when there is an overall loss, allocate this between the other two partners in the ratio of their loss shares up to that point.

Step 4   Then take the remaining 183 days of loss and apply the apportioning arrangements for the period after 31 March 1998.

Step 5   Finish off part (a) by totalling the loss share for each partner.

Step 6   Part (b) might be easy to overlook. Essentially all you need to say is that whether a loss is to be used under s.380 (as in part (a)) or under s.385 (as in part (b)) it is apportioned between the partners in exactly the same way.

The examiner's answer

(a) The loss will be appropriated to the partners in accordance with the profit sharing arrangements for the loss-making accounting period.

	C £	J £	M £	Total £
1.10.97 - 31.3.98				
$(^{182}/_{365} \times 20,000) = 9,973$				
Interest on capital 5% $\times$ $^{182}/_{365}$	299	399	449	1,147
Salary $\times$ $^{182}/_{365}$	2,992	-	-	2,992
	3,291	399	449	4,139
Balance (in PSR) 1:2:2	(2,822)	(5,645)	(5,645)	(14,112)
	469	(5,246)	(5,196)	(9,973)
Allocation of C's notional profits				
(5,246 : 5,196)	(469)	236	233	-
	-	(5,010)	(4,963)	(9,973)
1.4.98 - 30.9.98				
$(^{183}/_{365} \times £20,000) = 10,027$				
Interest on capital 4% $\times$ $^{183}/_{365}$	241	321	361	923
Balance (in PSR) 1:1:1	(3,650)	(3,650)	(3,650)	(10,950)
	(3,409)	(3,329)	(3,289)	(10,027)
Total for year	(3,409)	(8,339)	(8,252)	(20,000)

(b) If the partners had had no other income and wished, therefore, to carry the loss forward under S385 ICTA 1988 the loss would still have been appropriated to the partners in accordance with the profit-sharing arrangements for the basis period in which the loss was sustained ie, the year ended 30 September 1998.

DECEMBER 1995 QUESTIONS

43   (Question 1 of examination)

Unplugged Utensils Ltd (UUL) is a United Kingdom resident company which has been manufacturing kitchen appliances since 1988. It has no associated companies. The following is a summary of the company's results:

	Year ended 31.12.95 £	Year ended 31.12.96 £	6 months to 30.6.97 £	Year ended 30.6.98 £	Year ended 30.6.99 (forecast) £
Schedule D Case I Profit/(loss)	100,000	(50,000)	60,000	(400,000)	50,000
Schedule A	–	22,000	–	20,000	–
Chargeable gains/ (losses)	50,000	–	(6,000)	5,000	–
Bank interest receivable	–	–	–	–	4,000
Gift aid payment (net)	–	3,000	–	3,080	3,080
Patent royalties received (gross amount)	–	20,000	10,000	–	–
Patent royalties paid (gross amount)	2,000	2,000	1,000	2,000	8,000
Dividends received	1,600	1,500	–	–	–

Notes:

(1)   The gift aid payment was the actual amount paid. Payments were made on 31 March.

(2)   All dividends were received and paid on 31 March.

(3)   The company had no losses to carry forward at 31 December 1994.

(4)   All patent royalties were paid and received on 31 March.

You are required:

(a)   to calculate the corporation tax liabilities for all years in the question after giving maximum relief at the earliest time for the trading losses sustained and any other reliefs;   **(15 marks)**

(b)   to show any balances carried forward; and   **(4 marks)**

(c)   to calculate the amount of any repayments of income tax due to the company, ignoring repayment supplements.   **(4 marks)**
                (Total: 23 marks)

44   (Question 2 of examination)

Tom, aged 63, has been married to Mary, aged 66, for 40 years. Tom is employed at an annual salary of £18,000 and is provided with a house which is owned by his employers. The house cost £120,000 and had a gross rateable value of £2,000. Tom had been provided with furniture for the house, costing £8,000 on 6 April 1997. On 5 April 1999 he bought the furniture from his employers for £2,000 when its market value was £4,000. Tom paid no rent for the accommodation and there was no business use. Tom was not required by his employers to occupy the house.

Tom received bank interest of £40 from Midland Bank on 30 June 1998.

In the absence of a company pension scheme Tom had entered into a personal pension scheme with a UK insurance company and paid the maximum premiums permitted each year. He also paid £600 (net) in May 1998 in respect of private medical insurance for himself and Mary.

In 1998/99 Mary has the following income and capital gains:

	£
State retirement pension	3,600
Dividends (amount received)	10,320
Capital gains	23,700

There are no allowable capital losses brought forward from earlier years. No election has been made to transfer any of the married couple's allowance to Mary.

You are required to calculate the 1998/99 taxation liabilities of:

(a) Tom; and **(12 marks)**

(b) Mary. **(10 marks)**
(Total: 22 marks)

Assume an official rate of interest of 10% pa.

---

45 (Question 3 of examination)

You are required to prepare computations of the capital gains arising in the following four situations, providing explanations as appropriate (only the asset in (c) is a business asset for taper relief purposes).

(a) Aphrodite purchased a plot of land in July 1990 for £60,000. In November 1998 she sold part of the land for £15,000 when the value of the remainder was £55,000. No other disposals of land were made by Aphrodite in 1998/99. **(5 marks)**

(b) Andromeda purchased a diamond necklace for £50,000 in June 1998. In July 1998 it was stolen and the insurance company paid £60,000 compensation. In October 1998 Andromeda purchased another necklace for £65,000. **(3 marks)**

(c) Ariadne had been a full-time working director of Ajax Manufacturing Company Ltd since 1983 and a shareholder of the company since 1 July 1992 when she bought 20% of the company's ordinary shares. On 1 July 1998, her 57th birthday, she retired from the company and sold all her shares. The capital gain on the disposal was £400,000. The market value of the assets in the balance sheet at that date were:

	£
Land and buildings	1,200,000
Goodwill	500,000
Plant and machinery (75% costing more than £6,000 per item)	400,000
Motor cars	300,000
Investments	600,000
Stock	450,000
Debtors	600,000

(6 marks)

(d) In August 1984 Aristotle purchased a seaside cottage for £50,000. The cottage was not his principal private residence. In September 1987, when its value was £80,000, he gave it to his wife, Antigone. In May 1998 Antigone sold it for £120,000. From August 1984 until May 1998 they were living together. **(4 marks)**
(Total: 18 marks)

---

46 (Question 4 of examination)

(a) **You are required** to state the records and accounts which must be kept for VAT purposes and to state for how long they must be retained by the trader. **(6 marks)**

(b)   Antrobus Ltd had the following transactions in the quarter to 30 June 1998:

	£
Standard-rated supplies (excluding VAT)	150,000
Zero-rated supplies	50,000
Exempt supplies	100,000

Input tax had been paid as follows:

	£
Standard-rated supplies	12,000
Zero-rated supplies	5,000
Exempt supplies	9,000
General overheads	4,000

The general overhead input tax cannot be directly attributed to any of the listed supplies.

You are required to calculate the VAT payable for the quarter.

(5 marks)

(Total: 11 marks)

---

47   (Question 5 of examination)

You are required to state:

(a)   the normal due date of payment of mainstream corporation tax;   **(1 mark)**

(b)   the normal date when the corporation tax return (CT 200) must be submitted, the 'filing date';   **(1 mark)**

(c)   two situations when the filing date is postponed;   **(2 marks)**

(d)   the circumstances under which no penalty is charged for late submission of a return;

(1 mark)

(e)   the penalties for failing to submit a corporation tax return on time;   **(4 marks)**

(f)   the action a company chargeable to corporation tax should take if a corporation tax return is not received, and the penalty for not taking such action.   **(2 marks)**

(Total: 11 marks)

---

48   (Question 6 of examination)

(a)   **You are required** to name three taxable social security benefits.   **(3 marks)**

(b)   **You are required** to calculate the National Insurance contributions payable for 1998/99 by both employer and employee in the following situations:

(i)   Sergio is employed at an annual salary of £52,000. He is paid weekly and is not contracted out of the state pension scheme. He was provided with a 1900cc company car costing £15,000 when new on which the business mileage was 20,000. He had use of the same vehicle for the whole of 1998/99. It was two years old. Petrol for both business and private mileage is provided by his employer.

(6 marks)

(ii)   Antionette is employed at an annual salary of £10,400. She is paid weekly and is not contracted out of the state pension scheme.   **(2 marks)**

(Total: 11 marks)

49 (Question 7 of examination)

You are required to briefly contrast the income tax, National Insurance and pension funding consequences of a taxpayer commencing a trade in January 1999 as:

(a)   a sole trader; and
(b)   a director of his own company.

(11 marks)

50 (Question 8 of examination)

Rachel commenced in business as a fashion designer on 1 July 1997, and made up her first accounts to 30 April 1999. Her profit for the period, adjusted for taxation, was £33,000.

You are required:

(a)   to calculate the assessable profit for the first three years of assessment;   **(6 marks)**

(b)   to calculate the 'overlap profits';   **(1 mark)**

(c)   to state one disadvantage of having 'overlap profits'; and   **(1 mark)**

(d)   to state how Rachel could have avoided the creation of 'overlap profits', supporting your statement with a relevant example.   **(3 marks)**

Note: for this question your calculations should be made in days and not months using the calendar provided (at the end of this book).

(Total: 11 marks)

ANSWERS TO DECEMBER 1995 EXAMINATION

43   (Answer 1 of examination)

Examiner's comments and marking guide

(i)   This was a corporation tax question which tested:

(1)   Setting off losses against current, previous and later profits;
(2)   Repayment of Income Tax on UFII; and
(3)   Treatment of trade and non-trade charges in the context of losses.

(ii)   In general the performance of candidates on this question was very disappointing. In many cases candidates demonstrated a complete lack of knowledge of the treatment of corporation tax losses. Specifically:

(a)   Many candidates did not know whether losses were to be set off before or after charges.

(b)   Similarly many candidates failed to make any distinction between trade and non-trade charges for the purpose of off-setting losses.

(c)   Perhaps the major problem with many candidates was the lack of a systematic approach for dealing with the multi-period situation. Most surprisingly, many candidates failed to use a columnar approach, as in the question preferring instead to set out each year on a separate page. This appeared to cause some confusion in addition to a loss of time through repetition of the narrative descriptions.

(d)   Many candidates were confused over how chargeable losses could be offset.

(e)   Many of the weaker candidates spent some considerable time explaining the nature of the loss relief rules in broad descriptive terms, rather than applying them to the circumstances of the question.

(f)   The treatment of income tax by the vast majority of candidates was extremely poor.

Clearly the above is not an exclusive list of weak areas but highlights some of the major problems and difficulties in what was an extremely poor performance.

			Marks
(a)	CAP to 30.6.99		
	Loss b/f s.393(1)	£50,000	1
	Bank interest	£4,000	1
	CAP to 30.6.97		
	Trade charge b/f from		
	CAP to 31.12.96	£2,000	1
	CAP to 31.12.95:		
	Chargeable gains	£50,000	1
	CT liability	£35,000	2
	Charges on income:		
	'Trade' as in answer		2
	'Non-trade' as in answer		1
	Un-relieved 'non trade' as in answer		2
	Working 1a (Loss to 31.12.96):		
	CAP to 31.12.96	£42,000	1
	CAP to 31.12.95	£8,000	1
	Working to 1b (Loss to 30.6.98):		
	CAP to 30.6.98	£20,000	1
	CAP to 30.6.98	£67,000	1
			—
			15
(b)	(i) Capital losses carried forward		1
	(ii) Losses carried forward:		

Unrelieved trading loss £263,000			1
Unrelieved 'trade' charges:			
CAP to 30.6.98	£2,000		1
CAP to 30.6.99	£8,000		1
			—
			4

(c) Working 2 - Income tax repayable:

CAP to 31.12.96	£3,500		2
CAP to 30.6.97	£2,160		2
			—
			4

Total   23
                                                                                                              ——

(**Step by step answer plan**)

Overview

The first question on the paper is always on corporation tax. It should be obvious to you from a first glance that this one mainly concerns relief for trading losses. The fact that there are two trading losses and a capital loss thrown in for good measure should not put you off. As we show below, there is a relatively simple set of steps for relieving losses.

The examiner knows that trading losses questions are not easy for most candidates and tends to avoid setting too many other tasks in such a question.

The question and the examiner's comments etc have been heavily edited to exclude references to material now deleted from the syllabus.

Step 1   Read the question and its requirements carefully. Part (a) requires a standard spread sheet type PCTCT layout modified for losses. The loss entries on this must be supported by a Loss Memo working. Part (b) is just a statement of remaining balances from part (a). For part (c) you have to consider the means of recovering income tax suffered on any UFII - ie, the two amounts of patent royalties received.

Step 2   Head up a 5 column PCTCT layout and put in the labels down the LHS as appropriate - eg, start with Schedule D I followed by a s.393(1) loss line.

Step 3   Head up a Loss Memo working for both losses and slot in the two trading losses.

Step 4   As we are told to take 'maximum relief at the earliest time' we will first be setting losses where possible against 'total profit'. Therefore fill in the PCTCT layout with all the income and gains figures but don't yet total the columns.

Step 5   You will deal with the earlier loss first. This will be set first, by election, against 'total profits' of the loss year. So total that column and set-off £42,000 of loss, recording this simultaneously in the Loss Memo.

Step 6   The £8,000 remaining can, by election, be carried back against total profits of the previous 12 months but not to displace any trading charges (ie, the maximum set-off would have been £148,000). Again update Loss Memo.

Step 7   Now total PCTCT in the first 2 columns and carry forward the unrelieved charge of £2,000 from the year to 31.3.96 against Sch DI in the following period.

Step 8   Next attend to the second loss and repeat the technique in steps 5 & 6 above. This time the carry back set-off is restricted to leave the £1,000 trading charge covered. The loss could be carried back a further 6 months (ie, a total of 12 months c/b) but there is no profit left to use it. This illustrates the importance of using losses in chronological order.

Step 9   Total columns 3 & 4 and carry forward the remaining loss.

Step 10 Use the loss against Sch DI in column 5 under s.393(1), total column 5 and place any unrelieved trading charges from columns 4 & 5 into the Loss Memo for further c/f.

Step 11   Compute CT on any PCTCT remaining.

Step 12   Highlight any unrelieved non-trading charges - there is usually a mark or two for this.

Step 13   For part (b) restate the figure for loss remaining and review the question and your answer for any less obvious remaining balances. You should spot the capital loss which you need to show here.

Step 14   Finally, for part (c), compute the income tax suffered on the two amounts of patent royalties received and reduce for the tax withheld on charges paid in the same AP. The net figures are repaid because there is no CT payable in the years concerned.

The examiner's answer

(a)

Unplugged Utensils Ltd

	Year ended 31.12.95 £	Year ended 31.12.96 £	6 months to 30.6.97 £	Year ended 30.6.98 £	Year ended 30.6.99 £
Schedule D Case I	100,000	–	60,000	–	50,000
Losses b/f [S393(1)]	–	–	(2,000)	–	(50,000)
Schedule A	–	22,000	–	20,000	–
Bank interest	–	–	–	–	4,000
Patent royalties	–	20,000	10,000	–	–
Chargeable gains	50,000	–	–	–	–
Total profits	150,000	42,000	68,000	20,000	4,000
S393A(1) relief (12/96)	(8,000)	(42,000)	–	–	–
S393A(1) relief (6/98)	–		(67,000)	(20,000)	–
	142,000	–	1,000	–	4,000
Charges on income					
Trade	(2,000)	–	(1,000)	–	–
Non-trade	–	–	–	–	(4,000)
Profits chargeable	140,000	–	–	–	–
CT payable at 25%	35,000	–	–	–	–
Unrelieved non-trade charges	–	4,000	–	4,000	–

(b)   (i)   Capital losses carried forward

	£
Losses of six months to 30 June 1997	6,000
Utilised in year to 30 June 1998	(5,000)
Carried forward	1,000

   (ii)   Carried forward under S393(1)

Trading losses (W1) including unrelieved trade charges = £273,000

(c)   Income tax repayable (W2)

	£
CAP to 31 December 1996	3,500
CAP to 30 June 1997	2,160
	5,660

WORKINGS

(W1) Loss memoranda

			£
(a)	Year ended 31 December 1996		
	Loss		50,000
	CAP to 31 December 1996 [S393A(1)(a)]		(42,000)
			8,000
	CAP to 31 December 1995 [S393A(1)(b)]		(8,000)
			–

			£
(b)	Year ended 30 June 1998		
	Loss		400,000
	CAP to 30 June 1998 [S393A(1)(a)]		(20,000)
			380,000
	CAP to 30 June 1997 [S393A(1)(b)]		(67,000)
			313,000
	CAP to 30 June 1999 [S393(1)]		(50,000)
			263,000
	Unrelieved trade charges [S393(9)]		
	CAP to 30 June 1998		2,000
	CAP to 30 June 1999		8,000
	Carried forward [S393(1)]		273,000

(W2) Income tax

- CAP to:	Income tax withheld on payment £	Income tax suffered on receipt £	Income tax repayable £
31 December 1996	1,500 [1]	5,000 [3]	3,500
30 June 1997	240 [2]	2,400 [4]	2,160

[1]	£6,000 at 25% (patent royalties £2,000 + gift aid £4,000)
[2]	£1,000 at 24% (patent royalties £1,000)
[3]	£20,000 at 25% (patent royalties received £20,000)
[4]	£10,000 at 24% (patent royalties received £10,000)

Tutorial notes

1 When the question was set, a loss could be carried back for 36 months - not just 12 months - under s.393A(1)(b). The change applies from 2 July 1997 and the examiner states that the old rule is no longer examinable. Therefore, in updating the question we have changed the year ends and some of the earlier figures to ensure that only the 12 month carry back situation can apply. For example, the loss of the year to 31.12.96 could go back 36 months but we ensure full relief by just 12 month carry back.

2 The loss relief techniques described in the step by step guide above can be summarised:

(a) Deal with earlier losses before later losses.

(b) Apply s.393A(1) relief against total profits in the year of loss then carry back.

(c) On carry back don't displace trading charges.

(d) Remaining losses and unrelieved trading charges must be applied under s.393(1) as soon as future trading profits arise.

44	(Answer 2 of examination)

(**Examiner's comments and marking guide**)

(i)   This was a personal tax question aimed, in the earlier part, at testing the tax treatment of certain benefits-in-kind, bank interest received, pension premiums and private medical insurance.

The latter part of the question examined candidates' knowledge:

- •   in dealing with the age allowances and their restriction when income exceeds the statutory limit;

- •   of the distinction between dividends and capital gains when allocating the lower rate and basic rate bands before calculating the respective liabilities to income tax and capital gains tax.

(ii)   Overall this was a badly answered question and caused candidates many problems in dealing with nearly all aspects of personal tax computations examined by the question. The most common errors are itemised below:

Part (a): TOM

Transfer of furniture: The calculation of the charge arising on the transfer of furniture to Tom was very poorly handled. Many candidates did not show the 1998/99 charge (£1,600) and most candidates did not consider the two alternative methods of calculating the charge, the higher of the amounts being assessable.

Pension premiums: Many candidates based their calculation of the personal pension payment on salary only and ignored the benefits-in-kind. A large number of those who did manage to compute the correct payment ignored the adjustment to income tax liability for the tax deducted at source.

Married couple's age allowance (MCAA): Personal allowances seemed to create all sorts of problems for many candidates ranging from identifying the correct allowance to its appropriate relief. When calculating the MCAA, a surprisingly large number of candidates ignored the restriction and any reference to Tom's statutory total income.

Even if, due to an earlier error, STI is lower than £16,200 candidates ought to explain, by way of a note, why the restriction is not required. Other candidates failed to realise that Tom is entitled to the higher MCA.

Medical insurance premium: A very large number of candidates showed this as a charge on income, which it ceased to be from 1994/95 onwards. This error was further compounded by grossing-up errors.

Part (b): MARY

Income: Grossing up dividends using the wrong fraction is still a common error. A very high percentage of candidates included chargeable gains as income in the personal tax computation. It follows that at least a similar percentage did not know the order in which dividends and chargeable gains were to be taxed.

Personal age allowance: This was handled relatively better than other parts of the question; common errors were ignoring the restriction and allocating the allowance to Tom.

Calculation of income tax: Since there was no non-dividend income chargeable capital gains would claim the lower rate band and dividends would fall in the basic rate band, but attracting tax at only 20%. A common error made by candidates was to allocate the lower rate band against the retirement pension (£3,600) which was already covered by Mary's personal allowance (£5,260). The correct treatment may be summarised as follows:

Income Tax:

		£
Dividends	(£11,240 @ 20%)	2,248
Tax credit	(£12,900 @ 20%)	(2,580)
Repayment		(332)

Capital gains	£
Lower rate: £4,300 @ 20%	860
Basic rate: ranks after non-dividend (if any) and dividend income ie,	
(22,800 - 11,240) £11,560 @ 23%	2,659
Higher: 1,040 @ 40%	416
	3,935

				Marks	
(a)	Benefits-in-kind:				
	1	House		1	
	2	Excess charge on house		1	
	3	Use of furniture		1	
	4	Transfer of furniture		2	
	Pension premiums			1	
	Bank interest			1	
	Treatment of medical insurance premiums			1	
	Income tax retained on:				
	Pension premiums			2	
	Married couple's allowance			2	
				—	12
(b)	A	1	Chargeable to income tax (£16,500)	1	
			Personal allowance	2	
			Note	1	
		2	Chargeable to capital gains tax (£16,900)	1	
	B	1	Charge at basic rate	1	
			Tax credit	1	
		2	Capital gains tax (£3,925)	2	
	C	Repayment		1	
				—	10
Total					22

(Step by step answer plan)

Overview

Question 2 is the compulsory personal tax question - mainly income tax but with a levening of capital gains tax. The first sentence sets the scene. This is a husband and wife question many years past the year of marriage. Further reading shows neither separation nor death befalls them in the year concerned. Their ages are given as 63(H) and 66(W). Keep in mind, therefore, the relevance to the PA and MCA and the PPC maximum.

Step 1 For part (a) construct a Taxable Income/IT standard layout with working notes as necessary. A separate column for savings income is not strictly necessary in this situation.

Step 2 For part (b) compute Mary's Taxable Income and her gains net of the annual exemption.

Step 3 Compute Mary's income tax and CGT recognising that while capital gains are usually taxed 'on top of' taxable income, capital gains are entitled to any part of the lower rate band unoccupied by non-savings income.

Step 4 Although Mary has a CGT liability, there is a repayment of income tax to highlight.

The examiner's answer

(a)

Tom
Income tax computation 1998/99

	£	Total £	Non-savings £	Savings £
Salary		18,000	18,000	–
Benefits-in-kind:				
House benefit	2,000			
Additional charge on house (W1)	4,500			
Use of furniture (W2)	1,600			
Transfer of furniture (W3)	2,800			
		10,900	10,900	–
		28,900	28,900	–
Personal pension payments (40%)		(11,560)	(11,560)	–
		17,340	17,340	–
Bank interest $\left(40 \times \frac{100}{80}\right)$		50	–	50
		17,390	17,340	50
Personal allowance		(4,195)	(4,195)	–
		13,195	13,145	50

Income tax payable:

		£
On non-savings income:	4,300 at 20%	860
	8,845 at 23%	2,034
On savings income:	50 at 20%	10
		2,904
Income tax retained on payment of personal pension premium 11,560 × 23%		2,659
		5,563
Married couple's allowance 2,710 (W4) at 15%		(406)
Income tax liability		5,157

WORKINGS

(W1)   £(120,000 – 75,000) × 10% = £4,500 (excess of cost of house over £75,000 × official rate of interest)

(W2)   20% × £8,000 = 1,600 (annual value)

(W3)   Greater of:

		£
(a)	MV	4,000
	Paid	(2,000)
	Excess	2,000
(b)	Original cost	8,000
	Less: annual value for 1997/98 and 1998/99 (2 × 20%)	(3,200)
		4,800
	Paid	(2,000)
	Excess	2,800

(b) is greater

(W4)   £

Income   17,390
Limit   16,200
                                                                   ─────────
Excess   1,190
                                                                   ─────────
Allowance   3,305
Less: ½ excess   595
                                                                   ─────────
Net allowance   2,710
                                                                   ─────────

Note: Private medical insurance paid net after deduction of basic rate tax if it qualifies for tax relief. (TN1)

(b)   **Mary**
                              Income tax computation 1998/99

(A)   The amounts chargeable will be:

(1)   Income tax
                                                                      £

        Dividends $\left(10,320 \times {}^{100}\!/_{80}\right)$ 12,900
        Pension   3,600
                                                                   ─────────
                                                                   16,500
        Personal allowance (W1)   5,260
                                                                   ─────────
                                                                   11,240
                                                                   ─────────

Note: the personal allowance would first be set against the retirement pension leaving the whole of the £11,240 attributable to dividends.

(2)   Capital gains
                                                                      £

        Gain   23,700
        Exemption   (6,800)
                                                                   ─────────
                                                                   16,900
                                                                   ─────────

(B)   The liabilities will be:

(1)   Income tax on dividends
                                                                      £

        11,240 at 20%   2,248
        Tax credit   2,248
                                                                   ─────────
        Repayment due   Nil
                                                                   ─────────

Note: the dividends are treated as falling in the basic rate band leaving the lower rate band for capital gains.

    (2)   Capital gains tax

	£		£
	4,300 at 20%		860
	11,560 at 23% (W2)		2,659
	1,040 at 40%		416
	16,900	amount payable	3,935

(C)   Repayment

There will be a repayment in respect of the tax credit attaching to the dividends covered by personal allowances. This will be £12,900 – £11,240 = £1,660 at 20% = £332 (TN2).

WORKINGS

(W1)

	£
Income	16,500
Limit	16,200
Excess	300
Allowance	5,410
Less: ½ excess	150
	5,260

(W2)   Basic rate band

	£
Available	22,800
Utilised by dividends	11,240
Available for capital gains	11,560

Tutorial notes

1   Relief for private medical insurance for the over 60s is usually given at source. The premium does not reduce STI for purposes of age relief restriction. This relief is being phased out in any case. For relief, payments must be made on a contract entered into before 2 July 1997. As contracts can only run for a year at a time, no qualifying contract will exist after 1 July 1998 at the latest.

2   An alternative way of reaching this answer would be as follows:

Income tax on dividends

	£
11,240 at 20%	2,248
Tax credit (12,900 × 20%)	2,580
Repayment due	332

45 (Answer 3 of examination)

Examiner's comments and marking guide

(i) A capital gains tax question testing the treatment of:

(a) part-disposals of land;

(b) compensation for loss where proceeds were fully invested in a replacement asset;

(c) retirement relief on disposal of shares in a personal company where some assets in the balance sheet are non-chargeable business assets and some assets are chargeable but are non-business assets; and

(d) treatment of an asset transferred from a spouse and then sold.

(ii) (a) Very few candidates mentioned the 'small proceeds' rule and of those who did only a small proportion stated the correct monetary and percentage limits.

A number of candidates had conceptional difficulty in apportioning the cost between the part sold and the part retained.

Most candidates were aware that indexation cannot create or increase a loss.

(b) (Examiner's comment no longer relevant).

(c) Plant and machinery not eligible for the chattels exemption was frequently excluded from the calculation of chargeable business assets whereas cars were often included. Some candidates attempted to scale down their gain eligible for retirement relief by 6/10 × £1,000,000 (the upper limit) despite the chargeable gain being only £400,000 and the eligible gain being £307,692. Many candidates forgot to show the non-eligible part of the gain as chargeable.

(d) Candidates were generally aware that husband and wife are connected persons but mainly unaware that they can transfer assets to each other at a tax value of cost plus indexation allowance producing a no gain/no loss situation. Many candidates mentioned gift relief overlooking the fact that a seaside cottage is not a business asset.

		Marks	
(a)	Summary of small disposals procedure and why not appropriate	2	
	Cost	1	
	Indexation	1	
	Restriction of indexation	1	
		—	5
(b)	Initial gains £10,000 (no indexation)	1	
	Treatment of gain	1	
	Reduced cost of (£55,000)	1	
		—	3
(c)	Chargeable business assets	1	
	Chargeable assets	1	
	Proportion of gain eligible for retirement relief	1	
	1st tranche relief	1	
	2nd tranche relief	1	
	Remainder of gain chargeable	1	
		—	6
(d)	Transferred at £56,950	2	
	No gain/no loss	1	
	Gain £30,361	1	
		—	4
Total			18

Step by step answer plan

Overview

Knowledge of capital gains rules is normally tested in question 3 with 2 or 3 or, as here, sometimes 4 quite separate parts. Note carefully that you have to 'provide explanations as appropriate'.

Step 1 For part (a) state why the small part disposal treatment cannot apply. Consideration of this point is clearly required by the reference to 'no other disposals of land' given in the question.

Step 2 Then construct a capital gain part disposal calculation remembering to apply the formula 'A/(A + B)' to the cost.

Step 3 For part (b) calculate the gain on the 'disposal' and assume that the opportunity to roll-over the gain is taken. Again, ensure an adequate explanation is given.

Step 4 For part (c) produce an analysis of the company's assets between chargeable business assets and chargeable non-business assets. There is no harm in showing the non-chargeable assets as excluded from both categories but this does not seem to appear in the marking scheme.

Step 5 Show the part of the gain qualifying for retirement relief and compute the appropriate amount of relief. Don't forget to add back in the non-qualifying part of the gain.

Step 6 Part (d) requires two computations - one on the inter-spouse disposal on a no gain/no loss basis, and the other on the disposal to a third party using the base cost determined in the first calculation.

The examiner's answer

(a)   **Aphrodite**

Although total disposals of land in 1998/99 are less than £20,000 the consideration of £15,000 exceeds 20% of the value of the land immediately prior to the sale (20% × £70,000 = £14,000). The small disposals procedure, whereby the disposal proceeds may be deducted from cost, cannot therefore operate in this case.

	£
Sale proceeds	15,000
Cost $\dfrac{15,000}{15,000+55,000} \times 60,000$	12,857
Unindexed gain	2,143
Indexation $\dfrac{161.2-126.8}{126.8}$ 0.271 × 12,857 = 3,484 restricted to	2,143
No gain/no loss	–

(b)   **Andromeda**

	£
Compensation	60,000
Cost	50,000
Gain	10,000

No indexation is available as the purchase occured after April 1998.

As the whole of the compensation was utilised within 12 months on a replacement necklace, Andromeda can set off the gain against the cost of the replacement asset for capital gains tax purposes.

	£
Cost of new necklace	65,000
Set-off gain	(10,000)
Reduced cost	55,000

(c)   **Ariadne**

WORKING

	Chargeable business assets £'000	*Chargeable assets* £'000
Land and buildings	1,200	1,200
Goodwill	500	500
Plant and machinery	300	300
Motor cars	–	–
Investments	–	600
Stock	–	–
Debtors	–	–
	2,000	2,600

Gain on disposal of shares = £400,000

		£
Proportion eligible for retirement relief $\dfrac{2,000}{2,600}$		307,692
Retirement relief		
1st tranche $\left(£250,000 \times \dfrac{6}{10}\right)$	150,000	
2nd tranche $\dfrac{(307,692 - 150,000)}{2}$	78,846	
		228,846
		78,846
Remainder of gain (400,000 - 307,692)		92,308
		171,154
Gain tapered to 92.5%		158,317

Did you answer the question?

The examiner did not expect you to go into detail as to why the qualifying period was only 6 years nor why retirement relief was available. There seems to be a principle of explanations only being appropriate in less mainstream situations.

(d)   **Aristotle and Antigone**

   (i)   Aristotle

	£
Cost	50,000
Indexation allowance to September 1987 $\dfrac{102.4 - 89.94}{89.94} = 0.139 \times 50,000$	6,950
Transferred to Antigone	56,950

Treated as a no gain/no loss situation.

Note: transfer value of £80,000 ignored.

(ii)   Antigone

	£
Sale proceeds	120,000
Deemed acquisition price	56,950
	63,050
Indexation allowance $\dfrac{161.2-102.4}{102.4} = 0.574 \times 56,950$	32,689
	30,361

Tutorial notes

1   In part (c) retirement relief is available because Ariadne has been a full time working director and the company is her personal company - 5%+ ownership. The qualifying period is the lesser of the period of directorship and the period of share ownership.

---

46   (Answer 4 of examination)

Examiner's comments and marking guide

(i)   **A two-part VAT question testing in part (a) details of VAT records and in part (b) a calculation of VAT.**

(ii)   Most candidates made a reasonable attempt at part (a). Part (b) was poorly answered with only a few candidates attempting to calculate the deductible input tax on the general overheads.

			Marks
(a)	1.	1	
	2.	1	
	3.	1	
	4.	1	
	5.	1	
	6 years	1	
		—	6
(b)	Output tax	1	
	Input tax:		
	Taxable	1	
	Zero-rated	1	
	Overheads:		
	No de minimis relief as greater than £625 pa	1	
	Calculation	1	
		—	5
Total			11

Step by step answer plan

Overview

Question 4 always concerns aspects of VAT and, as here, can provide some fairly easy marks. Part (a) is on the basic VAT admin point of the records and accounts to be kept and part (b) requires a partial exemption calculation. Both of these requirements should be obvious from a first glance.

Step 1 Write down 4 types of records, 'the VAT account', and 'the 6 year retention period' for the 6 easy marks on offer.

Step 2 For part (b) prepare a VAT return summary showing the output tax and giving the three amounts of recoverable input tax. The key to this answer is to calculate the proportion of unattributable input tax which is recoverable by its deemed association with taxable supplies.

Step 3 Comment on the provisional nature of the apportionment.

The examiner's answer

(a) The following records should be kept and retained for six years.

      (i)   Copies of the invoices issued.
      (ii)   A record of all outputs.
      (iii)   A record of all payments made.
      (iv)   Supporting evidence of all claims for input tax.
      (v)   The VAT account

(b)

Antrobus Ltd

	£	£
Output tax 150,000 at 17.5%		26,250
Input tax		
Taxable	12,000	
Zero-rated	5,000	
Overheads (W)	2,680	
		19,680
VAT payable		6,570

WORKING

Recoverable input tax on overheads.

$$\frac{\text{Taxable supplies}}{\text{Total supplies}} - \frac{150,000+50,000}{150,000+50,000+100,000} = 67\% \times £4,000 = £2,680$$

Note: The calculation of the apportionment of the overhead input tax would be provisional until the end of the annual accounting period.

Tutorial notes

1   When computing the attributable portion as in the working above it is always rounded up to the next highest percentage point - ie, 66.66667% in the answer becomes 67% - unless it computes as an exact percentage.

---

47   (Answer 5 of examination)

Examiner's comments and marking guide

(i)   **This was a question on the compliance rules of the 'Pay and File' system of corporation tax.**

(ii)   There were six parts to the question and most candidates attempting the question only answered the part relating to the date of payment of mainstream corporation tax. The remaining parts were parts poorly answered if attempted.

			Marks
(a)			1
(b)			1
(c)	(i)		1
	(ii)		1
(d)			1
(e)	(i)		1
	(ii)		1
	(iii)		1
	(iv)		1
(f)			2
Total			11

Step by step answer plan

Overview

This is clearly a question on administrative aspects of corporation tax - under the Pay and File system. Make sure you answer each of the six parts. However, judging from the examiner's comments above this is a good example of the type of question to avoid in the real exam. Where you are faced with such a multi-part question you should ask yourself honestly how many of the marks you could score. Here the first 2 marks are easy but if that is all you will score out of 11 consider choosing another question.

Step 1   Answer each part noticing the number of marks given. For example, if only one mark is given you probably only have to make one point. This is well illustrated in parts (a) and (b).

Step 2   In part (e) 4 marks have to be earned so try carefully to remember all the relevant paragraph of your study text. Part (e) is probably the only part where you need to make a rough plan before writing out your answer.

The examiner's answer

(a)   9 months after the end of the accounting period.

(b)   12 months after the end of the accounting period.

(c)   (i)   When the notice requiring the return is issued more than nine months after the end of the accounting period, the filing date is postponed to three months after the notice was issued.

(ii)   When the period of account exceeds 12 months the filing date is postponed to 12 months after the end of the period.

(d)   No penalty is charged where the return is made not later than the deadline for submitting accounts to the Company Registrar.

(e)   (i)   £100 for a delay of up to three months.

(ii)   £200 for a delay exceeding three months.

(iii)   The £100 and £200 penalties are increased to £500 and £1,000 respectively if the return in question is the third consecutive one to be filed late.

(iv)   An additional tax-related penalty of 10% of the tax unpaid six months after the return was due, if the total delay does not exceed 12 months; and 20% if the total delay exceeds 12 months.

(f)   The company must notify its chargeability to corporation tax to the Inland Revenue within 12 months of the relevant accounting period. The maximum penalty for not so doing is the tax unpaid 12 months after the end of the accounting period.

48   (Answer 6 of examination)

Examiner's comments and marking guide

(i)   **This was a two-part question testing Social Security and National Insurance contributions.**

(ii)   The first part was well done with most candidates managing to mention three Social Security benefits which were taxable. The calculation of National Insurance contributions in the second part was also well done with most candidates managing to put up a creditable attempt. Particularly encouraging was the fact that most candidates managed to correctly calculate the benefit-in-kind which formed the basis of the Class IA contribution.

					Marks
(a)	3 from 6				3
(b)	(i)	Sergio			
		1.	£303	4	
		2.	£5,200	1	
		3.	£2,236	1	
				—	6
	(ii)	Antoinette			
		1.	£728	1	
		2.	£780	1	
				—	2
Total					11

Step by step answer plan

Overview

This is a relatively easy question on National Insurance requiring the statement of three taxable social security benefits and some straightforward Class 1 and Class 1A calculations.

Step 1   List down the three items required in part (a). You only need to give three of the six shown in the examiner's answer.

Step 2   Compute the figures required for part (a) (i). This will be the Class 1A employer's contribution on the employee's car and fuel benefit amounts and the primary and secondary Class 1 charge on his salary. It is fairly obvious that you need to show there is an upper earnings limit for employee contributions but not for employer's.

Step 3   Compute the figures needed to answer part (b) (ii). The less obvious point here is that the earnings are in the 7% band (not 10%) for secondary contributions.

The examiner's answer

(a)   (1)   Retirement pension.
       (2)   Widow's pension.
       (3)   Jobseeker's allowance.
       (4)   Statutory sick pay.
       (5)   Statutory maternity pay.
       (6)   Incapacity benefit.

(b)   (i)   (1)   Class 1A - payable by employer only

Benefits-in-kind:

	£
Car £15,000 at 35%	5,250
Mileage reduction $\left(\frac{2}{3}\right)$	(3,500)
	1,750
Fuel	1,280
	3,030

£3,030 at 10% = £303

Did you answer the question?

You are not required to state the Schedule E amount or calculate the income tax that Sergio would be likely to bear on his income and benefits.

---

             (2)   Class 1 - payable by employer

£52,000 at 10% = £5,200

             (3)   Class 1 - payable by employee

	£	£
Weekly	64 at 2%	1
	421 at 10%	42
		43

Annual 52 × £43 = £2,236

Did you answer the question?

You are not required to give the pay day for Class 1A NIC.

     (ii)   (1)   Class 1 - payable by employer

Weekly £200 at 7% = £14

Annual 52 × £14 = £728

             (2)   Class 1 - payable by employee

	£	£
Weekly	64 at 2%	1
	136 at 10%	14
		15

Annual 52 × £15 = £780

49 (Answer 7 of examination)

Examiner's comments and marking guide

(i) **The question required candidates to contrast the income tax, National Insurance and pension funding consequences of a taxpayer trading as a sole trader or the director of his own company.**

(ii) Rather surprisingly this was not a popular question and most of the answers were very superficial. Very few candidates mentioned income tax payment dates, treatment of assets for own use and the distinction between the deductibility of expenses for sole traders and employees. A large number of answers concentrated on National Insurance by reproducing the information provided on the question paper and many candidates outlined the corporation tax rules affecting the company which were not required.

		Marks
1	Income tax	
	(i)	
	(a)	1
	(b)	1
	(ii)	
	(a)	1
	(b)	1
	(iii)	1
	(iv)	
	(a)	1
	(b)	1
2	National insurance	
	(a)	1
	(b)	1
3	Pension funding	
	(a)	1
	(b)	1
Total		11

Step by step answer plan

Overview

Your answer will have to cover the three topics - viz, IT, NIC and pensions - for each of the two types of business status with emphasis on opening years. Can you be sure of mentioning all the points the examiner has in mind for 11 marks? A lot will depend on having a carefully thought out structure to your answer before starting, not least so the examiner can follow the points you make.

Step 1   Start with a main heading of 'income tax' and decide on the sub paragraphs that should be covered.

Step 2   Under each sub-heading cover in separate paragraphs the treatment as sole trader and the treatment as director/shareholder.

Step 3   Then have a heading each for 'NI' and 'Pension Funding' and repeat the approach in step 2.

The examiner's answer

(a) **Income tax**

    (i)   **Basis of assessment**

           –   As a sole trader the taxpayer will be assessed on the current year basis under Schedule D Case I ie, the accounting date being treated as coterminous with the following 5 April. There are special rules to be applied for the opening years.

> As a director the taxpayer will be assessed under Schedule E on his remuneration, and dividends received in the tax year.

(ii)   **Income tax payment dates**

> As a sole trader equal payments on account of the income tax due will be paid on 31 January in the year of assessment and on 31 July following the year of assessment. A balancing payment (or repayment) will then be due on the following 31 January.

> As a director the Schedule E tax will be collected under PAYE at the time of receipt of the remuneration.

> As a shareholder lower rate tax will be deemed to have been accounted for by the tax credit attaching to the dividend and any higher rate liability will remain payable by 31 January following the year of assessment at the latest.

(iii)   **Deductibility of expenses**

> As a sole trader all expenses of the trade would generally be allowable if they were incurred 'wholly and exclusively' for the purposes of the trade. This same rule will apply to the expenses of the trade for corporation tax purposes.

> The taxpayer's own expenses would have to be incurred 'wholly, exclusively and necessarily' in the performance of the duties of the employment in order to be deductible for Schedule E.

(iv)   **Treatment of assets for own use**

> As a sole trader it will be necessary to disallow the private use proportion of expenses incurred on assets used partially for private use. A similar proportion of capital allowances on the same assets will be disallowed.

> As a director any private usage of company assets will be taxed under the benefit-in-kind provisions. There will be no disallowance of expenses or capital allowances.

Did you answer the question?

The examiner does not ask for a discussion of the corporation tax aspects of trading through a company as oppose to trading as an individual.

(b)   **National Insurance**

(i)   As a sole trader the taxpayer will be liable to pay Class 2 contributions (flat rate) and Class 4 contributions according to the level of profit. The Class 4 contributions will be collected at the same time as the Schedule D Case I income tax.

(ii)   When the trade is carried on by the company Class 1 (primary) contributions will be payable by the director and Class 1 (secondary) by the company. The amounts payable will be determined by the level of earnings. In addition a Class 1A contribution will be payable by the company in respect of any company car and private fuel provided for the personal use of the director.

(c)   **Pension funding**

(i)   As a sole trader any pension would have to be provided by a personal pension plan funded by premiums paid by reference to relief limited by age-determined percentages of net relevant earnings.

(ii)   The company may decide to set up an Inland Revenue approved pension scheme under which contributions could be paid by both the company and the director. The company contributions would not be assessed on the director and the director's contributions would be allowed as a deduction in arriving at his taxable pay. Where there is no company pension scheme the director may take out a personal pension plan. Premiums would be paid by the director under deduction of basic rate income tax.

50 (Answer 8 of examination)

Examiner's comments and marking guide

(i) **The question tested the new rules for Schedule D, Case I as they affect new unincorporated businesses commencing after 5 April 1994.**

(ii) Most candidates had prepared themselves for a question of this nature and as a consequence scored highly. The calculation of the assessable profit for the first three years was very well done and the calculation of the 'overlap profits' only marginally less so. Very few candidates mentioned the fact that overlap profits are not indexed for inflation and consequently lose monetary value. It was very pleasing to note that most candidates were aware of the advantages of choosing a 31 March or 5 April accounting date.

					Marks
(a)	1997-98	£13,762		2	
	1998-99	£18,004			2
	1999-2000	£18,004			2
					—
					6
(b)	£16,770				1
(c)					1
(d)	by choosing 5 April			1	
	example			2	
					—
					3
					—
Total					11
					—

Step by step answer plan

Overview

This is primarily a simple application of the CYB opening year rules but there are two minor problems which you should consider before choosing this question. The first period of account ends in the third year of assessment. Are you sure you know how the opening years apply to that situation? Also, three marks are given (part d) for advice on avoiding the creation of overlap profits. Again do you know or can you work out how to answer this?

Step 1 Schedule out the answer to part (a) for all three years showing clearly the basis period for each and the fraction of profits taken.

Step 2 Double check the number of days you have calculated in each fraction in step 1.

Step 3 Calculate overlap profits for part (b) stating, for your own benefit, the dates of the overlap period.

Step 4 Note down your answer to part (c). One disadvantage is the need to keep a record of overlap profits to carry forward and the length of the overlap period. However, the main disadvantage is the effect of inflation as stated and that's the one you should give.

Step 5 For part (d) you should know - or be able to work out - that the choice of a 5 April y/e will avoid creating overlap profits. There are 3 marks to earn so don't forget to give a 'relevant example'.

The examiner's answer

(a) **Rachel**

Assessment:

1997/98 (1 July 1997 to 5 April 1998) $\dfrac{279 \text{ days}}{669 \text{ days}} \times £33,000 = £13,762$

1998/99	(6 April 1998 to 5 April 1999)	$\dfrac{365 \text{ days}}{669 \text{ days}} \times £33,000 = £18,004$
1999/2000	(1 May 1997 to 30 April 1998)	$\dfrac{365 \text{ days}}{669 \text{ days}} \times £33,000 = £18,004$

(b)   **Overlap profits**

The profits assessed twice are those for the period 1 May 1998 to 5 April 1999.

$$\dfrac{340 \text{ days}}{669 \text{ days}} \times £33,000 = £16,770$$

(c)   The disadvantage of utilising overlap relief in the future is that it will lose value as no allowance is being made for the effects of inflation.

(d)   **Avoidance of overlap profits**

By choosing an accounting date conterminous with the fiscal year it is possible to avoid the creation of 'overlap profits'. If Rachel had chosen 5 April as her accounting date instead of 30 April the assessments for the first three years would have been based on the following basis periods with a consequent absence of 'overlap profits'.

Year of assessment	*Basis period*
1997/98	1.7.97-5.4.98
1998/99	6.4.98-5.4.99
1999/2000	6.4.99-5.4.2000

Did you answer the question?

For a 'relevant example' in part (d) note that the examiner did not require you to make up any figures. He just wanted you to demonstrate that overlap profits cannot arise if a 5 April year end is used.

Tutorial notes

1   Using a 5 April and not a 30 April year end may make a significant difference to assessable amounts in the year of cessation. If Rachel ceases on 31 December 2010, for example, her 2010/11 basis period is 9 months from 6 April 2010 in the first instance, but is 20 months from 1 May 2009 in the second instance, albeit with 11 months of overlap relief brought forward. In 2010 values the overlap relief created over 10 years earlier may not be sufficient to give a 'fair' 9 months of assessable profits.

JUNE 1996 QUESTIONS

51   (Question 1 of examination)

Unquoted Untruths Ltd (UUL) is a publishing company. It is resident in the United Kingdom and has been trading since 1980. It has no associated companies. The company's results for the year ended 31 December 1998 are:

	£
Adjusted Schedule D Case I profit	382,000
Bank interest	4,000
Loan interest received (gross amount)	25,000
Debenture interest paid (gross amount)	17,000
Dividends received	43,000

Notes:

(1)   Income tax has been deducted from the loan interest received and the debenture interest paid at 20%.

(2)   There were no losses brought forward at 1 January 1998.

(3)   Dividends received from UK companies

The amounts of dividends received were:

	£
11.9.98	8,000
19.11.98	35,000
	43,000

(4)   Loan interest received

The gross amounts of loan interest received were:

	£	
28.2.98	15,000	3000
19.6.98	10,000	2000
	25,000	

The accrued amount for the year was £26,000.

(5)   Debenture interest paid:

The gross amounts of debenture interest paid were:

	£	
19.4.98	8,000	1600
19.9.98	9,000	1800
	17,000	

The accrued amount for the year was £18,000 which is the amount deducted in the adjusted profit.

(6)   The bank interest received during the year is the same as the amount accrued.

The company owns three properties which are let. All rents are receivable quarterly in advance on the calendar quarter days, 1 January, 1 April, 1 July And 1 October.

(i)   Property 1 is a shop which is let unfurnished on a tenant's repairing lease. The lease at an annual rental of £6,000 ended on 31 December 1997. The property was re-let from 1 July 1998 on a new lease at an annual rental of £5,000. Between April and June when the property was empty internal decoration work was carried out costing £3,500.

(ii)   Property 2, also a shop, is let un-furnished on a landlord's repairing lease. The shop was purchased in July 1998. Immediate remedial work costing £12,000 was required to repair the foundations which had slipped in May 1998. The property was then let from 1 October 1998 at an annual rental of £20,000. The incoming tenant also had to pay a premium of £5,000 in return for the granting of a seven-year lease.

(iii)   Property 3 is a house which is permanently let furnished on a landlord's repairing lease. The annual rental is £2,500.

Expenditure incurred during the year was:	£
Routine decoration and maintenance costs	2,000
Water rates	200
Council tax	400
	2,600

A 10% wear and tear claim for furniture and fittings was to be made rather than claim the renewals basis.

You are required

(a)   to prepare entries relating to income tax as they would appear on forms CT61 to be submitted to the Collector of Taxes for the quarterly periods to 31 December 1998 and

(3 marks)

(b)   to calculate the corporation tax payable for the year ended 31 December 1998.

(17 marks)
(Total: 17 marks)

---

52   (Question 2 of examination)

Mario and Marisa married in 1983. Mario is now 45 and Marisa is 42. No elections have been made by Mario and Marisa in respect of the married couple's allowance for 1998-99.

In 1998-99 Mario received a salary from his employer of £28,000. Mario was provided with a company car by his employer. Until 5 September 1998 he had the use of a 1800cc petrol car which was first registered on 1 January 1995 and whose list price was £14,000. On 6 September 1998 the car was changed for a 2300cc new diesel car with a list price of £16,000.

All fuel was paid for by his employer.

The car mileages were:

6.4.98 - 5.9.98 12,000 of which 9,000 was business use;

6.9.98 - 5.4.99 10,000 of which 8,000 was business use.

Mario was also provided with a mobile telephone costing £50, by his employer on 6 October 1997. The following costs were incurred in 1998-99 by Mario's employer:

	£
Connection charge	60
Monthly line rental	240
Telephone calls	200
	500

20% of all calls were private.

Mario received bank interest from Lloyds Bank of £120 on 30 June 1998. Mario and Marisa moved into a new home on 6 April 1998.

The purchase of the house was funded by two non-MIRAS loans:

(1)   A loan of £20,000 from Mario's employer on which annual interest of 4% was payable and

(2)   A loan of £6,000 from Marisa's mother on which annual interest of 3% was payable. Marisa pays the interest.

No capital repayments had been made on either loan at 5 April 1999. No elections concerning the allocation of interest paid have been made in respect of either loan. There were no other loans on the house.

Marisa has made capital gains totalling £17,000 in 1998-99.

Marisa had for many years carried on a garment manufacturing business and made up annual accounts to 31 March. Her adjusted Case I profit to 31 March 1999 was £40,000 before capital allowances and the capital allowances on plant and machinery were £2,500. On 1 April 1990 she purchased a new factory for £100,000 which was immediately brought into use. It was not in an Enterprise Zone. Between 1 January 1992 and 31 December 1993 the building was let to a mail order company as storage space. During this time Marisa's business was conducted from rented premises. Between 1 January 1994 and 30 September 1998 Marisa re-occupied the factory. On 30 September 1998 Marisa sold the factory for £55,000, again moving the business to rented premises.

You are required to calculate the tax payable for the year 1998-99 by:

(a)	Mario and	**(14 marks)**
(b)	Marisa	**(10 marks)**

Note that for businesses which commenced before 6 April 1994, profits were assessed on PYB and capital allowances were computed on PYB. Thus capital expenditure in the year to 31 March 1991 would attract CAs first in 1991/92. To change CAs from PYB to CYB, 1996/97 was a change over year with, here, a two year basis period ending 31 March 1997 - but with only one years worth of WDA.

(Total 24 marks)

---

53   (Question 3 of examination)

You are required to prepare computations of the capital gains arising in the following three situations, providing explanations as appropriate. No rebasing election has been made in any case.

(a)   Laurent purchased an antique table for £7,500 in July 1995. He sold the table in August 1998 for £4,000.

(2 marks)

(b)   Marco who has a dry-cleaning business, purchased a building for business use in June 1981 for £60,000. In September 1998 he sold the building for £150,000. Its value in March 1982 was £50,000. Marco had purchased a replacement building to carry on his business in December 1997 for £130,000. Marco claimed any available reliefs.

(5 marks)

(c)   Fabio had the following dealings in the shares of Casartelli Holdings plc, a quoted company.

		Number of shares	£
November 1980	bought	5,000	15,000
May 1985	bonus (1 for 5)	1,000	-
July 1992	bought	3,000	12,000
September 1993	rights (1 for 6)	1,500	5,250
November 1998	sold	5,000	28,000

The 31 March 1982 value adjusted for the bonus issue was £3.25p per share.

(13 marks)
(Total: 20 marks)

---

54   (Question 4 of examination)

You are required

(a)   to state when a VAT 'default surcharge' arises and for how long a 'default surcharge period' lasts.

(4 marks)

(b)   to state when a VAT 'serious misdeclaration' occurs, the limits above which a misdeclaration is regarded as serious and the maximum penalty and

(4 marks)

(c)   to state under what circumstances Customs and Excise may raise assessments for VAT 'default interest' and the period for which interest is charged.

(3 marks)
(Total: 11 marks)

---

55   (Question 5 of examination)

Ulysses Ltd, a manufacturing company, makes up annual accounts to 30 April.

In late March 1999 you were invited to the company's pre-year end meeting when the following matters were discussed. The company directors were particularly interested in hearing your advice on the *timing* of the proposed transactions.

(a)   The sale of an asset which was to be simultaneously replaced. Both assets are classified for capital allowances purposes as 'short-life' assets.

(b)   On 1 May 1974 the company had purchased a new industrial building for £30,000 which was brought into use immediately. A new and larger factory was purchased in December 1998 and the 1974 factory was now surplus to the company's needs. The 1974 factory was on the market for sale and would hopefully realise £150,000.

You are required to state your advice on all the matters raised:

(a)

(3 marks)

(b)

(4 marks)
(Total: 7 marks)

56   (Question 6 of examination)

(a)   Topic no longer examinable.

(b)   Sean began his car repair business from a rented workshop on 1 May 1996. His trading profits, as adjusted for taxation, were:

	£
Period to 30.6.97	18,000
Year ended 30.6.98	20,000
Year ended 30.6.99	25,000

Additions and sales of plant and machinery were:

		£
1.7.96	Additions	3,000
1.5.97	Additions	2,000
1.11.97	Sale proceeds	1,500
1.12.97	Additions	6,000

You are required

(i)   to calculate the assessable amounts for the years 1996-97 to 1999-00 inclusive and   **(7 marks)**

(ii)   to calculate the 'overlap' profits   **(1 mark)**

NB for part (b) of this question your calculations must be made in days and not months, using the calendar provided in the tax tables.

(Total: 8 marks)

57   (Question 7 of examination)

Norma, who had been in business as a confectioner since 1 May 1994, disposed of the business and retired on 31 May 1998 when she was 56 years old. She does not intend to start any other business.

Her trading profits/(losses), as adjusted for taxation were:

	£	
Period ended 31.12.94	21,000	profit
Year ended 31.12.95	17,000	profit
Year ended 31.12.96	14,000	profit
Year ended 31.12.97	11,000	profit
Period ended 31.5.98	(5,000)	loss

Norma had no other income

Required

(a)   to calculate the amount of any loss relief claim to which Norma is entitled and to show how this would be allowed and

(8 marks)

(b)   to state any reliefs from capital gains tax to which Norma would be entitled on disposal of the business assets.

(3 marks)

NB No calculations are required in part (b) nor need any reference be made to taper relief.

(Total: 11 marks)

58 (Question 8 of examination)

Fred has been a self-employed builder for 20 years. He was born on 31 August 1938 and is contemplating retirement in a few years time. He consults you in early June 1999 about the payment of premiums into a personal pension scheme. He has paid annual premiums of £5,000 for each of the past 7 years and assures you he has enough money to pay the maximum amount allowed.

Fred's agreed taxable profits for the past 7 years are:

	£
1992-93	18,000
1993-94	20,000
1994-95	22,000
1995-96	24,000
1996-97	26,000
1997-98	28,000
1998-99	30,000

He expects his taxable profits to be at least £30,000 for the next two tax years.

You are required to calculate the additional premiums which Fred is permitted to pay and to advise him when to pay the premiums to obtain the maximum tax advantage.

(11 marks)

(Assume that any tax relief should either be taken at 40% or at the basic rate, but not at the lower rate.)

ANSWERS TO JUNE 96 EXAMINATION

---

51   (Answer 1 of examination)

(**Examiner's comments and marking guide**)

(i)   **A two-part corporation tax question testing:**

(a)   the preparation of entries in relation to income tax as they would appear on forms CT61 for the year ended 31 December 1998; and

(b)   the calculation of the corporation tax liability for the year ended 31 December 1998, including an income from property calculation.

(ii)   In general terms the performance of candidates on this relatively straightforward question was a little disappointing. In particular, many candidates demonstrated little knowledge of the rules governing properties. In mitigation however, the CT61 computations had improved from the previous occasion this type of question was set.

Common errors included the following:

In part (a), many candidates failed to express the relevant calculations in the format required by form CT61. This was the case even for those candidates who ultimately calculated the net amounts of income tax correctly. The income tax computations frequently showed quarterly UFII and charges rather than tax deducted and suffered.

Bank interest was frequently grossed up.

A number of the weaker candidates continue to include FII in the calculation of profits to corporation tax.

There were many errors in the treatment of property income. Some examples were as follows:

*   In the case of Property 2, many candidates correctly calculated the lease premium, but then ignored the rental income.

*   Many candidates were confused over the deductibility of expenses.

On a more positive note, a large number of candidates calculated the wear and tear allowance on Property 3 correctly.

(iii)   Overall, while there were some positive aspects to candidates' performance on this question, there remain a number of weaknesses in core areas of corporation tax.

			Marks
(a)	Total tax deducted		1
	Total tax suffered		1
	To be deducted against CT		1
			— 3
(b)	Bank interest £4,000		1
	Debenture interest paid treated as an expense		1
	Working 1		
	Property 1 -		
	Rent	£2,500	1
	Repairs	£3,500	1
	Property 2 -		
	Rent	£5,000	1
	Premium	£4,400	1
	Repairs - not allowable		1
	Property 3 -		
	Repairs and expenses		1

Wear and tear allowance	1	
Summary	1	
Working 2		
Calculation of 'P'	1	
Determination of rate	1	
Charge at 31%	1	
Taper relief calculation	1	
	—	14
Total		17

Step by step answer plan

Overview

As usual, question 1 requires a CT computation but this time 3 marks are also given for form CT 61 entries - ie, quarterly accounting for income tax. This much is obvious from the requirements. A glance through the question then shows the normal PCTCT elements, the information for quarterly accounting and detailed notes on property income.

Step 1   There is no good reason not to start with part (a). In fact, the quarterly accounting conclusion will probably be needed later in your answer so should be done first in any case.

Step 2   Head up a CT61 standard layout IT.

Step 3   Notes 4 and 5 give the detail for IT accounting. However, remember each year stands alone for IT accounting - no balances b/f to look out for. Also bank interest, being received gross, is irrelevant and only the tax suffered/withheld on other items need be considered - gross amounts are not needed.

Step 4   Highlight any conclusions from part (a), especially figures needed later in part (b).

Step 5   Head up a PCTCT layout for part (b) and fill in from the question.

             As the notes in the question are not cross-referenced to the general results block, take care that all required adjustments are identified.

Step 6   Produce workings for the property income figures either property by property or as a single working. As the results are combined at the end it does not matter.

Step 7   Compute CT on PCTCT using a separate working to consider 'profits' and FY straddle etc. and deduct IT recoverable figure generated in part (a).

Step 8   Check that you have cross-referenced all workings to your answer and have explained why you treated items in a particular way. For example, why the FY straddle has no impact on the CT calculation. Use your judgement on how much explanation is needed.

Step 9   Re-read the question to ensure nothing has been overlooked.

(The examiner's answer)

(a)

Unquoted Untruths Ltd

CT61 forms

Income Tax

	Tax deducted on payment £	Tax suffered on receipt £	IT payable/ (repayable) £
1.1.98 - 31.3.98	-	3,000	-
1.4.98 - 30.6.98	1,600	2,000	-
1.7.98 - 30.9.98	1,800	-	-
1.10.98 - 31.12.98	Nil return		
	3,400	5,000	

The excess of the income tax suffered over the income tax deducted (1,600) will be set-off against the corporation tax.

Unquoted Untruths Ltd

(b)

Corporation tax computation

Chargeable accounting period ended 31 December 1998

	£
Schedule D Case I profit	382,000
Bank interest	4,000
Unfranked investment income (loan interest)	26,000
Schedule A (W1)	8,110
Chargeable profits	420,110
Corporation tax payable (W2)	107,490
Income tax suffered (part (a) (ii) of answer)	(1,600)
Corporation tax payable	105,890

WORKING 1

Income from property

Schedule A

	Property 1 £	Property 2 £
Rent receivable	2,500	5,000
Premium assessable	-	4,400*
Repairs	(3,500)	- **
	(1,000)	9,400

	£
* Premium	5,000
$2\% \times (7 - 1) \times 5,000$	(600)
	4,400

**not allowable as remedial work necessary before purchase

Property 3

	£
Rent receivable	2,500
Repairs	(2,000)
Expenses	(600)
W and T allowance	(190)*
	(290)

* 10% × (2,500 – £600 water rates and council tax)

Total under Schedule A: 9,400 - 1,000 - 290 = **£8,110**

WORKING 2

Corporation tax payable

Although the accounting period is partly in financial year 1997 (1/4) and partly in financial year 1998 (3/4) there is no need to apportion the chargeable profits as the upper and lower limits and the rates of CT are the same for each financial year. The figure of 'P' (£420,110 + FII £53,750) £473,860 lies between the lower and upper limits and therefore the marginal rate will apply.

	£
420,110 × 31%	130,234
Marginal relief	
$(1,500,000 - 473,860) \times \dfrac{420,110}{473,860} \times 1/40 =$	(22,744)
	107,490

Tutorial notes

1   As the full corporation tax rate and the marginal relief fraction remain unchanged between FY97 and FY98 it is not necessary to calculate the full rate of tax and the marginal relief in two separate parts.

2   You are given the 'Adjusted Schedule D Case I profit'. This will be after deducting debenture interest paid using the correct accruals basis so no further adjustment is needed.

3   IT items for quarterly accounting are always dealt with on an actual paid/received basis whereas loan interest received is dealt with for PCTCT purposes on an accruals basis.

4   Bank and building society interest is always received gross by a company and shown in PCTCT on the normal accruals basis. There is usually a mark allocated for not grossing up bank interest.

5   It would be perfectly acceptable to calculate the Schedule A income as if all the property letting was a single business - which it is for tax purposes.

---

52   (Answer 2 of examination)

(**Examiner's comments and marking guide**)

(i)   **A personal tax question testing the calculation of car and fuel benefits, the treatment of loan interest on property outside the MIRAS scheme and industrial buildings allowance where the property was sold for less than cost after a period of non-industrial use.**

(ii)   (a)   *Car benefit*

Most candidates managed to pick up good marks in this area, although many had problems in calculating the correct mileage reduction in respect of the first car. A large number of candidates time-apportioned the benefits using days which though more accurate is also more time consuming and not essential in this instance. It is quite acceptable and normal practice in examinations to time-apportion the car and fuel benefits to the nearest month for Schedule E computations.

Mobile telephone

Many candidates, quite incorrectly entered an additional charge (£40) for private use, showing a total charge of £240 (200 + 40). The maximum benefit is equal to the standard charge of £200 per annum.

Beneficial loan

This was badly dealt with by the majority of candidates. Although the calculation of the actual benefit was fairly straightforward, the calculation of the relief (in the form of a tax reducer) was beyond most candidates.

Personal allowances and tax liability

The relief for married couples allowances was generally well handled, although some candidates applied the wrong rate (20% instead of 15%) in calculating it.

(b)   This computation, compared to the income tax computation in part (a) was badly done, largely due to the treatment of industrial buildings allowances, capital gains and the loan from Marisa's mother.

Industrial buildings allowances

Answers in this area were rather messy and showed a clear lack of understanding of the basic principles. A very large number of candidates were unable to identify the first tax year when IBAs would become available (ie, 1991/92) which in turn led to errors in the calculation of notional WDAs and the residue of expenditure before sale. Only a few candidates progressed beyond this point and calculated adjusted net cost and the balancing allowance. Many candidates, strangely, treated the net cost (proceeds minus cost) as a capital loss and set it against Marisa's capital gains.

CGT calculation

A surprising number of candidates incorrectly included the capital gains in Marisa's personal tax computation in arriving at her 'taxable income'.

(iii)   In general, the answers to this question were satisfactory and there was a definite improvement on the personal tax question in the December 1995 diet. Overall part (a) was better answered than part (b).

			Marks	
(a)		Mobile phone	1	
		Assessment on beneficial loan	1	
		Bank interest	1	
		Income tax calculation	1	
		Married couple's allowance	1	
		Loan interest relief	1	
			—	6
(b)	(i)	Net Case I assessment	1	
		Loan interest relief	1	
	(ii)	Annual exemption	1	
		Capital gains tax calculation	1	
			—	4

Working 1

Car 1		
35%	½	
Mileage reduction	1	
Age reduction	1	
Time reduction	1	
Car 2		
35%	½	
Mileage reduction	1	
Time reduction	1	
Fuel benefit		
Car 1	1	
Car 2	1	
	——	8

Working 2

Total allowances claimed	1	
Residue of expenditure before sale	1	
Net cost	1	
Non-industrial use	1	
Adjusted net cost	1	
Balancing allowance	1	
	——	6

Total   24

(Step by step answer plan)

Overview

Question 2 invariably concerns the personal taxation of a married couple - mainly computing taxable income and income tax but with a CGT computation on a supplied gains figure. Here the husband is an employee with benefits to calculate. Ages are given as usual but age relief is clearly ruled out and the other main age-sensitive factor - maximum relief for PPCs - does not seem to be present. Also there is no apparent tax interaction between the spouses. For example, the MCA has not been elected away from the husband and he clearly has enough income to use the MCA credit in full. Turning to the wife, she is clearly assessable under Schedule D I with IBAs to compute. After one read through of the question you should have picked up most of these points and have a good idea of the shape your answer will take.

Step 1   Part (a) concerns the husband, Mario. Produce a Taxable Income/IT layout for him with separate workings for the benefits.

Step 2   Review the question down to and including the notes on the loans to ensure nothing has been overlooked. Have you remembered to give a tax reducer for the non-MIRAS interest including the amount assessable on Mario as a benefit?

Step 3   The key to part (b) is an IBA working. Unfortunately we have had to give some guidance on working out past IBAs as earlier years were under PYB and this is no longer examinable. Essentially there were 7 basis periods giving 4% WDAs up to the year of sale but only 5 lots of WDAs were given. The other 2 were only 'notional' on account of non-industrial use.

Step 4   Produce a Taxable Income/IT layout for Marisa again not forgetting the relief for non-MIRAS interest.

Step 5   Conclude with Marisa's CGT computation treating the gains as taxable on top of the taxable income.

Step 6   Review the part of the question concerning Marisa to ensure nothing overlooked.

Step 7   Cross reference all workings into the main part of your answer.

The examiner's answer

(a) Mario

Income tax computation for 1998/99

	£
Earned income	
Salary	28,000
Benefits-in-kind:	
Car and fuel (W1)	4,268
Mobile phone	200
Beneficial loan	
(£20,000 × (10% – 4%))	1,200
Investment income	
Bank interest (£120 × $^{100}/_{80}$)	150
Statutory income	33,818
Personal allowance	(4,195)
Taxable income	29,623

	£
Non savings income	
4,300 at 20%	860
22,800 at 23%	5,244
2,373 at 40%	949
29,473	7,053
Savings income	
150 at 40%	60
	7,113
Married couple's allowance	
(£1,900 at 15%)	(285)
Interest on home loan (£20,000 at 10% =	
£2,000 at 10%)	(200)
Income tax liability	6,628

(b) Marisa

(i)

Income tax computation 1998/99

	£	£
Schedule D Case I profit	40,000	
Capital allowances		
- P and M	(2,500)	
- IBA (W2)	(14,412)	23,088
Personal allowance		(4,195)
Taxable income		18,893

£

4,300 at 20%	860
14,593 at 23%	3,356
18,893	4,216
Interest on home loan (£180 at 10%)	(18)
Income tax liability	4,198

Capital gains tax computation 1998/99

£

Gains	17,000
Annual exemption	(6,800)
	10,200

£

8,207 (27,100 – 18,893) at 23%	1,888
1,993 at 40%	797
10,200	2,685

Working 1 - Car and fuel benefits

	£	£
Car 1		
35% × £14,000	4,900	
Mileage reduction		
(equivalent of more than 18,000)	3,267 (2/3)	
	1,633	
Age reduction (over four years old at 5.4.99)	544 (1/3)	
	1,089	
Time reduction (7/12)	635	454
Car 2		
35% × £16,000	5,600	
Mileage reduction		
(equivalent of between 2,500 and 17,999)	1,867 (1/3)	
	3,733	
Time reduction (5/12)	1,555	2,178
Fuel Car 1		
1400cc to 2000cc (petrol)	1,280	
Time reduction (7/12)	747	533
Fuel Car 2		
over 2000cc (diesel)	1,890	
Time reduction (5/12)	787	1,103
		4,268

Working 2

Industrial Building Allowance

	£	Allowance claimed £
Cost	100,000	
1991-92 (y/e 31.3.91) (PYB)		
WDA 4%	4,000	4,000
	96,000	
1992-93 (y/e 31.3.92) (PYB)		
WDA 4% (notional)	4,000	
	92,000	
1993-94 (y/e 31.3.93) (PYB)		
WDA 4% (notional)	4,000	
	88,000	
1994-95 (y/e 31.3.94) (PYB)		
WDA 4%	4,000	4,000
	84,000	
1995-96 (y/e 31.3.95) (PYB)		
WDA 4%	4,000	4,000
	80,000	
1996-97 (2 y/e 31.3.97) ('Transitional')		
WDA 4%	4,000	4,000
	76,000	
1997-98 (y/e 31.3.98) (CYB)		
WDA 4%	4,000	4,000
Total allowances claimed		20,000
Residue of expenditure before sale	72,000	

Calculation of balancing adjustment

	£
Cost of building	100,000
Proceeds	(55,000)
Net cost	45,000
Period of non-industrial use:	
$£45,000 \times \dfrac{24\ *}{102\ **}$	(10,588)
Adjusted net cost	34,412
Allowances claimed	20,000
Balancing allowance	14,412

* 1.1.92 - 31.12.93 period of non-industrial use
** 1.4.90 - 30.9.98 total period of ownership

Did you answer the question?
There was no need to explain why you correctly ignored the peripheral information on the mobile telephone. Showing the £200 figure in your answer was sufficient.

Did you answer the question?
You were not asked to give tax paydays.

Did you answer the question?
There was no requirement to compute WDAs for the secondhand user of the building although you had enough information to do so.

Tutorial notes
Although the IBA principles above are still examinable, the PYB treatment for businesses which commenced before 6 April 1994 is no longer required knowledge. A footnote in the question explains how to deal with this aspect.

53   (Answer 3 of examination)

Examiner's comments and marking guide

(i)   **A capital gains tax question testing:**

    (a)   the treatment of the disposal of a chattel costing more than £6,000 but sold for less than £6,000;

    (b)   the sale of an asset preceded by the purchase of a replacement asset within 12 months and a consequent roll-over claim; and

    (c)   the calculation of a gain on the sale of quoted securities following bonus and rights issues.

(ii)   (a)   The rules on the restriction of losses on disposal of chattels were not as well known as they should have been with candidates attempting to restrict the cost by 5/3 of the excess over £6,000. By contrast the fact that indexation cannot enhance an unindexed loss was much better known.

    (b)   This part of the question was much better done than the other two parts. Most candidates correctly computed the gain. The majority then went on to recognise the application of roll-over relief, but a much smaller proportion picked up the fact that the roll-over was restricted because the full proceeds were not reinvested.

    (c)   The principles that were tested in this part of the question have been tested frequently in recent examinations at this level. Candidates are still failing to recognise the fact that the FA85 pool and the FA82 frozen pool are separate assets and that rights and bonus issues are not, but that they relate back to the shareholdings from which they derive. As a result this part of the question was, on the whole, poorly done.

(iii)   Again there were many positive aspects in the answers submitted but many aspects of basic capital gains tax knowledge need to be tightened up.

		Marks
(a)	Deemed sale proceeds - £6,000	1
	No indexation allowance	1
		—
		2

(b)			
	Unindexed gain	1	
	Indexation allowance	1	
	Lower gain taken	1	
	Gain chargeable (£18,500)	1	
	Gain 'rolled over' (£8,260)	1	
		—	5

(c)			
	FA 1985 pool -		
	Sale proceeds	1	
	1982 holding -		
	Sale proceeds	1	
	Indexation allowance (1.029)	1	
	Calculation (£4,300)	1	
	Indexation allowance (0.136)	1	
	Calculation (£102)	1	
	No gain/no loss	1	
	Working 1 -		
	Indexation £268	1	
	Indexation £1,907	1	
	Working 2 -		
	Cost of shares sold £3,964	2	
	MV of shares sold £4,929	2	
		—	13

Total			20

Step by step answer plan

Overview

This is the conventional three part capital gains question. Part (c), being for 13 of the 20 marks, will clearly need the bulk of your time. Part (a) clearly involves a chattel sold at a loss with the 'minimum £6,000 proceeds' rule to apply. Part (b) is slightly less transparent but the words 'business' and 'replacement' are the clear hallmarks of roll-over relief. Again relatively easy marks. Part (c) is a share disposal with two 'assets' - the FA 1985 pool and the 1982 holding - and the complications of a bonus and a rights issue. Difficult but not impossible! Don't overlook the instruction in the requirements for 'providing explanations as appropriate'.

Step 1 Part (a) should take seconds.

Step 2 For part (b), produce a cost/March 1982 value pair of computations and show clearly which gain applies - ie, the lower gain.

Step 3 Then show the twin effects of roll-over where only part of the proceeds are reinvested - ie, gain deferred (and not tapered) and reduced base cost of replacement asset.

Step 4 For part (c) start by constructing a share history - one working for the FA 1985 pool and one for the 1982 holding - remembering that bonus and rights shares are always related back to the shares which gave the right to the additional shares.

Step 5 Start the main part of your answer with a gain calculation of the entire FA 1985 pool this implies correct knowledge of the order of disposal - ie, from the FA 1985 pool in priority.

Step 6 Then calculate the gain on the part disposal from the 1982 holding computing IA on the rights element separately. This is a conventional, if slightly involved, two column computation and the conclusion 'no gain /no loss' should be shown.

Step 7 Summarise your results for part (c).

Step 8 Review all parts to ensure appropriate explanations have been given. This is a fairly subjective requirement so it might be wise to provide more rather than less detail in the hope of meeting what the examiner has in mind.

The examiner's answer

		£
(a)	Deemed sale proceeds	6,000
	Cost	7,500
	Loss	1,500

No indexation allowance available.

Did you answer the question?

The examiner did not seem to expect an explanation of why £6,000 was used in place of actual proceeds.

(b)   Marco

	Cost £	MV £
Sale proceeds	150,000	150,000
Cost/MV	60,000	50,000
	90,000	100,000

Indexation allowance (to April 1998)

$$\frac{161.2 - 79.44}{79.44} = 1.029 \quad \text{(on £60,000)}$$

	Cost £	MV £
	61,740	61,740
Indexed gain	28,260	38,260
The lower gain is taken	£28,260	

The amount of sale proceeds not re-invested, £20,000 (£150,000 – £130,000) is immediately chargeable to capital gains tax. Provided it is not relieved by losses it will be tapered at 92.5% to £18,500.

The balance of £8,260 (£28,260 – £20,000) is 'rolled over' against the cost of the replacement building.

(c)   Fabio

(i)   Sale from FA 1985 pool

	£
Sale proceeds $\dfrac{3,500}{5,000} \times £28,000$	19,600
Indexed cost (W1)	(15,925)
Indexed gain	3,675

(ii)   Sale from 1982 holding

	Cost £	MV on 31.3.82 £
Sale proceeds $\dfrac{1,500}{5,000} \times £28,000$	8,400	8,400
Cost (W2)	(3,964)	(4,929)
Unindexed gain	4,436	3,471

Indexation allowance

- original shares and bonus issue

$$\frac{161.2 - 79.44}{79.44} = 1.029$$

On $\frac{1,500}{7,000} \times £19,500$ (4,300)   (3,471)

- rights issue

$$\frac{161.2 - 141.9}{141.9} = 0.136$$

On $\frac{1,500}{7,000} \times £3,500$ (102)   Nil

                                          34   Nil

No gain/no loss

Summary

FA 1985 pool	3,675
1982 holding	-
	3,675

Working 1

FA 1985 pool

	No. of shares	Unindexed pool £	Indexed pool £
July 1992	3,000	12,000	12,000
September 1993			
Indexation			
$\frac{141.9 - 138.8}{138.8} \times £12,000$	-	-	268
	3,000	12,000	12,268
Rights issue	500	1,750	1,750
	3,500	13,750	14,018
November 1998			
Indexation (to April 1998)			
$\frac{161.2 - 141.9}{141.9} \times £14,018$	-	-	1,907
	3,500	13,750	15,925
Sale	3,500	13,750	15,925
	-	-	-

Note: Indexation in the FA 1985 pool after April 1985 is not rounded to three places.

Working 2

1982 Holding

	No. of shares	Cost £	MV on 31.3.82 £
November 1980 (purchase)	5,000	15,000	19,500
May 1985 (bonus issue)	1,000	-	-
	6,000	15,000	19,500
September 1993 (rights issue)	1,000	3,500	3,500
	7,000	18,500	23,000
November 1998 (sale)	1,500*	3,964	4,929
	5,500	14,536	18,071

* 5,000 - FA 1985 pool (3,500)

---

54   (Answer 4 of examination)

Examiner's comments and marking guide

(i)   A VAT question covering default surcharge, serious misdeclaration and default interest.

(ii)   Many candidates attempted the question with little detailed knowledge of the relevant rules. Part (a) was the best answered part whereas many candidates displayed only superficial knowledge in their answers to parts (b) and (c).

(iii) A very disappointing performance bearing in mind that a VAT question is a permanent feature of the paper.

		Marks	
(a)	Late return	1	
	Late payment	1	
	12 months	1	
	End after continuous 12 month period	1	
		—	4
(b)	30%	1	
	Definition of 'gross amount of tax'	1	
	£1,000,000	1	
	15%	1	
		—	4
(c)	(i)		
	(ii) two from three	2	
	(iii)		
	Calculation	1	
		—	3
Total			11

(**Step by step answer plan**)

Overview

Being question 4, this is always the VAT question. This one concerns the three main penalty topics mentioned in the syllabus and provides some fairly easy marks for remembering the appropriate paragraphs of your study text. For each part, once you have identified the requirements you don't need to plan an essay! A carefully crafted sentence or paragraph will suffice in most instances.

Step 1   There are two answers to give for part (a). Make sure your answer states them both clearly.

Step 2   Similarly don't lose sight of the precise requirements for part (b) - there are three of them and all three must be given for the full mark.

Step 3   Approach part (c) in the same way ensuring both parts of the question are answered.

(**The examiner's answer**)

(a)   A 'default surcharge' arises when a late VAT return is submitted or late payment of VAT due is made. The 'surcharge default period' will initially be for 12 months and will only come to an end when no defaults have occurred for a continuous 12 month period.

(b)   A 'serious mis-declaration' occurs when a VAT return seriously understates VAT payable or overstates VAT repayable. A mis-declaration is regarded as serious when the amount of tax which would have been lost is the lower of:

(i)   at least 30% of the 'gross amount of tax' for the period which is defined as the aggregate of input and output tax which should have been included on the VAT return for the period, or

(ii)   £1,000,000.

The maximum penalty is 15% of the tax lost.

(c)   Customs and Excise may assess taxpayers to VAT where:

(i)   no returns have been submitted
(ii)   evidence to back up the returns is deficient or
(iii)   the returns and/or information are considered to be incorrect.

Such assessments bear 'default interest' which runs from the original due date of payment of the VAT until the payment is made.

Did you answer the question?

In each part, particularly part (a) your study text would contain more detail on the topic of the question. For example, for part (a) you probably know the rates of surcharge (2%, 5% etc). But these was not asked for. The examiner has clearly spelt out his requirements and they should be followed to the letter.

---

55   (Answer 5 of examination)

(**Examiner's comments and marking guide**)

(i)   **A question providing candidates with the opportunity to participate in the decision-making process concerning.**

(a)   Simultaneous replacement of a short-life asset; and
(b)   Sale of a redundant industrial building.
(c)   (Topic no longer examinable).

(ii)   The main focus of the question was, of course, the proximity of the year-end and whether action in relation to the various points had to be taken before or after, the year end date.

    (a)   The balancing adjustment on the sale of the short-life asset, which is of course its 'raison d'etre', was largely overlooked.

    (b)   Most candidates were aware of the roll-over implications and some recognition that the building was near the end of its tax life. There was, however, little attempt to relate the answer to the year-end, 30 April.

(iii)   The question was an attempt to introduce a thought provoking element into Section B. Candidates did not find the question attractive, although it was optional. In most cases no advice at all was given. A very disappointing response from candidates.

				Marks	
(a)	(i)			1	
	(ii)			1	
	(iii)			1	
				—	3
(b)	(i)			1	
	(ii)			1	
	(iii)	(1)		1	
		(2)		1	
				—	4
Total					7
					—

Bonus mark for stating (b) (iv)

Step by step answer plan

Overview

This question clearly requires some simple tax planning advice on capital allowances for a company approaching its year end. The examiner knows that Tax Planning proper is left to paper 11 later in your studies and is therefore unlikely to require anything complicated in a planning context. In fact, the question emphasises that you need consider only the timing of the proposed transactions.

Step 1   There are two proposed events in part (a) but the examiner makes life easier by specifying that they are to occur simultaneously.

Step 2   You have to identify the possible different tax results of these events and comment on whether they should occur in the current or the following accounting period.

Step 3   For part (b) the proposed sale will have both an IBA and a capital gain consequence to consider. Did you spot that the buildings tax life of 25 years has almost expired and timing is therefore quite crucial?

Step 4   You can probably think of most of the points in part (b) for 4 marks. Note that the examiner's point (iv) in his answer is a general commercial point rather a pure tax matter and he has not actually awarded it a mark in his marking scheme.

Step 5   Re-read the question with particular attention to the requirement for 'advice on all the matters raised' - have you done so?

The examiner's answer

(a)   (i)   If the sale of the asset were to result in a balancing allowance it should be sold before the year end.

    (ii)   If the sale of the asset were to result in a balancing charge it should be sold after the year end.

(iii)   An advantage in favour of replacing the asset in April 1999 would be that capital allowances on the new asset would be obtained one year earlier. The company should note that a higher initial rate of 40% FYA applies (instead of 25% WDA) for expenditure on plant before 2 July 1999 but not thereafter.

(b)   (i)   The tax life of the building comes to an end on 30 April 1999 and any sale after that date will not result in a balancing charge (in this case £30,000).

(ii)   A sale after 30 April 1999 will mean, of course, that the purchaser will not receive any Industrial Buildings Allowances and may ask for a compensating adjustment to the purchase price.

(iii)   A sale shortly after 30 April 1999 will have two advantages from a capital gains standpoint:

    (1)   any gain, subject to roll-over relief, will be taxed a year later (in the CAP to 30 April 2000) and

    (2)   any increase in the Retail Prices Index to the ultimate date of sale will result in a higher indexation allowance.

(iv)   If the purchaser wishes to occupy the building immediately, a short rental period could be arranged.

Did you answer the question?

You were only required to comment on timing for the factors given. For example, you were not told whether there were different marginal tax rates in the two years concerned so there was no need to discuss this aspect.

---

56   (Answer 6 of examination)

Examiner's comments and marking guide

(i)   **A question concentrating on the capital allowances aspect of the new current year basis assessment regime for sole traders and partnerships.**

The question was in two parts. Part (a) required candidates to contrast the new treatment with the old treatment and part (b) was a practical example.

(ii)   Most candidates correctly stated that capital allowances will be calculated by reference to accounting periods rather than years of assessment. Many of them then went on to calculate the capital allowances by reference to years of assessment. Part (b) of the question rewarded candidates who practised what they had stated in part (a).

(iii)   Candidates who did calculations on the year of assessment basis did not pick up as many marks on this question. The material covered in this question is new core material and needs to be mastered thoroughly.

			Marks	
(a)	(No longer examinable)			
(b)	(i)	Basis periods (no fiscal years)	1	
		Additions and sales in correct periods	1	
		WDA (1.5.96 - 30.6.97)	1	
		Assessable profits (all years)	1	
		Assessable amounts 1996-97	1	
		1997-98	1	
		1998-99 and		
		1999-00	1	
			—	7
	(ii)	'Overlap profits'	1	
			—	
Total				8
				—

Step by step answer plan

Overview

Part (a) has been excluded because it was based on knowledge now outside the syllabus. This makes the examiners comments above difficult to follow. As he seems concerned that many candidates had used the old rules by mistake, the less you know about them the better! Part (b) is clearly a Schedule D I opening year situation with capital allowances on plant. The first period is for 14 months ending in the second year of assessment so we are spared the fringe situations such how to compute CAs for a > 18 month period or how to identify assessment basis periods when there is no profit period ending in the second year. Don't forget to compute apportionment where needed on a daily (not monthly) basis.

Step 1   For part (b) start with the capital allowance computations for the first three periods. These are given as expenses for the corresponding periods of account so they must be deducted from the adjusted profit figures before any further steps.

Step 2   Deduct the CAs to arrive at the final adjusted profits for each of the three periods.

Step 3   Compute the assessments for the first four years showing clearly both your workings and the basis periods.

Step 4   Don't overlook the 1 easy mark for stating the overlap profits. It is not strictly asked for but it is good practice to state also the overlap period.

The examiner's answer

(a)   Topic no longer examinable.

(b)   (i)

Sean

A. Capital allowances claim

	Pool 25% £	Allowances £
1.5.96 - 30.6.97		
Additions	3,000	
Additions	2,000	
	5,000	
WDA $(25\% \times \frac{426}{365})$	(1,459)	1,459
	3,541	
1.7.97 - 30.6.98		
Sales	(1,500)	
	2,041	
WDA (25%)	(510)	510
Additions qualifying for FYA	6,000	
FYA (50%)	(3,000)	3,000
	4,531	3,510
1.7.98 - 30.6.99		
WDA (25%)	(1,133)	1,133
	c/f 3,398	

Did you answer the question?

There is no need to annotate your CA workings to explain such matters as the dates taken for the periods (ie, corresponding to the profit periods).

B. Profits for the accounting periods

		£
1.5.96 - 30.6.97	18,000 - CAs 1,459 =	16,541
1.7.97 - 30.6.98	20,000 - CAs 3,510 =	16,490
1.7.98 - 30.6.99	25,000 - CAs 1,133 =	23,867

C. Assessable amounts

Tax year	Basis period	Assessable £
1996-97	1.5.96 - 5.4.97	13,202 (W1)
1997-98	1.7.96 - 30.6.97	14,172 (W2)
1998-99	1.7.97 - 30.6.98	16,490
1999-00	1.7.98 - 30.6.99	23,867

Workings

W1 $£16,541 \times \dfrac{340}{426} = £13,202$

W2 $£16,541 \times \dfrac{365}{426} = £14,172$

(ii) 'Overlap' profit
'Overlap' period 1.7.96 - 5.4.97
$£16,541 \times \dfrac{279}{426} = £10,833$

Tutorial notes

For opening year basis periods the first year is always based on the actual profits to the first 5 April. If there is a > 12 month period ending in the second year, the basis period for that year is the 12 months to that accounting date. Thereafter, CYB applies as normal

57 (Answer 7 of examination)

Examiner's comments and marking guide

(i) **The question was a standard terminal loss question with marks available in part (b) for stating the capital gains tax relief to which the taxpayer may be entitled on ceasing to be in business.**

(ii) Most candidates were not aware of the procedure for calculating the terminal loss. The majority of candidates assumed that the terminal loss was £5,000 (5 months to 31 May 1998) and omitted the second part of the calculation. Several candidates even suggested that the loss be carried forward against future trading income. In part (b) most candidates mentioned retirement relief.

(iii) As this was the last time terminal loss could be examined (under the old PYB rules) it was perhaps surprising that candidates had not made more of an effort to familiarise themselves with the somewhat complex rules. A very disappointing performance.

Marks

(a)	A.	Losses 1.	6.4.98 - 31.5.98	1
		Losses 2.	1.6.97 - 31.12.97	1
			1.1.98-5.4.98	1

		No effect	1
		Overlap relief	2
	B.	Utilisation of terminal loss	1
		Utilisation of balance of loss	1
			—
			8
(b)	(i)	Retirement relief	1
	(ii)	Gift relief	1
	(iii)	Enterprise Investment Scheme deferral relief	1
			—
			3

Total   11

Step by step answer plan

Overview

This is clearly a question on terminal loss relief for a sole trader. We are given the whole profit history of the business so overlap relief will have to be determined and added to the terminal loss. Remember that for paper 7 all Schedule D I income tax questions require apportionment on a daily, not monthly, basis. Care must be taken not to overlook part (b) which provides 3 easy marks for brief remarks on capital gains reliefs.

Step 1 Calculate the terminal loss including the overlap relief.

Step 2 Apply the terminal loss against the 1997/98 Case I income.

Step 3 Explain how s.380 relief is available for the part of the loss excluded from the terminal loss amount.

Step 4 List the three capital gains reliefs as your answer to part (b).

The examiner's answer

(a)   A. Calculation of terminal loss

Losses

			£
(1)	6.4.98 - 31.5.98 ($\frac{56}{151}$ × £5,000)		1,854
(2)	1.6.97 - 31.12.97 ($\frac{214}{365}$ × £11,000)	6,449 P	
	1.1.97 - 5.4.97 ($\frac{95}{151}$ × £5,000)	3,146 L	
		3,303 P	

As profit arises this is treated as   Nil
Add overlap relief:
1.1.95 - 5.4.95: 17,000 × $\frac{95}{365}$ =   4,425

Terminal loss   6,279

B. Utilisation of terminal loss

The terminal loss of £6,279 will be allowed against the 1997-98 assessable amount:

	£
Case I	11,000
Terminal loss relief	6,279
Net amount assessable	4,721

The balance of the loss £3,146 (£5,000 − £1,854) would be allowed under S380 against STI of 1998/99 and/or 1997/98.

(*Tutorial note:* This question was originally set as the cessation of a pre 6 April 1994 business. It has been updated to reflect the fact that this is no longer examinable.)

(b) Norma would be entitled to the following reliefs from capital gains tax:

    (i) Retirement relief on the sale of the business to a third party or a sale at undervalue or a gift of the business assets.

    (ii) Gift relief on a sale at undervalue or a gift of the business assets.

    (iii) Enterprise investment scheme (EIS) deferral relief of the sale proceeds in ordinary shares in a qualifying unquoted trading company, which exists wholly for the purpose of carrying on one or more qualifying trades (excluding banking and dealing in land or commodities).

(*Tutorial note:* Any gain remaining chargeable in 1998/99 will be reduced to 92.5% by taper relief. Any gain deferred (ie, using EIS) rather than exempted (ie, by retirement relief) or rolled over (ie, gift relief) will be tapered to 92.5% but only when it becomes finally chargeable.)

Did you answer the question?

You are only required to state the reliefs, not explain them in any detail nor discuss how they interact with taper relief.

---

58   (Answer 8 of examination)

Examiner's comments and marking guide

(i) **The question required candidates to calculate the additional personal pension contributions to be paid and to advise on the best time to pay the premiums from a tax point of view.**

(ii) Although an 'in-depth' knowledge of the subject was required to gain full marks, marks were available for demonstrating the percentage allowances and a basic knowledge of the 'unused relief' rules. Most candidates seemed to have attempted the question as a 'stop-gap' measure without having seriously thought how to provide a meaningful answer.

(iii) The question was the least popular of the optional questions. More awareness of the rules would have provided many candidates with the opportunity to have scored many more marks on this question.

	Marks
Unused relief	2
£5,500 in 1999-2000 with c/b to 1998-99	1
Working showing how much unused relief can be utilised in 1998-99 at 23%	3
Recognition of:	
(1) Maximum marginal rate is 23% for all years	1
(2) Earlier relief always better than late relief (marginal rates being equal)	1
Correct utilisation of unused relief	1
1997-98 unused relief to be utilised in 1999-2000, provided maximum payment for 1999-2000 is made	1
Summary	1
	—
Total	11

Step by step answer plan

Overview

This question concentrates solely on relief for pension premium contributions for a self-employed individual. As he consults you in June 1999 (ie, in 1999/2000), he is still in time to pay a premium and relate it back a year to 1998/99. The maximum relief for premiums paid or deemed paid in that year is the relief for 1998/99 plus any unused relief for the past 6 years on a FIFO basis. As he was born in 1938 he will qualify for the higher percentages of NRE applying to older taxpayers. If you understand these basic rules the answer is quite straightforward.

Step 1 Produce a tabular working to show any unused relief for the 7 years up to and including 1998/99.

Step 2 Identify the additional premiums Fred could pay.

Step 3 Identify in a working the maximum amount of premiums which would generate relief at 23% for 1998/99.

Step 4 Discuss the choices and optimum set-off of additional pension contributions.

The examiner's answer

Fred consults you in June 1999 which is in the year 1999-2000. If the maximum premium for 1998-99 is paid in 1999-00 and related back to 1998-99 it is then possible to start using up unused relief for the six preceding years ie, 1992-93 to 1997-98 inclusive on a FIFO basis. Unused relief is calculated:

	1992-93	1993-94	1994-95	1995-96	1996-97	1997-98	1998-99
	£	£	£	£	£	£	£
Net relevant earnings	18,000	20,000	22,000	24,000	26,000	28,000	30,000
Maximum paid	5,400 (30%)	6,000 (30%)	6,600 (30%)	8,400 (35%)	9,100 (35%)	9,800 (35%)	10,500 (35%)
Premium paid	5,000	5,000	5,000	5,000	5,000	5,000	5,000
Unused relief	400	1,000	1,600	3,400	4,100	4,800	5,500

The maximum additional premiums which Fred can pay are:

(1)   £5,500 paid in 1999-2000 for relief in 1998-99. An election should be made before 31 January 2001 to carry back this premium to 1998-99.

(2)   As the maximum payment has now been made for 1998-99 unused relief for the preceding six years can be utilised, ie, 1992-93 to 1997-98 inclusive. To achieve maximum tax advantage premium payments for the years 1992-93 to 1997-98 can be made in 1999-2000 and carried back to 1998-99 by an election made before 31 January 2001. There are two advantages to this:

(i)   relief is obtained at 23% (provided the 1997-98 relief is not used in full) (W1) and
(ii)   relief is obtained against an earlier tax year with a repayment of tax already paid.

(3)   Relief for the remaining unused relief for 1997-98 of £4,295 (4,800 − 505) can be obtained at 23% by a premium payment in 1999-2000 in addition to the maximum 35% premium payment for that year of £10,500 (35% × £30,000).

(4)   To summarise additional premiums to be made in 1999-2000 are:

A.   Premiums to relate back to 1998-99

		£
1998-99		5,500
1997-98 (part)		505
1996-97		4,100
1995-96		3,400
1994-95		1,600
1993-94		1,000
1992-93		400
		16,505

B.   Premiums to use in 1999-2000

	£
35% of net relevant earnings for 1999-2000	10,500
1997-98 (part)	4,295
	14,795

Working 1

1998-99

	£	£
Net relevant earnings		30,000
Personal allowance	4,195	
Lower rate limit	4,300	(8,495)
		21,505
Premium paid in 1998-99		(5,000)
		16,505
Premium paid 1999-2000 and related back		(5,500)
		11,005

To pay in 1999-2000 in respect of relief from

	£	£
1992-93	400	
1993-94	1,000	
1994-95	1,600	
1995-96	3,400	
1996-97	4,100	
1997-98 (part)	505	(11,005)
		-

Premiums of £11,005 are relieved at 23%.

DECEMBER 1996 QUESTIONS

59   (Question 1 of examination)

Upbeat Ukuleles Ltd (UUL) is a United Kingdom resident company which has been manufacturing musical instruments for many years. It has no associated companies. The company has previously made up accounts to 30 June but has now changed its accounting date to 30 September.

The company's results for the 15 month period to 30 September 1998 are as follows:

	£
Trading profits (as adjusted for taxation before capital allowances)	1,250,000
Debenture interest receivable (notes 3 and 6)	20,000
Bank interest receivable (note 4)	6,000
Patent royalties receivable (notes 5 and 6)	70,000
Chargeable gain (notes 7 and 8)	10,000
Deed of covenant payment (notes 6 and 9)	5,000
Dividends received from UK companies (note 10)	30,000

Notes:

(1)   Capital allowances

On 1 July 1997 the tax written-down value of plant and machinery in the capital allowances pool was £100,000.

There were no additions or sales in the period of account to 30 September 1998.

(2)   On 1 July 1997 the company had trading losses brought forward of £800,000.

(3)   Debenture interest receivable

	£
22.9.98 received	18,000
30.9.98 accrued	2,000
	20,000

The debenture had been acquired in July 1998.

(4)   Bank interest receivable

31.12.97 received	3,000
30.6.98 received	2,000
30.9.98 accrued	1,000
	6,000

(5)   Patent royalties receivable

	£
31.12.97 received	30,000
30.6.98 received	25,000
30.9.98 accrued	15,000
	70,000

(6)   The gross amounts of debenture interest receivable, patent royalties receivable and the deed of covenant payment are shown.

Income tax has been deducted at source.

(7)   Chargeable gain

The chargeable gain of £10,000 is in respect of shares disposed of on 31 December 1997.

(8)   On 1 July 1997 the company had capital losses brought forward of £12,500.

(9)   Deed of covenant

£5,000 was paid to a charity on 31 December 1997.

(10)   Dividends received

25.3.98	18,000
29.9.98	12,000
	30,000

You are required to calculate the mainstream corporation tax liabilities for the 15 month period ended 30 September 1998 after setting off and income tax. You should also state what unrelieved amounts are to be carried forward.

NB. All apportionments may be made to the nearest month.

(22 marks)

---

60   (Question 2 of examination)

Dietrich, who is 58, has been married to Marlene, who is 57, for many years. On 1 May 1996 Dietrich started a road haulage business. The profits, as adjusted for income tax but before capital allowances, are:

	£
1.5.96 to 31.12.96	25,000
1.1.97 to 31.12.97	45,000
1.1.98 to 31.12.98	50,000

Capital additions and disposals were as follows:

Additions

		£
1.5.96	Lorry (1)	40,000
1.6.96	Car (1)	8,000
1.6.96	Car (2)	20,000
1.2.97	Lorry (2)	45,000
1.12.97	Car (3)	22,000
1.3.98	Lorry (3)	25,000

Disposals

1.12.97	Car (2)	12,500
1.3.98	Lorry (1)	20,000

Car (1) was purchased new and was for the use of Marlene. The annual mileage is 10,000 miles of which 5,000 is private.

Cars (2) and (3) are for the use of Dietrich whose annual mileage is 20,000 of which 8,000 is private.

No claim is to be made to treat any of the assets as 'short-life' assets. Marlene was employed by her husband at an annual salary of £15,000 which has already been charged in arriving at the adjusted profit figure given. PAYE of £2,600 was deducted. Although Marlene had private use of car (1) no fuel was provided for private motoring.

Other relevant information is:

(1)   Marlene had purchased a life annuity in 1996 from which she receives an income each month of £200 (gross). The capital element of each payment has been agreed with the Inland Revenue at £125. Income tax is deducted from the income element.

(2)   Marlene has an account with the Halifax Building Society and £200 interest was credited on 31 January 1999.

(3)   Marlene received dividends in 1998-99 of £1,200.

(4)   Marlene paid the maximum personal pension contribution for 1998-99.

You are required to calculate:

(a)   the income tax assessable amounts for Dietrich for the years 1996-97, 1997-98 and 1998-99

(10 marks)

(b)   the 'overlap' profits and

(1 marks)

(c)   Marlene's taxation payable for 1998-99

(12 marks)

NB. Apportionments should be made in days.   **(Total: 23 marks)**

61	**(Question 3 of examination)**

(a)   Jun Ying had the following dealings in Chinatown plc a UK quoted company.

	Date	Number of shares	£
Purchase	15.8.77	1,000	1,500
Purchase	15.10.81	2,000	3,500
Purchase	15.7.83	3,000	12,000
Purchase	15.6.89	2,000	7,000
Sale	15.7.98	6,000	42,000

The 31 March 1982 value of the shares was £3.70 per share. No election is being made to 're-base' the cost of all assets held on 31 March 1982 at their value on that date.

You are required to calculate Jun Ying's 1998-99 capital gain before the annual exemption.

(9 marks)

(b)   Jin Ming had been a full-time working director of Porcelain Products Ltd since 1 December 1981 and had owned 10% of the company's ordinary shares since 1 December 1993. He retired from the company on 1 December 1998 when aged 58. The agreed capital gain on the disposal of the shares was £600,000, after indexation allowance but before taper relief.

The market values of the assets in the balance sheet at that date were:

	£
Land and buildings	250,000
Goodwill	100,000
Plant and machinery	200,000
Motor cars	80,000
Investments	50,000

All the items of plant and machinery cost more than £6,000.

You are required to calculate Jin Ming's 1998-99 assessable capital gain before the annual exemption.

(5 marks)

(Total: 14 marks)

62 (Question 4 of examination)

(a) You are provided with the following information relating to Portia, who is a practising solicitor, for the quarter ended 30 November 1998:

	£
Fees (standard-rated and exclusive of VAT)	60,000
Rent received from sub-letting part of her offices	6,000
Car purchase (exclusive of VAT)	18,000
Overheads (standard-rated and exclusive of VAT)	9,000
VAT attributable to taxable supplies	2,000

The car was purchased on 1 September 1998 and had an engine capacity of 1900cc. Petrol for both private and business motoring was charged through the business and not refunded. The VAT inclusive quarterly scale charge figure relevant for this car was £268.

Bad debts of £550 (exclusive of VAT) were written off during November 1998; the date payment was due for the services was January 1998.

You are required to calculate the VAT payable for the quarter ended 30 November 1998 and to state when this will be payable to HM Customs and Excise.

(9 marks)

(b) **You are required** to advise Portia on the VAT consequences of (i) purchasing a computer on hire-purchase and (ii) renting a computer.

(2 marks)

(Total: 11 marks)

63 (Question 5 of examination)

(a) Alphabetic Ltd makes up annual accounts to 30 June. It paid corporation tax of £100,000 on 1 May 1998 in respect of the accounting period to 30 June 1997. It subsequently transpired that the actual liability was £90,000 and £10,000 was subsequently repaid on 28 August 1998.

You are required to state:

(i) the interest already charged on overdue tax which is now repayable to the company and

(1 mark)

(ii) the repayment supplement payable to the company

(1 mark)

NB. Apportionments should be made in days and interest should be charged or paid at 10% pa..

(b)   **You are required** to state what action a company should take if it does not receive a corporation tax return and the penalty for not taking such action.

(2 marks)

(c)   **You are required** to state:

      (i)   the fixed rate penalties for failing to submit a corporation tax return on time and

(4 marks)

      (ii)   the tax-geared penalties for falling to submit a corporation tax return on time.

(3 marks)

Your answers to (c) (i) and (c) (ii) should indicate under what circumstances these penalties are triggered.

(Total: 11 marks)

---

64   (Question 6 of examination)

Lucien Buysse, a married man aged 25, commenced trading as a chiropodist on 1 July 1996. His trading results adjusted for income tax and capital allowances were:

		£	
Year ended 30.6.97		(15,000)	Loss
Year ended 30.6.98		5,000	Profit

Lucien had not previously been employed or been in business. He had inherited shares in April 1995 which have produced the following dividend income:

1995-96	12,200	(net)
1996-97	9,000	(net)
1997-98	10,000	(net)
1998-99	11,000	(net)

You are required to show how the loss sustained in the year ended 30 June 1997 can be utilised in the most tax-efficient manner and calculate Lucien's taxable income for the years 1995-96, 1996-97, 1997-98 and 1998-99.

(11 marks)

NB.

(1)   You may assume income tax rates and allowances for 1998-99 apply to all years in the question.

(2)   Apportionments should be made in days.

---

65   (Question 7 of examination)

There are many advantages in being treated as 'self-employed' rather than 'employed'.

You are required to state what tests are applied by the Inland Revenue and Department of Social Security in deciding a taxpayer's status.

(11 marks)

66   (Question 8 of examination)

Set out below is the 1998-99 PAYE coding of one of your clients, James Matthews.

PAYE Coding Notice 1998-99

Allowances	£	*less amounts taken away to cover items shown below*	£
Personal pension	945	Benefits (car)	4,700
Personal allowance	4,195	Benefits (car fuel)	1,890
Married allowance	1,900	Untaxed interest	910
		Allowance restriction	1,188
		Unpaid tax	230
Total allowances	7,040	Total reductions	8,918
		Net allowances used to work out your tax code	(1,878)

Code for the year to 5 April 1999 is K186

You are required to state:

(a)   the information you need to know in order to check the accuracy of all the items in James's coding notice and

(10 marks)

(b)   how 'K' codes are utilised in the collection of tax under the PAYE system.

(1 marks)
(Total: 11 marks)

ANSWERS TO DECEMBER 1996 EXAMINATION

59   (Answer 1 of examination)

(Examiner's comments and marking guide)

(i)   this was a corporation tax question which included the following matters to be considered by candidates:

    (1)   a 15 month accounting period;

    (2)   the new treatment of debenture interest receivable;

    (3)   the treatment of trading and capital losses brought forward;

    (4)   the chargeable accounting period straddling 31 March;

    (5)   capital allowance computations covering plant and machinery;

    (6)   marginal relief on a three month accounting period;

    (7)   treatment of income tax suffered on unfranked investment income.

(ii)   Whilst there were a number of interacting elements to this question a well-prepared candidate should have been able to pick up the majority of the marks. Specific points to note were:

    (a)   Many of the weaker candidates failed to split the long accounting period or did not correctly split it into 12 month and 3 month periods.

    (b)   Many candidates failed to apportion correctly debenture interest, bank interest, royalties and charges into the 12 month and 3 month periods. This frequently appeared to be the case even where trading profits had been correctly apportioned.

    (c)   In a similar vein there appeared to be much confusion over whether accruals should or should not be included.

    (d)   Capital losses brought forward were often allowed against income. Similarly, trading losses were frequently split between the two periods and/or set off against non-trading income.

    (e)   The treatment of income tax was poor. Many of the weaker candidates either ignored it altogether or failed to split the period correctly.

The above is not an exhaustive list of errors but covers large areas which are core to the syllabus and thus should be considered as aspects of corporation tax of which the average candidate has a firm grasp. Disappointingly candidates at this session did not appear to have such a grasp.

(iii)   The overall performance was disappointing but many candidates did perform reasonably well.

	Marks	
Apportionment of trading profit	1	
Trading loss set-off	1	
Debenture interest	1	
Bank interest received	1	
Patent royalties received	1	
Charge on income	1	6
Working 1		
Capital allowances to 30.6.98	1	
Capital allowances to 30.9.98	1	2
Working 2		
Chargeable gains		1

Working 3

Recognition of 'P'	1	
Calculation of corporation tax	1	2

Working 4

Calculation of upper and lower limits	1	
Recognition of 'P'	1	
Calculation of corporation tax	2	4

Working 5

Calculation of FII for 30.6.98	1	
Calculation of FII for 30.9.98	1	2

Working 6

Income tax suffered on patent royalties	2	
Income tax withheld on deed of covenant	1	
Set-off against MCT	1	4

Working 7

Income tax suffered on debenture interest		1

Total		22

(Step by step answer plan)

Overview

This is a CT computation for a > 12 month period of account. It is crucial therefore to realise that there are two chargeable accounting periods to compute for - a 12 month AP followed by a 3 month AP. As long as the results are correctly apportioned between the two APs and the computations are kept separate it should be possible to earn most of the 22 marks available.

Step 1 Read through the question and try to visualise where each bit of information will impact on your answer. It might be helpful to high light key words such as 'trading losses b/f' in note 2 and 'capital losses b/f' in note 8. Also, if you risk overlooking FII when finding the CT rate then write 'Profits' or something similar against note 10.

Step 2 Head up your main PCTCT layout with a column for each of the APs concerned. A tabular layout is much to be preferred if only for the time saved in writing out the labels.

Step 3 Apportion the trading profit on a time basis.

Step 4 Produce a working note for the capital allowances for each AP and transfer the figures to your main working.

Step 5 Subtract in each column to find the Schedule D I figures and deduct the trading loss b/f - but only from the first column as that is sufficient to absorb all the loss.

Step 6 Continue filling in the layout by apportioning interest on an accruals basis but patent royalties received on a paid basis.

Step 7 Show the net-off of the gain and the capital loss - best in a working - with a nil figure in the PCTCT layout and a loss remaining to highlight for the final part of your answer.

Step 8 Allocate charges on a paid basis and total the PCTCT for each period.

Step 9 Compute CT for each AP in a separate working.

Step 10 Use a separate working to identify the recoverable income tax for each AP.

Step 11 Transfer the figures generated in steps 9 and 10 above to your main working to give the two CT figures.

Step 12 Finally ensure that the unrelieved amounts being carried forward are clearly labelled in your answer. The examiner seems to be content if these figures are left in your workings but it is good practice to state them separately as part of your main answer. After all, your workings may not be tidy enough for the relevant figures to be easily identified in the marking.

The examiner's answer

Upbeat Ukuleles Ltd
Corporation tax computations

	12 month CAP to 30.6.98 £	3 month CAP to 30.9.98 £
Trading profit	1,000,000	250,000
Capital allowances -		
Plant and machinery	(25,000) (W1)	(4,688) (W1)
	975,000	245,312
Trading losses brought forward	(800,000)	-
	175,000	245,312
Debenture interest receivable	-	20,000
Bank interest receivable	5,000	1,000
Patent royalties received	55,000	-
Chargeable gains	Nil (W2)	-
Total profits	235,000	266,312
Charge on income	(5,000)	-
Profits chargeable	230,000	266,312
Corporation tax payable	48,300 (W3)	80,340 (W4)
Income tax	(11,500) (W6)	(3,600) (W7)
CT payable	36,800	76,740

Notes:

(1)   Trading profit is apportioned on a time basis.
(2)   Bank interest and debenture interest is allocated on the accruals basis.
(3)   Chargeable gains are allocated according to the date of disposal of the chargeable asset.
(4)   Royalties are allocated according to the date of receipt.
(5)   Deed of covenant payments are allocated according to the date of payment.

Did you answer the question?

Although the examiner has given a list of 5 notes explaining the apportionment rules for a "long" period of account it does not feature in the marking scheme and it seems unlikely that you would need to include it in your answer.

Working 1

	Capital allowances		
CAP to 30.6.98	25% of £100,000	=	£25,000
CAP to 30.9.98	6¼%* of £75,000**	=	£4,688
*	$\frac{3}{12}$ × 25%		
**	£100,000 - £25,000		

Working 2

Chargeable gains

CAP to 30.6.98   £

    Gain for period   10,000
    Losses brought forward   12,500
    ———
    Losses carried forward   2,500
    ———

Working 3

Corporation tax payable

CAP to 30.6.98   £

I   (Chargeable profits) $=$ 230,000
P   (Chargeable profits +
           Franked investment income W5) $=$ 252,500

As P is below the lower limit the small companies rate applies. Because there was no change in the small companies rate at 1 April 1998 the corporation tax payable will be calculated as follows.

                              £

£230,000 × 21%   48,300
                              ———

Working 4

Corporation tax payable

CAP to 30.9.98   £

I   (Chargeable profits) $=$ 266,312
P   (Chargeable profits +
           Franked investment income W5) $=$ 281,312
The reduced limits are:
Upper ($\frac{3}{12}$ × £1,500,000) $=$ 375,000
Lower ($\frac{3}{12}$ × £300,000) $=$ 75,000

As 'P' is between the reduced limits the marginal rate of corporation tax applies.

                              £

£266,312 at 31% $=$ 82,557
Marginal relief
$(375,000 - 281,312) \times \dfrac{266,312}{281,312} \times \frac{1}{40}$ (2,217)
                              ———
                            80,340
                            ———

Working 5

Franked investment income

CAP to 30.6.98: 18,000 × $\frac{100}{80}$ 22,500
                              ———

CAP to 30.9.98: 12,000 × $\frac{100}{80}$ 15,000
                              ———

Working 6

Income tax

CAP to 30.6.98
Income tax suffered on royalties

	£	£
£30,000 at 23%	6,900	
£25,000 at 23%	5,750	12,650

Income tax withheld on deed of covenant
£5,000 at 23%   =   1,150

                                                     11,500
Set-off against MCT   11,500

To be repaid   -

Working 7

Income tax

CAP to 30.9.98
Income tax suffered on debenture interest
£18,000 at 20%   =   £3,600

To be set-off against corporation tax

Did you answer the question?

As neither quarterly accounting nor tax paydays are asked for, income tax recoverable is simply calculated as a single exercise for each AP without using the more formal CT61 type layout.

Tutorial notes

Although the whole of the debenture interest receivable credited to the profit and loss account is chargeable to corporation tax, only income tax deducted from interest received is set off against the corporation tax payable.

---

60   (Answer 2 of examination)

Examiner's comments and marking guide

(i)   This was an income tax question testing:

   (a)   the calculation of income tax assessments, including capital allowances computations, for the first three years of a business commencing to trade after 5 April 1994;

   (b)   the calculation of 'overlap' profits for the business; and

   (c)   the calculation of income tax liability including a car benefit-in-kind, personal allowances, pension premiums, purchased life annuity, building society interests and dividends including the new rates on the deduction of income tax from savings income.

(ii)   The main problems encountered by candidates are itemised below.

   (a)   Assessments

          When calculating the assessments, many candidates either did not adjust for capital allowance so they deducted them, incorrectly, after first relating the profits to tax years (as under the old regime). The 1996/97 assessment presented problems to most candidates.

Although the tax tables included a calendar, specifically for apportionment purposes, many candidates chose to ignore this and calculated the 1996/97 assessment to the nearest month.

Capital allowances

Overall, this part was well attempted by most candidates. However, as in the past candidates did experience some difficulties with computing capital allowances for the first period 1.5.96 to 31.12.96 eg, incorrect apportionment of writing down allowances (WDAs) and confusion over restrictions applicable on the expensive car (ie, the maximum amount and private use). In addition, on expensive cars the amount deducted from the qualifying expenditure should be the full amount of WDAs available (ie, before restriction for private use) when carrying forward the balance for future WDAs.

Quite a significant number of candidates applied private use restriction on Marlene's car, when it was clearly stated that she was an employee in her husband's business - an employee's private use does not affect the business' capital allowances. The employee, if higher paid, will be assessed on the car as a benefit-in-kind under Schedule E.

Whilst additions and disposals were handled well by most candidates, some candidates could not perform this task, indicating that they are not up to date with the new rules.

A surprisingly large number of candidates produced Dietrich's personal tax computations for years 1996/97, 1997/98 and 1998/99, when they were only asked for Schedule D Case 1 assessments. Some candidates also wasted valuable time in calculating car benefits, which clearly does not apply in Dietrich's case since he is not an employee of the business.

(b) Overlap relief

Candidates who computed the assessments correctly in part (a) had no problems with this.

(c) Marlene's personal tax computation was handled competently by a good number of candidates and the car benefit, in particular, was well done. Some candidates continue (despite comments in the June 1996 Examiner's Report) to time-apportion the benefit using days which though more accurate is also more time consuming and not essential in this instance. It is quite acceptable and normal practice in examinations to time-apportion the car and fuel benefits to the nearest month.

There was still plenty of evidence of grossing-up errors in respect of investment income. Calculation of income from the purchased life annuity also presented problems to many candidates. A significant number of candidates excluded benefits-in-kind when calculating the personal pension premium.

Calculation of the income tax liability was, in general, well handled by the majority of candidates - the main problem noted was the restriction to 20% of income tax chargeable on savings income falling within the basic rate band.

(iii) The answers to this question were satisfactory.

		Marks
(a)	1996-97 assessment	2.
	1997-98 and 1998-99 assessments	1
	Capital allowances	
	1.5.96-31.12.96	
	WDA 245/365	1
	£3,000 restriction on car (1)	1
	1.1.97-31.12.97	
	Additions and sale	1
	WDAs and car (2) restriction	1
	Balancing allowance	1
	1.1.98-31.12.98	
	Addition and sale	1
	WDAs and car (2) restriction	1
		—
		10

(b)   1

(c)   Benefit-in-kind on car   2
           Personal pension premium   1
           Purchased life annuity   1
           Building society interest   1
           Dividends   1
           Personal allowance   1
           Income tax on non-savings income   1
           Income tax on savings income   1
           Basic rate tax on pension premiums   1
           Tax suffered:
           PAYE   ½
           Purchased life annuity   ½
           Building society interest   ½
           Dividends   ½
                                                                                    —   12

Total   23

(Step by step answer plan)

Overview

Question 2 is always a husband and wife personal tax computation. Usually it includes a minor CGT computation but that is omitted this time. Also there is no start or end of marriage situation as can sometimes be tested.

On a quick initial read through of the question the following points should occur to you. Their ages are given and this will be relevant for Marlene paying maximum PPCs (note 4). The husband has commenced a business and employs his wife - opening years CA and profit rules to apply for him and Sch E benefits for her.

Step 1   For part (a) produce a P & M CA standard layout with a Main Pool, Car Pool and 2 expensive car columns covering the first three periods of account. Don't forget daily apportionment for the WDA calculations in the first period.

Step 2   Deduct the CA amounts from the profit figures and compute the assessable amounts for the first 3 years of assessment - again daily apportionment where necessary.

Step 3   Claim that 1 easy mark for calculating overlap profits for part (b).

Step 4   For part (c) produce Marlene's Taxable Income/IT computation not forgetting the special rate for savings income and the fact that employees are entitled to pay their PPCs net of basic rate tax. As the gross PPC is deducted against NRE, the tax withheld has to be added into the IT liability or relief will have been taken twice.

(The examiner's answer)

(a)

Dietrich
Income tax assessments

		£	£	£
1996-97 (1.5.96 - 5.4.97)				
1.5.96 - 31.12.96	Adjusted profit	25,000		
	Capital allowances	(9,262)	15,738	
1.1.97 - 5.4.97	Adjusted profit	45,000		
	Capital allowances	(26,328)		
	95/365 ×	18,672	= 4,860	20,598

1997-98 (1.1.97 - 31.12.97)

Adjusted profit	45,000	
Capital allowances	(26,328)	18,672

1998-99 (1.1.98 - 31.12.98)

Adjusted profit	50,000	
Capital allowances	(25,228)	24,772

	Main pool £	Car pool £	Capital allowance Expensive car (1) (Pte 40%) £	Expensive car (2) (Pte 40%) £	Claim £
1.5.96 - 31.12.96					
Additions	40,000	8,000	20,000		
Claim					
WDA 25% × $\frac{245}{365}$	(6,712)	(1,342)	(2,014) * 806		9,262
	33,288	6,658	17,986		
1.1.97 to 31.12.97					
Additions	45,000			22,000	
Sale			(12,500)		
	78,288		5,486		
Claim					
Balancing All	-	-	(5,486) 2,194	-	3,292
WDA 25%	(19,572)	(1,664)	-	(3,000)*1,200	23,036
	58,716	4,994	-	19,000	
					26,328
1.1.98 to 31.12.98					
Sale	(20,000)				
	38,716				
Claim					
WDA 25%	(9,679)	(1,249)		(3,000)*1,200	12,728
Addition	25,000				
FYA @ 50%	(12,500)				12,500
WDA c/f	41,537	3,745		16,000	25,228

* Maximum allowance is at the rate of £3,000 per annum.

'Overlap' profits

(b)   Period 1.1.97 - 5.4.97 = £4,860

(c)

Marlene
1998-99 income tax liability

		£	£
Non-savings income			
Employment			15,000
Benefits-in-kind	- car 35% × 8,000	2,800	
	- mileage reduction (1/3)	(933)	1,867
			16,867
Personal pension premium (35%)			(5,903)
			10,964

		£	£
Savings income			
Building society interest $\left(£200 \times \dfrac{100}{80}\right)$		250	
Purchased life annuity 12 × £75 (£200 – £125)		900	
Dividends $\left(£1,200 \times \dfrac{100}{80}\right)$		1,500	2,650
Total income			13,614
Personal allowance			(4,195)
Taxable income			9,419

		£
Tax on non-savings income		
£4,300 at 20%		860
£2,469 at 23%		568
£6,769 (£10,964 – £4,195)		1,428
Tax on savings income		
£2,650 at 20%		530
		1,958
Basic rate tax on pension premiums (£5,903 at 23%)		1,358
Income tax liability		3,316

	£	£
Income tax suffered:		
PAYE	2,600	
Purchased life annuity		
(£900 at 20%)	180	
Building society interest		
(£250 at 20%)	50	
Dividends		
£1,500 at 20%)	300	3,130
Income tax payable		186

Did you answer the question?

You are not required to comment on the paydays of any amounts of tax.

61	(Answer 3 of examination)

(Examiner's comments and marking guide)

(i)   This was a two-part capital gains tax question testing:

(1)   the sale of quoted shares out of both the 1982 holding and the Finance Act 1985 pool; and
(2)   the calculation of retirement relief following the sale of shares in the taxpayer's family company.

(ii)   In part (a) many candidates failed to correctly pool the shares. The most common mistake in calculating the gain on the 1982 holding was not to restrict the indexation allowance to the amount of the unindexed gain. Part (b) was very poorly attempted with many candidates overlooking the second tranche maximum of £500,000. Many candidates had very little idea how to calculate retirement relief.

(iii) The overall performance was disappointing even though part (a) was relatively straightforward.

			Marks	
(a)	(i)	FA 1985 pool		
		Proceeds £35,000	1	
		Indexation to April 1985	1	
		Indexation to June 1989	1	
		Indexation to April 1998	1	4
	(ii)	1982 holding		
		Proceeds £7,000	1	
		Cost £1,667	1	
		1982 market value £3,700	1	
		Indexation allowance	1	
		£Nil gain	1	5
(b)		First tranche retirement relief	1	
		Second tranche retirement relief	1	
		Taper relief	1	
		Working 1	1	
		Working 2	½	
		Working 3	½	5
Total				14

(Step by step answer plan)

Overview

The compulsory capital gains question, number 3, always consists of 2, 3 or 4 quite separate parts - here there are just two parts. Part (a) is a relatively straightforward question on a share disposal. It involves the creation of two 'assets' - the FA 1985 pool and the 1982 holding but avoids the complications of rights or bonus issues and the new post 5.4.98 matching rules. Part (b) clearly involves retirement relief for a full-time director disposing of shares in his personal trading company.

Step 1   For part (a) use a working note to produce each of the FA 1985 pool and the 1982 holding showing the 6,000 shares sold as coming primarily from the FA 1985 pool.

Step 2   Compute the gain on the disposal of the entire FA 1985 pool and the part disposal of the 1982 holding and summarise. The shares are clearly not business assets for taper relief purposes.

Step 3 For part (b) use a working note to schedule out the chargeable assets and the chargeable business assets of the company.

Step 4 Use the figures from step 3 to find the portion of the gain on the shares qualifying for retirement relief.

Step 5 In your main answer show the full gain and reduce it for the retirement relief available. Finally, the gain remaining, being in respect of shares in a qualifying company, should be tapered at the rate for business assets.

The examiner's answer

(a)

Jun Ying
1998-99 capital gain

(i) Disposal out of FA 1985 pool

		£	£
Proceeds 5,000/6,000 × £42,000 =		35,000	
Indexed cost (W1)		32,452	2,548

(ii) Disposal out of 1982 holding (W2) | | Nil | |

Total gain | | | 2,548 |

Did you answer the question?

Strictly you should show the FA 1985 pool disposal gain by deducting cost then deducting IA but since a loss is clearly not generated it is acceptable just to deduct the indexed cost.

Working 1

FA 1985 pool	Number of shares	Cost £	Indexed cost £
July 1983	3,000	12,000	12,000
Indexation to April 1985 $\frac{94.78-85.30}{85.30} = .111 \times £12,000$	-	-	1,332
	3,000	12,000	13,332
Indexation to June 1989 $\frac{115.4-94.78}{94.78} \times £13,332$	-	-	2,900
	3,000	12,000	16,232
June 1989 purchase	2,000	7,000	7,000
	5,000	19,000	23,232
Indexation to April 1998 $\frac{161.2-115.4}{115.4} \times £23,232$	-	-	9,220
	5,000	19,000	32,452
July 1998 sale	5,000	19,000	32,452
	-	-	-

Working 2

1982 holding	Number of shares	Cost
		£
July 1977	1,000	1,500
October 1981	2,000	3,500
	3,000	5,000
July 1998	(1,000)	(1,667)
carried forward	2,000	3,333

Calculation of gain	Cost	31.3.82 value
	£	£
Proceeds 1,000/6,000 × £42,000	7,000	7,000
Cost	(1,667)	-
31.3.82 value		
(1,000 at £3.70)		(3,700)
	5,333	3,300
Indexation allowance		
$\dfrac{161.2 - 79.44}{79.44}$		
= 1.029 × £3,700	(3,807)	(3,300) restricted
	1,526	Nil

Gain is £Nil

(b)

Jin Ming
1998-99 assessable capital gain

	£	£
Gain on disposal of shares		600,000
Retirement relief		
First tranche		
£250,000 × $\dfrac{5}{10}$	125,000	
Second tranche		
$\dfrac{(£500,000\ (W1) - £125,000)}{2}$	187,500	312,500
Assessable gain		287,500
Tapered to 92.5%		265,937

Working 1

The maximum proportion of the gain eligible for retirement relief is prima facie £550,000

$\left(£600,000 \times \dfrac{£550,000\ (W2)}{£600,000\ (W2)} \right)$ but the second tranche maximum cannot exceed 50%

$\dfrac{(5\ years)}{(10\ years)} \times £1,000,000 = £500,000.$

Did you answer the question?

You are not required to explain why the qualifying period is 5 years. By using 5 years, you show in any case your awareness that the QP can only run if the share ownership and the employment conditions are concurrently satisfied.

Working 2

Chargeable business assets	£
Land and buildings	250,000
Goodwill	100,000
Plant and machinery	200,000
	550,000

Working 3

Chargeable assets	£
Land and buildings	250,000
Goodwill	100,000
Plant and machinery	200,000
Investments	50,000
	600,000

62	**(Answer 4 of examination)**

(**Examiner's comments and marking guide**)

(i)   **This was a two-part value added tax question testing candidates' ability to calculate value added tax and offer advice on the value added tax consequences of acquiring a computer on hire purchase or rental.**

(ii)   In part (a) candidates' main errors were not apportioning overheads and not calculating the car fuel charge. The partial exemption point was over-looked by all but a few candidates. The wrong date of payment was frequently supplied. In part (b) there was general confusion about the value added tax tax point.

(iii) The performance was very poor on this question.

		Marks	
(a)	Fees - £10,500	1	
	Fuel - £40	1	
	Bad debts - £96	1	
	Attributable to taxable supplies - £2,000	1	
	Overheads - £1,433	2	
	Exempt VAT - £142	2	
	Due date - 31 December 1998	1	9
(b)	(i)	1	
	(ii)	1	
			2
Total			11

Step by step answer plan

Overview

As expected, question 4 tests your knowledge of VAT. Part (a) is relatively straightforward as long as you know the rules for bad debts, partial exemption and the car scale charge for private use fuel. Part (b) offers 2 marks for 2 fairly obvious comments on entitlement to input tax.

Step 1   Head up your main answer 'VAT payable for q/e 30.11.98'.

Step 2   Slot in the output tax figures not forgetting the liability for output tax on a scale basis for private use petrol.

Step 3   List the recoverable input tax showing the amount of the general overheads input tax attributable to taxable supplies and the entitlement to recover the VAT element in bad debts written off.

Step 4   Show the balance of the input tax on overheads as allowable being within the de minimis limit.

Step 5   Summarise the VAT payable and don't forget to state the due date.

Step 6   Answer part (b).

The examiner's answer

(a)

Portia
VAT payable - quarter to 30 November 1998

	£	£
Output tax		
Fees - £60,000 at 17½%		10,500
Car fuel charge - £268 × $^7/_{47}$		40
		10,540
Input tax		
Bad debts - £550 at 17½%	96	
Attributable to taxable supplies	2,000	
Overheads		
£9,000 × $\left(\dfrac{60,000*}{66,000}\right)$ ie, 91% = £8,190 at 17½% =	1,433	
Exempt VAT - (£9,000 - £8,190) at 17½%**	142	
		3,671
VAT payable		6,869

Due and payable on 31 December 1998

$*$ $\dfrac{\text{Taxable supplies}}{\text{Total supplies}}$

$**$ The balance of VAT on overheads will be deductible as exempt VAT as it is less than £625 per month

---

Did you answer the question?

You are not required to mention that if Portia chooses not to claim input tax on any car fuel - business or private - by concession, the car fuel charge (£40 per quarter) would be waived.

You are not required to state the rounding requirements of the partial exemption formula - (see TN 1 below).

Partial exemption is dealt with quarter by quarter but with an annual adjustment after the year end. On the assumption that this is not likely to arise on these figures - they show no risk of exceeding the de minimis limit - the examiner required no mention of it.

(b)   (i)   If Portia purchased the computer on hire-purchase she would be able to reclaim the input tax immediately.

    (ii)   If Portia rented the computer, VAT would be chargeable periodically on the rental payments and she could claim the input tax accordingly.

Tutorial notes

1   In the partial exemption formula the percentage must be a whole number. If the formula does not produce a whole number, it is rounded up to the next whole number.

2   Bad debt relief for VAT charged on outputs but not received requires the debt to be written off in the supplier's books and the payment date to be overdue at least 6 months by the end of the return quarter. There are other conditions but it is reasonable to assume that these have been satisfied.

63   (Answer 5 of examination)

Examiner's comments and marking guide

(i)   **A corporation tax 'Pay and File' question in three parts.**

(ii)   In part (a) many calculations were wrongly based on tax of £100,000 rather than tax overpaid of £10,000. Apportionments were made in months rather than days as required by the question. Many answers to part (b) made vague references to contacting the Inland Revenue by the 'required date', without supplying any dates. Similar references were made to 'fixed rate' penalties. There were a few correct answers to part (c) but most answers were combinations of any percentage or amount together with a period of lateness from 3 months to 2 years.

This was frequently the last question to be attempted and was not a popular question.

(iii)   The poor performance of candidates on this question reflected the reluctance of candidates to learn or revise this topic.

				Marks
(a)	(i)			1
	(ii)			1
				2
(b)				2
(c)	(i)	1		1
		2		1
		3		2
				4
	(ii)	Additional to c (i)		1
		10%		1
		20%		1	3
Total				11

(**Step by step answer plan**)

Overview

This is a question on corporation tax administration under the Pay and File system. It starts with a relatively easy 2 mark part which most candidates should manage. However, the rest of the 11 marks are given for knowing the main penalty provisions and it would be unwise to choose this question if you were only confident of answering part (a) properly.

Step 1 Work through parts (a), (b) and (c) in that order.

Step 2 In parts (b) and (c) decide exactly what is asked for and write it as briefly and accurately as you can. There are no marks for answering some other CT admin question which you wish had been set.

(**The examiner's answer**)

(a) (i) *Repaid interest on overdue tax*
£10,000 (W) at 10% for 30 days (April 1998)

$$= \quad £10,000 \text{ at } 10\% \times \frac{30}{365} = £82$$

W. £100,000 - £90,000 = £10,000

(ii) *Repayment supplement*

£10,000 at 10% for 1 May to 27 August 1998.

$$= \quad £10,000 \text{ at } 10\% \times \frac{119}{365} = £326$$

(b) The company must notify the Inland Revenue of its liability to corporation tax within 12 months of the end of the relevant accounting period. The maximum penalty for non-notification is 100% of the corporation tax due for the relevant accounting period.

(c) (i) (1) £100 where the return is up to three months late

(2) £200 where the return is more than three months late

(3) Where the return in question is the third consecutive one to be filed late the £100 and £200 penalties are increased to £500 and £1,000 respectively.

(ii) Tax-geared penalties operate in addition to fixed rate penalties where the return is more than six months late ie, more than 18 months from the end of the return period.

These are 10% of the corporation tax unpaid six months after the return was due where the delay was more than six but less than 12 months and 20% where the delay was 12 months or more.

64 (Answer 6 of examination)

(**Examiner's comments and marking guide**)

(i) **An income tax loss relief question.**

(ii) The loss relief could have been claimed under Sections 380, 381 or 385, a fact appreciated by most candidates. Many candidates did not apply the new Section 380 rules as an alternative to Section 381 in 1995/96. In many instances the dividend income was wrongly grossed-up.

(iii) The question was reasonably well attempted but with a little more thought candidates could have appreciably increased their score on the question.

1995-96	
Investment income	1
Claim under either s380 or s381	1
Part personal allowance lost	1
1996-97	
Claim under s380 or s381	1
1997-98	1
1998-99	1
Working 1 -	
1996-97	1
1997-98	1
Working 2	1
Explanation	2
	——
Total	11

Step by step answer plan

Overview

This is a question on opening year trading losses with consideration of how to make best use of the loss. By asking for taxable income for earlier years there is a strong hint that s.381, three year carry back, should be claimed although as it turns out s.380 would achieve the same result in this situation. This is the 'thinking' question on the paper. The examiner is well aware that such questions must not be made too difficult. Consequently there may be some easy marks for just a little careful thought.

Step 1   Compute the amounts of loss available for s.380 or s.381 using a working note. Under the opening year rules two separate losses arise - one for 1996/97 and one for 1997/98. Don't forget the exam requirement for daily apportionment for Schedule D I under the income tax rules.

Step 2   Consider how to use these two losses without wasting PAs or with minimum wastage of PAs but balance this with the preferment to achieve relief sooner rather than later. You have to assume that he had no income prior to 1995/96. It would help to note down in rough the income before PAs for 1995/96 to 1997/98. The optimum result seems to be achieved by using s.380 to carry back both losses. A small wastage of PAs in 1995/96 is preferable to waiting till 1998/99 to achieve loss relief.

Step 3   Schedule out the taxable income for the 4 years concerned using the losses as discussed in step 2.

Step 4   Explain briefly why you have used the losses in this manner and comment on the transferability of the MCA.

The examiner's answer

Lucien Buysse
Income chargeable to income tax

	£
1995-96	
Investment income	
(£12,200 × 100/80)	15,250
Claim under either s380 or s381	(11,466) (W1)
	——
	3,784
Personal allowance	(3,784)
	——
Income chargeable	-
	——

Personal allowance lost £411
   (£4,195 - £3,784)

1996-97	£
Investment income	
(£9,000 × 100/80)	11,250
Claim under s380 or s381	(3,534)
	7,716
Personal allowance	(4,195)
Income chargeable	3,521

1997-98	
Investment income	
(£10,000 × 100/80)	12,500
Personal allowance	4,195
Income chargeable	8,305

1998-99	
Investment income	
(£11,000 × 100/80)	13,750
Case II income	5,000 (W2)
	18,750
Personal allowance	(4,195)
	14,555

Did you answer the question?

You are not required to use rates or allowances other than those applying for 1998/99.

Accepting the small loss of personal allowance for 1995-96 is more cost-effective than carrying the losses forward under s385 against profits for future years where there may be a larger loss of personal allowance. Furthermore the unused 1995-96 married couple's allowance could be transferred to Lucien's wife.

Working 1

1996-97 (1.7.96 to 5.4.97)	£	
279/365 × £15,000	(11,466)	Loss

No Case II assessments

1997-98 (1.7.96 - 30.6.97)		
£15,000 - £11,466	(3,534)	Loss

Working 2

1998-99 (1.7.97 - 30.6.98)	5,000	Profit

---

65   (Answer 7 of examination)

Examiner's comments and marking guide

(i)   The question required candidates to state the tests applied by the Inland Revenue and Department of Social Security in deciding a taxpayer's status.

(ii)   Many candidates, particularly those from overseas, discussed the income tax and national insurance consequences of being employed/self-employed rather than the factors which determine the taxpayer's status. A minority of candidates wrongly described the 'badges of trade'.

(iii)   The question was generally well answered.

	Marks
1	1
2	1
3	1
4	1
5	1
6	1
7	1
8	1
9	1
10	1
11	1
Total	11

Step by step answer plan

Overview

The contrast between employed and self-employed is a regularly tested - topic area. However, you must be careful to read the question. Although the first sentence mentions 'advantages' the question actually requires a statement of the tests for determining which status applies.

Your answer should aim to provide at least 11 tests since 11 marks are available. It is better to give 11 tests in outline rather than, say, 4 or 5 tests in some detail. The courts are likely to view the tests in their totality rather than give undue weight to one or two of the tests. In theory therefore it is more important to list a test than to put the tests into any particular order.

Step 1   List out 11 tests describing them in just sufficient detail to indicate your awareness of their significance.

The examiner's answer

The Inland Revenue and Department of Social Security will consider the following matters in arriving at their decision.

Answers in the affirmative to the following specific questions will usually mean the individual is self-employed.

(1)   Do you decide how the business is run?

(2)   Is your own money at risk?

(3)   Do you bear the financial risk for losses as well as taking profits?

(4)   Are you responsible for providing the main items of equipment used in the business?

(5)   Can you hire other people on your terms to do the work for you?

(6)   Does unsatisfactory work have to be corrected by you without payment?

In addition the following factors will be taken into account.

(7)   Exclusivity. The greater the number of people for whom an individual does work the more likely the individual is self-employed.

(8)   Insurance. Self-employed individuals will normally have to make their own insurance arrangements.

(9)   Integration. An employed person will be to a large extent integrated in the fabric of an organisation whereas a self-employed person will stand apart as an independent person.

(10)   An employee will normally have a contract of service with his employer whereas a self-employed person will normally have a contract for specific services to be carried out.

(11)   In reaching a decision all the relevant factors will need to be taken into account and a common-sense approach adopted.

Did you answer the question?

You are not required to discuss the tax or NIC advantages of being self-employed as opposed to being under employee status.

You might know some relevant case names but these are not asked for.

---

66   (Answer 8 of examination)

Examiner's comments and marking guide

(i)   **Candidates were presented with a taxpayer's coding notice and asked to state the information required to check its accuracy.**

(ii)   A significant number of candidates made the mistake of assuming self-employment although PAYE was clearly mentioned. Candidates listed documents required without indicating how they would use the documents to check the coding notice. Most candidates picked up marks by referring to age, date of marriage and car benefits but other areas were weak. In part (b) although it should have been obvious from the coding notice that the 'K' code given would increase the tax payable, only a very few candidates spotted this.

(iii)   A disappointing performance to an unusual type of question.

			Marks
(a)	Personal allowance		1
	Married allowance		1
	Allowance restriction		1
	Personal pension		2
	Benefits (car) -		
	35%	½	
	One-third between 2,500 and 17,999	½	
	Two-thirds 18,000 and over	½	
	Four years old	½	2

Benefits (car fuel)		1	
Untaxed interest		1	
Unpaid tax		1	10

(b)   'K' codes   1

Total   11

Step by step answer plan

Overview

This question requires a commonsense application of personal tax knowledge. For part (a) it would not have been entirely clear in the exam how the 10 marks would be allocated. It would be safe to assume that some items will require more detail than others and therefore attract more marks.

Step 1   For part (a) use a separately labelled paragraph for each of the 8 elements in the coding notice.

Step 2   Don't forget to claim the easy mark for answering part (b)

The examiner's answer

(a)   The following information would be required to check James's 1998-99 coding notice.

(1)   *Personal allowance*

Is £4,195 the correct allowance for 1998-99? How old is James?

(2)   *Married allowance*

Was James married throughout 1998-99 or at least prior to 6 May 1998 and is £1,900 the correct allowance for 1998-99? How old is James's wife?

(3)   *Allowance restriction*

This restriction applies to restrict the married allowance to £1,900 at 15% = £285. As £1,900 − 1,188 = 712 @ 40% = £285, the Revenue have assumed James to be a 40% taxpayer in 1998-99. Is this the case?

(4)   *Personal pension*

Relief for pension contributions in an employer's scheme is given by reducing the gross pay by the amount of the contributions before PAYE is applied. If relief is given in the coding notice the pension premium will be a free-standing additional voluntary contribution. For Schedule E taxpayers the premiums are paid net of the basic rate tax and for higher rate taxpayers the amount of relief in the coding notice must be such an amount as will provide relief of 17% (40% - 23%). The amount of the premium payable in 1998-99 would appear to be £945 $\times \dfrac{40}{17}$ = £2,224. (Check: £2,224 $\times$ 40% = £890. Deduct £2,224 $\times$ 23% = £512 is £378 saving due, which equals £945 $\times$ 40%).

Is this correct?

(5)   *Benefits (car)*

Where there is private use of a company car the annual benefit-in-kind is calculated at 35% of the price of the car. Any contribution by the employee will reduce the amount of the benefit. This amount is reduced by one-third if the annual business mileage is between 2,500 and 17,999 and by two-thirds if the annual business mileage is 18,000 miles or over. There is a further one-third reduction for cars which will be four years old at the end of the tax year. Is the figure of £4,700 correct taking the above factors into account?

(6)   *Benefits (car fuel)*

If any fuel is provided by the employer for an employee's private motoring and the total cost of such fuel is not reimbursed an annual table rate benefit applies calculated by reference to the car's engine size and whether it uses petrol or diesel. Is the figure of £1,890 correct based on the facts as applied to the table rate ie, a petrol or diesel driven car over 2000cc?

(7)   *Untaxed interest*

Interest received gross (eg, from the National Savings Bank) is assessable under Schedule D Case III, but is usually set against allowances in a coding notice for comparatively small amounts. Is £910 the amount of interest likely to be received in 1998-99? If James is a higher-rate taxpayer no adjustment to the interest figure is required in the coding notice.

(8)   *Unpaid tax*

Underpayments of tax arising from Schedule E are sometimes collected under self-assessment, but are often set against allowances in a coding notice for comparatively small amounts. The coding restrictions will vary according to the taxpayer's marginal rate of tax. For a 40% taxpayer the restriction will be 'underpayment' × 100/40. Is the underpayment which is being collected £230 × 40/100 ie, £92?

(b)   *'K' codes*

A 'K' code, as in James's case, is applied where there are negative allowances in the coding notice. In such a case 'negative allowances' are added to the taxable amount rather than being deducted as normal.

Did you answer the question?

You are not required to explain the make up of the coding notice other than to comment on how the accuracy of an item would be checked.

JUNE 1997 QUESTIONS

67 (Question 1 of examination)

Unbeatable Undercarriages Ltd (UUL) is a United Kingdom resident company which has been trading for many years and manufactures aircraft components. It has no associated companies. The company had always made up accounts to 31 December. The company's results for the year ended 31 December 1998 are as follows:

	£
Trading profits (as adjusted for taxation but before capital allowances and loan interest)	1,300,000
Payment under deed of covenant to a national charity (gross amount) (note 4 and 7)	5,000
Loan interest payable on trade loan (gross amount) (notes 5 and 7)	10,000
Bank interest receivable (note 6)	7,000
Dividends received from UK companies	50,000

Notes:

1. On 1 January 1998 the tax written-down values of plant and machinery were:

	£
Pool	78,000
Car pool	27,000
Short-life asset (purchased 1.6.95)	4,000

    On 1 August 1998 a car was sold for £7,000 and replaced by one costing £14,000.

    The short-life asset was sold on 1 July 1998 for £2,000.

2. The company had purchased a new industrial building on 1 July 1990 for immediate use for £200,000. During a period of recession from 1 April 1992 to 30 September 1994 the building was rented out for the storage of furniture. On 1 October 1994 manufacturing recommenced. On 31 May 1998 the building was sold for £400,000.

    The building was not situated in an enterprise zone.

3. On 1 January 1998 the company had trading losses brought forward of £300,000.

4. The deed of covenant payment was made on 1 June 1998.

5. Included in the figure of £10,000 for loan interest payable is a closing accrual of £2,000. The £8,000 was paid on 1 July 1998. The loan was taken out in 1998.

6. Included in the figure of £7,000 for bank interest receivable is a closing accrual of £2,440. The £4,560 was received on 30 September 1998. The bank account was opened in 1998.

7. The gross amounts of loan interest payable and the deed of covenant payment are shown. Income tax has been deducted at source.

You are required:

(a)   to calculate the corporation tax liability for the accounting period to 31 December 1998, and

      (17 marks)

(b)   to state the amount of income tax withheld by the company on payment of:

      (i)   loan interest and
      (ii)   deed of covenant.

      (2 marks)
      (Total: 19 marks)

NB. All apportionments may be made to the nearest month.

---

68   (Question 2 of examination)

Bruce died on 31 May 1998 when he was 66. He had been married to Sheila, aged 57, for many years. No elections have been made by Bruce and Sheila in respect of the married couple's allowance for 1998-99.

Bruce had the following income in 1998-99, up to his death

	£
Retirement pension	700
Income from employment (PAYE deducted £1,380)	5,600
Dividends	9,000
Capital gains (prior to death, before annual exemption)	12,000
Bank interest	40

Sheila started a wholesale soft furnishing business on 1 July 1996. The profits as adjusted for income tax, but before capital allowances, were as follows:

		£
1.7.96 - 31.5.97		14,000
1.6.97 - 31.5.98		20,000
Capital additions were:		
1.7.96	Shelving and furniture	3,500
4.7.96	Computer	2,500
1.10.97	Car	10,000

The car was also used by Sheila privately. The private mileage was 50% of the total mileage.

No claim is to be made to treat any of the assets as 'short-life' assets.

Sheila paid the maximum personal pension contribution for 1998-99 and received a widow's pension of £2,750 in that tax year.

You are required:

(a)   to calculate any income tax and capital gains tax payable or repayable on Bruce's income and capital gains for 1998-99,   **(12 marks)**

(b)   to calculate the Schedule D Case I income tax assessment on Sheila for the years 1996-97, 1997-98 and 1998-99,   **(6 marks)**

(c)   to calculate Sheila's 'overlap' profits and   **(1 mark)**

(d)   to calculate Sheila's income tax and NIC Class 4 liabilities for 1998-99.   **(6 marks)**
      (Total: 25 marks)

NB. All apportionments in parts (b) and (c) should be made in days.

---

69   (Question 3 of examination)

(a)   Galibier Limited sold one of its factories in May 1998 for £300,000. It did not intend to replace the factory which had been purchased in July 1989 for £160,000. Fixed plant and machinery costing £250,000 had been purchased in March 1998 and the company have asked you whether it is possible to defer the gain on the building against the cost of the fixed plant and machinery.

You are required:

(i)   to calculate the capital gain on the sale of the building and   **(1 mark)**

(ii)   to advise the company, with supporting computations, on the possibility and consequences of a deferral claim.   **(7 marks)**

(b)   Stephen had the following dealings in the shares of Glandon Limited, an unquoted company:

	Date	Number of shares	£
Purchase	1.7.79	6,000	15,000
Purchase	1.9.81	2,000	5,500
Bonus (1 for 4)	1.8.86	2,000	-
Purchase	1.8.88	3,000	12,750
Purchase	1.10.94	4,000	20,000
Sale	1.6.98	10,000	60,000

Relevant share valuations are:

31.3.82	(adjusted for bonus issue)	£3.50 per share
1.6.98	(remaining shares)	£4.00 per share

No election is being made to 're-base' the cost of all assets held on 31.3.82 at their value on that date.

Glandon Limited is not a qualifying company in relation to Stephen for taper relief purposes.

You are required to calculate Stephen's capital gain for 1998-99 before annual exemption.

(9 marks)
(Total: 17 marks)

---

70   (Question 4 of examination)

You have been asked by your tax partner to prepare briefing notes for a meeting with Mr Dalton, the owner of a hardware store, to advise on the following matters:

(a)   the appeals procedure for value added tax.

. **(7 marks)**

(b)   the determination of the VAT tax point in the following situations:

(i)   goods supplied on a sale or return basis,
(ii)   fuel supplies for private motoring and
(iii)   continuous supplies (eg, electricity)

(4 marks)
(Total: 11 marks)

---

71   (Question 5 of examination)

You are required to calculate the National Insurance contributions payable for 1998-99 by both employer and employee in the following situations:

(a)   Alma receives a gross weekly salary of £500. She is not contracted out of the state pension scheme. Alma is provided with a company car by her employer. Until 5 October 1998 the car was a 1,800cc petrol car which was first registered on 1 August 1997 with a list price of £15,000. On 6 October 1998 the car was exchanged for a new 2,500cc petrol car whose list price was £18,000. Petrol for both business and private mileage is provided by Alma's employer. The car mileages were:

6.4.98	- 5.10.98	16,000 of which 10,000 was business
6.10.98	- 5.4.99	12,000 of which 7,000 was business

(9 marks)

(b)   Albert is paid £220 per week gross and is not contracted out of the state pension scheme.

(2 marks)
(Total: 11 marks)

---

72   (Question 6 of examination)

You are required to briefly describe PAYE (Pay as you Earn) and outline the operation of the PAYE system for tax collection, including the procedures to be followed at the end of the tax year and when a taxpayer changes jobs.

(11 marks)

---

73   (Question 7 of examination)

(a)   Jocelyn owned a furnished cottage in the United Kingdom which was available for commercial letting when not occupied by Jocelyn and her family.

In the tax year 1998-99 it was let for 18 weeks on a weekly basis and was available for letting throughout the tax year apart from the whole of August when it was occupied by Jocelyn. In 1998-99 the total rent received was £4,900 and the following expenditure was incurred in respect of the property:

	£
Insurance (note 1)	500
Repairs and decorating	700
Water rates	250
Accountancy	100
Cleaning	300
Interest on loan to purchase property	1,200
Advertising	300

Note 1 (Cottage)

The insurance of £500 was paid on 1 October 1998. The insurance paid on 1 October 1997 had been £450.

Capital allowances on furniture and fittings in the cottage amounted to £400, before restriction for private use.

You are required:

(i)   to state the reasons the letting of the holiday cottage qualified as a 'commercial letting of furnished holiday accommodation'.   **(3 marks)**

(ii)   to calculate the amount assessable on the holiday cottage letting for 1998-99.   **(3 marks)**

(b)   Jocelyn also owns 2 flats

Flat 1.

The flat was purchased on 1 May 1998 and was first let on 24 June 1998 on a landlord's repairing lease at an annual rental of £5,000.

Flat 2.

The annual rental was £3,600 on a tenant's repairing lease which expired on 23 June 1998. The property was re-let on 29 September 1998 at an annual rental of £3,000 on a 5 year tenant's repairing lease. The incoming tenant was required to pay a premium of £2,000. Details of expenditure in the year ended 5 April 1999 were:

	Flat 1	Flat 2
	£	£
Insurance	300 (note 1)	400
Repairs and decorating	4,200 (note 2)	1,500 (note 3)
Accountancy	50	60

Notes (Flats)

1.   The insurance was taken out on 1 June 1998 on an annual basis.
2.   £3,000 of the expenditure was incurred in making good damage caused by flooding on 29 May 1998
3.   £1,200 of the expenditure was spent on normal re-decorating work between leases in July 1998.

The rent for both properties was due in advance on the usual quarter days, 25 March, 24 June, 29 September and 25 December.

You are required to calculate the amount assessable on Jocelyn for 1998-99 in respect of income from the flats.

(5 marks)

NB. Calculations may be made to the nearest month.
(Total: 11 marks)

---

74   (Question 8 of examination)

Rainier's annual salary from Excalibur Limited is £40,000. He was re-located by Excalibur Limited on 6 April 1998 and was required by the company to live in a company-owned house; the annual value of this job-related accommodation was £4,000. He was re-imbursed relevant re-location expenditure incurred of £10,000.

Ancillary services provided by the company in 1998-99 were:

	£
Electricity	400
Council tax	800
Gas	800
Water	300
Decorating	4,200

Rainier is required to make an annual contribution of £1,000 towards the cost of these services.

In addition Rainier was provided with furniture for the house by his employer on 6 April 1998. The furniture cost £15,000. On 5 April 1999 Rainier bought the furniture from his employer for £7,500 when its market value was £10,000.

Excalibur Limited provided Rainier with a loan of £30,000 on 6 April 1998 on which annual interest of 5% was payable.

Rainier pays superannuation contributions each year amounting to 6% of his basic salary.

You are required to calculate the amount assessable under Schedule E on Rainier for 1998-99.   **(11 marks)**

ANSWERS TO JUNE 1997 EXAMINATION

67   (Answer 1 of examination)

Examiner's comments and marking guide

A straight forward corporation tax question testing:

(a)   the calculation of corporation tax where the chargeable accounting period straddles 31 March,

(b)   the calculation of capital allowances, both plant and machinery and industrial buildings, and a consequential capital tax liability,

(c)   the treatment of loan interest payable.

In many cases candidates demonstrated a reasonable knowledge of the basic corporation tax rules and layout but were unable to deal with a number of issues raised by the question.

(a)   As in previous examinations the IBA part of the question was generally badly done. This was despite the computation being relatively simple in this case, with the only complication being a period of non-industrial usage. Common errors included calculating allowances on a reducing balance basis and pro rating allowances for partial use within a year.

(b)   The capital allowances for plant and machinery was generally well done.

(c)   The chargeable gain on the building was calculated correctly by many candidates, although many weaker candidates omitted the calculation altogether.

(d)   Losses brought forward were not deducted from trading profits.

(e)   Dividends paid and received were sometimes included in the calculation of 'I'.

(f)   Corporation tax payable was sometimes calculated on 'P'.

(g)   Income tax withheld on payment of the deed of covenant and loan interest was then deducted from the figure of corporation tax payable.

(h)   Bank interest was often grossed-up.

(i)   Loan interest was deducted as a charge on income.

The above is not an exhaustive list of errors but covers areas which are core to the syllabus and thus should be considered as aspects of corporation tax over which the average candidate should have a firm grasp.

(Then comments have been edited to remove points not currently relevant.)

			Marks
(a)	Trading losses brought forward		1
	Deed of covenant payment		1
	Loan interest payable		1
	Bank interest		1
	Working 1		
	Additions and disposals	1	
	WDA's	1	
	Balancing allowance	1	
		—	3

Working 2

WDA's to 31.12.90 and 31.12.91	1	
Notional WDA's to 31.12.92 and 31.12.93	1	
WDA's for 4 years to 31.12.97	1	
Balancing charge	1	
	—	4

Working 3

Unindexed gain	1	
Indexation allowance	1	2

Working 4

Calculation of 'P'	1	
Significance of 'P'	1	
Calculation of corporation tax	2	
	—	4
(b) (i) loan interest	1	
(ii) deed of covenant	1	
	—	2

Total   19

Step by step answer plan

Overview

As expected, part (a), for the bulk of the marks, is a 'compute CT' type question. This invariably requires a standard PCTCT layout followed by a standard corporation tax layout. It is important to read the question and break it down into manageable pieces. For example, Note 1 is clearly asking for a standard P & M CA computation and Note 2 concerns IBAs. You know the figures generated from this detail are deductible against trading profits. As you read the other items in the Notes you should make a mental note of their likely position in your standard layout.

Part (b) concerns the withholding of income tax on two payments. This would only be relevant to the CT comp if the company received income net of income tax - and it does not. Don't forget to earn these two easy marks.

Step 1   Head up the main part of your answer - ie, the PCTCT / CT layout.

Step 2   Slot in the figure for trading profits at the top and deal with the related items - ie, CAs on P & M (Note 1), IBAs (Note 2), and the accrued loan interest payable (Notes 5 & 7) - using separate workings where necessary.

Step 3   You know trading losses b/f (Note 3) can only be set against Sch D I profits - in fact, there is no choice inasmuch as the loss must be used as soon as future trading profits appear - so set them off next.

Step 4   In dealing with IBAs (Note 2) you spotted that a capital gain arose and you headed up another working to make that calculation. Transfer the gain figure to the PCTCT layout but check if there are any capital losses b/f or if roll-over relief is available.

Step 5   The PCTCT layout is fast taking shape and all the other figures needed are found in the remaining notes.

Step 6   Read through the question just to ensure that no points relevant to the PCTCT figure have been overlooked.

Step 7   The rest of your answer - ie, converting PCTCT to CT - covers more predictable ground and you need only consider the rate of CT and whether there is any income tax to recover.

Step 8 The examiner generally likes to see the CT figure in a separate working even if it is easy to compute as in this question. Here there is a FY 'straddle' but, exceptionally, without a change in rates etc. If the rates change you would start with the PCTCT figure, add in the FII (don't forget to gross-up the dividend received figure) and then time apportion into the two FYs and calculate the tax and marginal relief in two stages. This is not difficult but requires care. Show clearly what you are trying to do so you can still be given credit for correct technique even if the arithmetic comes to grief! Fortunately this complication did not arise here.

Step 9 Finally (for CT) is there any income tax to recover in respect of unfranked investment income? There is no UFII so there cannot be any income tax to recover. For part (b) you have to show the income tax withheld on amounts paid but don't make the common mistake of trying to recover it. It would be akin to asking for a tax credit for PAYE deducted on salaries to employees. In both situations the company is merely acting as an unpaid tax collector on behalf of the recipient's tax liability.

The examiner's answer

(a)

Unbeatable Undercarriages Limited
Corporation tax computation for the Chargeable
accounting period to 31 December 1998

		£
Trading profit		1,300,000
Capital allowances -		
Plant and machinery	(W1)	(29,500)
Industrial buildings	(W2)	48,000
Loan interest payable	(TN 2)	(10,000)
		1,308,500
Trading losses brought forward		(300,000)
		1,008,500
Chargeable gains	(W3)	145,600
Bank interest receivable	(TN 2&3)	7,000
		1,161,100
Total profits		1,161,100
Charge on income - Deed of covenant payment		(5,000)
Profits chargeable to corporation tax		1,156,100
Corporation tax payable	(W4)	351,717

(b)   Income tax deducted from

(i)   loan interest
       £8,000 at 20%   1,600

(ii)   Deed of covenant
       £5,000 at 23%   1,150

WORKING 1

Plant and machinery allowances

	Main pool £	Car pool £	Short-life asset £	Expensive car £	Total £
WDV b/f 1.1.98	78,000	27,000	4,000		
Disposals		(7,000)	(2,000)		
Additions				14,000	
	78,000	20,000	2,000	14,000	
WDA 25%	19,500	5,000	-	3,000*	27,500
Balancing Allce.	-	-	2,000	-	2,000
WDV c/f 31.12.98	58,500	15,000	-	11,000	

* restricted   29,500

WORKING 2

Industrial building allowance

	£	£
Cost		200,000
Allowances -		
CAP to 31.12.90 - 4%	8,000	
CAP to 31.12.91 - 4%	8,000	
CAP to 31.12.92 - 4% (notional)	8,000	
CAP to 31.12.93 - 4% (notional)	8,000	
(The building was not in industrial use on 31.12.92 and 31.12.93)		
CAP to 31.12.94 - 4%	8,000	
CAP to 31.12.95 - 4%	8,000	
CAP to 31.12.96 - 4%	8,000	
CAP to 31.12.97 - 4%	8,000	64,000
Residue before sale		136,000
CAP to 31.12.98		
Balancing charge - allowances actually given		48,000

WORKING 3

Chargeable gain on disposal of industrial building (TN 1)

	£
Sale proceeds	400,000
Cost	200,000
Unindexed gain	200,000
Indexation allowance	
$\frac{161.3-126.8}{126.8}$ (.272)	(54,400)
Indexed gain	145,600

WORKING 4

Corporation tax payable

		£
'I' (chargeable profits)		1,156,100
Franked investment income 50,000 × $^{100}/_{80}$		62,500
'P'	=	1,218,600

As 'P' is between the lower and upper limits for both financial year 1997 and financial year 1998 the marginal rate of corporation tax applies. As rates etc for FY 1997 and FY 1998 are these same it is not necessary to separately calculate the corporation tax payable for each financial year.

	£
£1,156,100 × 31%	358,391
Marginal relief	
$(1,500,000 - 1,218,600) \times \dfrac{1,156,100}{1,218,600} \times \dfrac{1}{40}$	(6,674)
	351,717

Tutorial notes

1   For the IBA calculation the cost/sale proceeds of the building is deemed to exclude the land. In the capital gain calculation it has to be assumed that the value of the land is included. This is a common exam convention to reduce complexity.

2   The 'loan relationship' rules apply to all loans or borrowings either made by or to a company. Thus bank or debenture interest receivable or payable will normally be included in the financial accounts on an accruals basis and should remain on that basis for tax purposes.

3   Bank or building society interest is always received gross by a company and the examiner frequently tests this point.

68   (Answer 2 of examination)

(**Examiner's comments and marking guide**)

An income tax question testing:

(a)   the calculation of income tax liabilities involving savings income, non-savings income and capital gains with restricted age allowance,

(b)   the calculation of income tax assessments, including capital allowances computations, for the first three years of a business commencing to trade after 5 April 1994 and

(c)   the calculation of NIC Class 4 liability.

The main problems encountered by candidates are itemised below

Part (a) Non-savings income. Some candidates either omitted retirement income or showed it (incorrectly) as savings income. A large number of candidates added PAYE tax, £1,380 to the income from employment without giving any explanation or assumption regarding their treatment.

Savings income. Although the dividend income was computed correctly, there were the usual grossing-up errors in computing the bank interest ie, using the fraction 100/77 instead of 100/80. Some candidates did not bother to gross up at all. Despite comments in several previous Examiner's Reports many candidates still treat capital gains as income liable to income tax.

Personal allowances. Age related allowances still tend to present problems to many candidates, ranging from identifying the correct allowance to its appropriate restriction and relief. Some candidates go on to restrict the age related MCA even where the restriction has been fully utilised against the higher personal allowance. Some candidates failed to distinguish between the relief for the personal allowance and the MCA, the latter being a deduction from the income tax liability. This weakness was also evident in part (d) of the answer.

Calculation of tax liability. There was a definite improvement in the calculation of tax liabilities (income tax and CGT) in a situation where the tax bands have to be correctly allocated between non-savings income, savings income and chargeable gains. However, this still appears to be the worst aspect of many candidates' personal tax computations. Many candidates included retirement income as savings income when allocating the bands. A large number of candidates failed to allocate part of the lower rate band against chargeable gains.

Capital allowances. Although, a distinct note to the question clearly asks for apportionments to be in days, a very large number of candidates either did not read the note or simply ignored it. Despite a note that a 'short life assets' claim has not been made, some candidates went on to treat the computer as a short life asset.

Assessments. Again, the above comments regarding apportionment in days, instead of months, applies in respect of the assessments for 1996/97 and 1997/98. A significant number of candidates made the fundamental error of apportioning profits before deducting capital allowances when computing the assessments. There still appears to be a lot of confusion regarding the treatment of capital allowances as between the old regime and the new regime of business taxation.

Part (c) Overlap profits. A surprisingly large number of candidates failed to identify the second overlap period (1.6.97 - 30.6.97).

Part (d) Income tax computation. The inclusion of widow's pension in the NRE when computing the private pension deduction was a common error. Many candidates gave basic rate tax relief against Sheila's income tax liability assuming quite incorrectly, that self employed persons pay private pension premiums net of basic rate tax. This relief only applies to individuals in employment. A significant number of candidates gave relief for both WBA and MCA, when only the former applied.

Class 4 NIC. Generally, well done by most candidates. Common errors were: basing the contribution on 'taxable income' or 'STI' instead of Sch D Case I profits; using, incorrectly, the upper limit (£25,220) even when the trading profits, as computed by the candidate, were clearly below the limit; ignoring the exempt limit (£7,310).

			marks
(a)	(i)	Non-savings income	1
		Dividends	1
		Bank interest	1
		Personal allowance	1
		Restriction on personal allowance	1
		Income tax on non-savings income	1
		Income tax on savings income	1
		Married couple's allowance	1
		Income tax suffered	1
	(ii)	Annual capital gains exemption	1
		Lower rate CGT liability	1
		Basic rate CGT liability	1
(b)	A.	1.7.96 - 31.5.97 WDA	1
		1.6.97 - 31.5.98 WDA	1
	B.	Profits for the accounting periods	1
	C.	Assessments - 1996-97	1
		- 1997-98	1
		- 1998-99	1
(c)		Overlap profits	1

(d)	(i)	Personal pension premium	1
		Widow's pension	1
		Personal allowance	1
		Income tax payable	1
		WBA	1
	(ii)	Class 4 NIC liability	1

Total 25

(**Step by step answer plan**)

Overview

Part (a) is clearly a 'husband and wife year of death' question with age relief to consider and parts (b), (c) and (d) involve 'commencement to trade'. This is obvious both from reading the question and the stated requirements. There is some limited interaction between the separate parts of the question in as much as parts (c) and (d) depend on figures computed for part (b) of the answer. The important point is not to overlook any part of the requirements and to make a special effort in parts (c) and (d) to show any point of principle you use in case you are having to use incorrect figures generated in part (b).

Step 1 Complete a standard Taxable Income layout for Bruce distinguishing between savings and non-savings income and showing the income adjusted age relief PA.

Step 2 Then compute the income tax showing why it is all at 20% and not forgetting the age relief MCA.

Step 3 Do not go on to part (b) until you have computed the CGT - it is easy to overlook even though it is clearly asked for in part (a).

Step 4 Part (b) asks for Schedule D I assessments but the adjusted profit figures in the question must first be reduced by the capital allowances. Hence, first compute these for the two periods of account.

Step 5 Next, reduce the profits by the capital allowances and produce the assessable amounts for the years of assessment concerned by applying the opening year rules.

Step 6 Don't forget to identify the overlap profits for the mark in part (c) - a lot to do for just one mark but easy enough following your calculations in part (b).

Step 7 Part (d) requires another standard taxable income/income tax layout. Note that the maximum PPC is age related - hence another reason to highlight a taxpayer's age. Also, widow's pension is taxable and WBA should not be overlooked.

Step 8 Finally don't waste the opportunity for an easy mark for calculating the Class 4 liability.

(**The examiner's answer**)

(a) (i)

Bruce's income tax liability 1998-99
(up to date of death 31.5.98)

	£	£
Non-savings income		
Retirement income	700	
Employment income	5,600	6,300
Savings income		
Dividends (£9,000 × $\frac{100}{80}$) (TN 1)	11,250	
Bank interest (£40 × $\frac{100}{80}$) (TN 1)	50	11,300

Total income		17,600
Personal allowance (65 - 74)	5,410	
Restriction 1/2 (17,600 - 16,200)	(700)	4,710
Taxable income		12,890
Income tax on non-savings income		
£1,590 at 20%		318
Income tax on savings income		
£11,300 at 20%		2,260
		2,578
Married couple's allowance (65 - 74)		
£3,305 at 15%		(496)
Income tax liability		2,082
Income tax suffered:		
PAYE	1,380	
Tax credit on dividends (£9,000 × $\frac{80}{20}$)	2,250	
Tax withheld on bank interest		
(£50 at 20%)	10	3,640
Income tax repayment due		1,558

(ii)

1998-99 Capital Gains tax liability
(up to date of death 31.5.98)

	£
Capital gains	12,000
Annual exemption	6,800
	5,200
Capital gains tax payable	
£2,710 at 20%	542
£2,490 at 23%	573
5,200	1,115

Allocation of bands (TN 2)

	Non-savings £*	Savings £	Gains £	Total £
Lower (20%)	1,590	-	2,710	4,300
Basic (23%)	-	11,300	2,490	13,790
	1,590	11,300	5,200	18,090

* Income £6,300 - PA £4,710 = £1,590

Did you answer the question?

The examiner did not ask for the CGT payday so don't waste time including it in your answer.

(b)

A.

Capital allowances claim

	Pool £	Car £	(50% (pte)) £	Claim £
1.7.96 - 31.5.97				
Additions	3,500			
	2,500			
	————			
	6,000			
WDA $(25\% \times \frac{335}{365})$	1,377			1,377
	————			————
	4,623			
1.6.97 - 31.5.98				
Additions		10,000		
WDA (25%)	1,156	2,500	(1,250)	2,406
	————	————		————
WDV c/f	3,467	7,500		

B.

Profits for the accounting periods

	£
1.7.96 - 31.5.97 14,000 - CA's 1,377 =	12,623
1.6.97 - 31.5.98 20,000 - CA's 2,406 =	17,594

C.

Assessments

Tax year	Basis period	Assessments £	
1996-97	1.7.96 - 5.4.97	10,513	(W1)
1997-98	1.7.96 - 30.6.97	14,069	(W2)
1998-99	1.6.97-31.5.98	17,594	

WORKINGS

		£
W1	$12,623 \times \frac{279}{335} =$	10,513
		————

W2	1.7.96 - 31.5.97	
	as in B	12,623
	1.6.97 - 30.6.97	
	$17,594 \times \frac{30}{365} =$	1,446
		————
		14,069
		————

(c)   Overlap profits
'Overlap' periods are 1.7.96 - 5.4.97 and 1.6.97 - 30.6.97.
'Overlap' profits are £10,513 + £1,446 = £11,959.

(d)   (i)

Sheila
1998-99 income tax liability

	£
Case I profits	17,594
Personal pension premium (35%)	(6,158)
	11,436
Widow's pension	2,750
	14,186
Personal allowance	(4,195)
Taxable income	9,991

Income tax payable

£4,300 at 20%	860
£5,691 at 23%	1,309
9,991	2,169
Widow's bereavement allowance £1,900 at 15%	(285)
	1,884

(ii)   NIC Class 4 liability

	£
Profits	17,594
Lower limit	7,310
	10,284
£10,284 at 6% =	617

Did you answer the question?

Your answer should exclude any mention of how Sheila would have to account for income tax and Class 4 NIC as this is not asked for. Similarly she would have to pay Class 2 NIC but this point is not required so don't waste time mentioning it.

Tutorial notes

1   Dividends and bank interest are usually shown net in the question and must be grossed up - with a tax credit to deduct lower down.

2   The capital gains tax computation illustrates a peculiarity of the legislation. Usually capital gains are taxed by placing them on top of taxable income regardless of whether it consists of savings or non-savings income. However, if there is insufficient non-savings income to utilise the lower rate band, gains take up the difference in priority to non-savings income.

69	**(Answer 3 of examination)**

(Examiner's comments and marking guide)

A two-part capital gains tax question testing:

(a) **calculation on the sale of a building giving rise to a liability and advising on the possibility of a part-deferral against fixed plant and machinery purchased within the relevant four year period together with supporting computations and**

(b) **calculation of a capital gain arising on the sale of part of a holding of unquoted shares, some of which were acquired prior to 31 March 1982, with a bonus issue after 31 March 1982, where no re-basing election has been made in respect of all assets held on 31 March 1982.**

The question was not popular and was not well done:

(a)   many candidates confused hold-over and roll-over reliefs. The minority of candidates who were aware of hold-over relief scored all or most of the marks available.

(b)   most candidates, except the very weak ones, recognised the need for two pools and so earned most of the marks. Most candidates seemed to be unaware that the shares were unquoted and that therefore the FA 1982 pool cost had to be calculated using the part-disposal formula.

				Marks
(a)	(i)	Calculation of gain		1
	(ii)	Depreciating asset to be 'held-over'		1
		A. disposal of plant		1
		B. March 2008		1
		C. Cessation of use of plant		1
		4 - year time limit		1
		immediate charge		1
		Held-over gain		1
(b)	(i)	Sale from FA 1985 pool		
		Sale proceeds		1
	(ii)	Sale from 1982 holding		
		Sale proceeds		1
		MV at 31.3.82 (£10,500)		1
		Indexation allowance (on £10,500) with restriction		1
		Working 1		
		Indexation to October 1994	1	
		Indexation to April 1998	1	2
				—
		Working 2		
		Allocated shares - 3,000 shares		1
		Working 3		
		Allocated cost - £8,022		2
				—
Total				17
				—

(**Step by step answer plan**)

Overview

Question 3 is always made up of 2 or 3 separate questions on capital gains tax. It is usually very easy to spot the technical points being tested. Part (a) clearly concerns a simple CG computation with the possibility of deferring the gain using a recently acquired depreciating asset - fixed plant and machinery. Part (b) is a standard share history construction with a 1982 holding - shares acquired before 6 April 1982 - and a FA 1985 pool - shares acquired since 5 April 1982 and before 6 April 1998. There are two complications. Firstly there is a bonus issue and secondly the examiner has invoked the part disposal rules for the 1982 holding. We discuss these in more detail below.

[**Step 1**]   In part (a), (i) requires a straightforward CG computation. Just ensure that you don't waste this one easy mark by being careless - eg, computing the IA on the unindexed gain rather than the cost, a common error when you are in a hurry.

[**Step 2**]   In part (a), (ii) offers 7 marks for a mainly written answer so care is needed to mention all the required detail. Essentially the company purchased a depreciating asset within the 4 year 'window'. It was one of the right sorts of assets but, being depreciating, only allowed hold-over, not roll-over. Not all of the sale proceeds amount has been reinvested. The implications of these facts have to be included in the advice you give.

[**Step 3**]   In part (b) a working is needed for each of the two assets involved - the FA 1985 pool and the 1982 holding. The bonus issue has to be related back to the shares that gave the right to the bonus.

[**Step 4**]   Finally gains on the 'two' disposals are calculated - ie, on all the FA 1985 pool and part of the 1982 holding

(**The examiner's answer**)

(a)   (i)

Galibier Limited
Capital gain

	£
Proceeds	300,000
Cost	160,000
	——————
Unindexed gain	140,000
Indexation allowance	
$\dfrac{161.3-115.5}{115.5}$ (.397)	63,520
	——————
Indexed gain	76,480
	——————

(ii)   As plant and machinery is a depreciating asset it is not possible to 'roll-over' the gain on the building, but it may be 'held over' and becomes chargeable on the earliest of:

A.   disposal of plant,

B.   March 2008 (ie, 10 years after acquisition of the plant)

and

C.   the date the plant and machinery ceases to be used in the company's trade.

The time limit within which the replacement must be purchased is one year prior to the disposal of the asset sold and three year afterwards. March 1998 falls within this four-year period. There will be an immediate charge to the extent that £50,000 (£300,000 - £250,000) of the sale proceeds have not been re-invested.

The amount of the gain to be 'held-over' will therefore be:

	£
Indexed gain	76,480
Chargeable	50,000
	26,480

The £26,480 will become chargeable on the earliest of the three events mentioned above.

(b)

Stephen

(i)   Sale from FA 1985 pool

	£
Sale proceeds $\frac{7,000}{10,000} \times £60,000$	42,000
Indexed cost (W1)	41,253
Indexed gain	747

(ii)   Sale from 1982 holding

	Cost	MV on 31.3.82
	£	£
Sale proceed $\frac{3,000}{10,000} \times £60,000$	18,000	18,000
Cost (W2)	(8,022)	
MV 3,000 at £3.50		(10,500)
	9,978	7,500
Indexation allowance		
$\frac{161.2 - 79.44}{79.44} = 1.029 \times £10,500$	9,978*	7,500*
	Nil	Nil

* The indexation allowance is restricted as this would create an unallowable loss.

Summary

	£
Sale from FA 1985 pool	747
1982 holding	-
	747

WORKING 1

FA 1985 pool	Shares	Unindexed pool £	Indexed pool £
August 1988	3,000	12,750	12,750
Indexation to October 1994			
$\frac{145.2 - 107.9}{107.9} \times £12,750$	-	-	4,408
	3,000	12,750	17,158

Addition	4,000	20,000	20,000
	7,000	32,750	37,158
Indexation to April 1998			
$\dfrac{161.2 - 145.2}{145.2} \times \text{£}37,158$	-	-	4,095
	7,000	32,750	41,253
Sale	(7,000)	(32,750)	(41,253)
	-	-	-

Indexation in FA 1985 pool after April 1985 is not rounded to three places.

WORKING 2

	Shares	Cost
		£
July 1979	6,000	15,000
September 1981	2,000	5,500
August 1986 (bonus issue)	2,000	-
	10,000	20,500
Allocated cost (10,000 - 7,000)	3,000	8,022 (W3)
Carried forward	7,000	12,478

WORKING 3

Allocated cost (TN 1)

$$\text{£}20,500 \times \frac{\text{(Sale proceeds)}}{\text{(Sale proceeds} + \text{Value of remaining shares)}}$$

$$\text{£}20,500 \times \frac{(18,000)}{(18,000 + 28,000**)}$$

$* * \ 7,000 \times \text{£}4$

Tutorial notes

1   Usually the 1982 holding cost is taken on an average pool basis. Here, for example, it would be 3/10ths of £20,500 (ie, £6,150). However, these are unquoted shares and the examiner's practice is to require an "A/A + B" part disposal approach. If he gives the 'B' value - ie, the value of the 1982 holding after the disposal - then you have to use the technique shown in working 3.

---

70   (Answer 4 of examination)

(Examiner's comments and marking guide)

This is a VAT question covering in part (a) the VAT appeals procedure and in part (b) the determination of VAT tax points.

This was not a popular optional question - in fact many candidates seem now not to have studied VAT.

(a)   Many candidates confused VAT tribunals with Inland Revenue Commissioners. Not many candidates knew the appeals procedure or the time limits required. Many candidates wrote on the need for registration which was not required.

(b)   Many candidates continued to muddle their way through part (b) much as they had done part (a) by stating generalisations eg, comments about VAT fuel charges in sub-section (ii).

		Marks
(a)	30 days	1
	21 days	1
	Further 30 days	1
	All returns and payment to have been made	1
	Public hearings	1
	Appeal to higher courts	1
	Award of costs	1
(b)	(i)	2
	(ii)	1
	(iii)	1
Total		11

Step by step answer plan

Overview

Question 4 is always on VAT. Provided you know enough of the points required (and you do not have to fall back on guessing) this question represents easy marks. Similar VAT topics have been asked before; in fact an almost identical question on appeals was set in June 1995. Thus a good knowledge of past questions is always potentially useful.

Step 1   In part (a) you have to think of at least 7 separate points for the 7 marks on offer.

Step 2   Plan out your answer to cover the chronological order of steps in an appeal - ie, first with the local VAT office, then the tribunal, then the courts.

Step 3   For part (b), if you know the tax point for each of the three situations then state it succinctly. Otherwise, however much you write will be in vain.

The examiner's answer

(a)   The taxpayer has 30 days to appeal in writing against a decision of the local VAT office. The local VAT office may then either confirm the original decision, in which case the taxpayer has a further 21 days to appeal in writing to a VAT tribunal, or send a revised decision, in which case the taxpayer has a further 30 days to appeal in writing to a VAT tribunal. Before the VAT tribunal will hear the appeal, all VAT returns and payments (including the tax in dispute) must have been made. Tribunal hearings are normally in public. An appeal on a point of law can be made to the courts. The tribunal may award costs.

Did you answer the question?

The answer covers appeal procedure in purely general terms. It is unnecessary to try to invent some contentious VAT point relevant to the hardware business run by the trader in the question.

(b)   (i)   Goods on sale or return
                The tax point is the earlier of the date when the sale is adopted by the customer or 12 months after dispatch of the goods.

       (ii)   Fuel for private motoring
                The tax point is the date the fuel was put into the vehicle's petrol tank.

       (iii) Continuous supplies
                The time of supply (in the absence of a natural tax point) is the earlier of the issue of the tax invoice or the receipt of payment.

71   (Answer 5 of examination)

(Examiner's comments and marking guide)

This was a question requiring the calculation of national insurance contributions, in part (a) by an employee provided with a company car.

The question was generally well done with many candidates scoring high marks. It was not generally realised that 6 October was half-way through the fiscal year, 5 months and 7 months being quite common conclusions. The most frequent mistakes were:

(a)   not checking the age of car 1 and failing to give a time reduction;
(b)   forgetting the upper limit of £485 for employees' contributions;
(c)   calculating the first £64 of the employer's contributions at 2% and
(d)   utilising all the different bands provided and charging only the balance over £210 at 10%.

			Marks
(a)	(i)	Car 1	
		35%	½
		Mileage reduction	½
		Time reduction	½
		Car 2	
		35%	½
		Mileage reduction	½
		Time reduction	½
		Fuel benefit	
		Car 1	1
		Car 2	1
		Class 1A	1
	(ii)	Class 1 - employer	1
	(iii)	Class 1 - employee	2
(b)	(i)	Class 1 - employer	1
	(ii)	Class 1 - employee	1
Total			──
			11
			──

(Step by step answer plan)

Overview

In each part you have to compute the primary and secondary Class 1 NIC amounts, the difference being that in part (a) the earnings are above the upper earnings limit thereby capping the primary contributions. Part (a) also required knowledge of how the Class 1A liability on company cars and fuel is calculated. This question is a comparatively easy source of marks if you take sufficient care over the calculations.

Step 1   In part (a) keep the Class 1 and Class 1A calculations quite separate and construct the benefit amount in a clearly laid out working.

Step 2   The inclusion of part (b) to the question is a gift provided you can do part (a). It requires the same Class 1 steps but without the complication of the upper earnings limit. It would be unfortunate if these two easy marks were overlooked.

(**The examiner's answer**)

(a)   **Alma**

(i)   Class 1A - payable by her employer only
        Benefits-in-kind (Workings)
        £4,560 at 10% = £456.00

(ii)   Class I - payable by employer
        52 × £500 = £26,000 at 10% = £2,600

(iii)   Class I - payable by employee

Weekly	£	£
64 at 2%	1.28	
421 at 10%	42.10	
485 (maximum)	43.38	

Annual 52 × £43.38 =   £2,255.76

Working - Car and fuel benefits

	£	£
Car 1		
35% × £15,000	5,250	
Mileage reduction		
(equivalent of more than 18,000 pa)	3,500 (2/3)	
	1,750	
Time reduction	875 (1/2)	
	875	875
Car 2		
35% × £18,000	6,300	
Mileage reduction		
(equivalent of between 2,500 and		
17,999 pa)	2,100 (1/3)	
	4,200	
Time reduction	2,100 (1/2)	
	2,100	2,100
Fuel - Car 1		
1400cc to 2000cc (petrol)	1,280	
Time reduction	640 (1/2)	
	640	640
Fuel - Car 2		
over 2000cc (petrol)	1,890	
Time reduction	945 (1/2)	945
		4,560

(b)   **Albert**

(i)   Class 1 - payable by employer
                         Weekly £220 at 10%   £22.00
                         Annual 52 × £22.00   £1,144.00

(ii)   Class I - payable by employee
                         Weekly

	£	£
64 at 2%		1.28
156 at 10%		15.60
220		16.88

Annual 52 × £16.88 =   877.76

---

72   (Answer 6 of examination)

(**Examiner's comments and marking guide**)

The question required a brief description of PAYE and its operation.

The question was reasonably well attempted by candidates who appeared to know most of the forms and who had probably had some personal experience of PAYE. The lack of experience of PAYE by some candidates was evident and the quality of answers disappointing.

	Marks
Description of PAYE	1
Payment to Collector of Taxes by employer	1
Purpose of code numbers	1
Compilation of code numbers	1
Tax tables	1
'K' codes	1
P60	1
P9D	1
P11D	1
P45	1
P.35/P.14	1
	—
Total	11
	—
	marks

(**Step by step answer plan**)

Overview

This is a difficult question to satisfy the examiner on because although he specifies some of the aspects of the PAYE system to discuss it remains slightly open ended (see the Tutorial Note following the answer for further advice on what material to include).

Step 1   This requires a wholly written answer for 11 marks so an outline answer plan is needed covering the obvious requirements of the question.

Step 2 The main plan headings should include
- What is PAYE?
- How does it operate?
- What are the year end procedures?
- What is required when an employee changes jobs?

Step 3 Within each main heading jot down briefly all the relevant points and arrange them in a sensible order. For example, when an employee changes jobs a multipart P45 is raised. You then describe what happens to the different parts and their purpose in serving the PAYE system.

Step 4 Not until you have a roughed out answer plan should you actually start writing your answer. The time spent on a plan is not wasted and you should practice this technique whenever you have to prepare a written answer.

The examiner's answer

PAYE is a system of tax collection whereby tax is collected under Schedule E by the employer from employees earning more than the weekly or monthly equivalent of a single person's allowances. For most employees the tax deducted under PAYE will constitute the final liability without adjustment.

The tax is remitted by the employer to the Collector of Taxes within 14 days of the end of the tax month (5th day) ie, 19th of the month. Code numbers, based on the taxpayer's allowances, operate on a cumulative basis ie, a proportion of the allowances is given each period and a proportion of the total liability is payable each period.

The code numbers are issued by the Inspector of Taxes showing the allowances and reliefs to which a person is entitled including personal allowances, relief for certain pension contributions, certain interest paid and business expenses, where these are deductible. Deductions in the code number include amounts of benefits-in-kind, comparatively small amounts of interest received gross and adjustments to collect comparatively low amounts of income tax underpaid in previous years.

The net allowances are converted into a code number which is notified to the employer.

In accordance with the tax tables, supplied by the Inland Revenue, a proportion of these allowances will be given each payment period. This is referred to as 'free pay'.

The free pay is then deducted from the employee's total pay to provide taxable pay.

Where the deductions in the code number exceed the allowances a so-called 'K' code is applied. In this situation the employer adds the negative allowances to the employee's pay before applying the tax tables.

At the end of each tax year a form P60 is completed by the employer and handed to the employee by May 31. This provides the employee with a permanent record of pay and tax deducted during the tax year, together with details of National Insurance contributions made.

Returns of any taxable non-cash benefits provided by the employer during the tax year are made to the Revenue by July 6 following the end of the tax year and copies provided for employees.

The forms are P9D for employees earning less than £8,500 pa and P11D for employees earning £8,500 pa and over.

When an employee changes job a form P45 is completed showing details of pay, tax deducted, code number and date of leaving. The new P45 is in four parts: part 1 is forwarded to the employer's tax district and parts 1A, 2 and 3 are given to the employee. The employee retains part 1A and gives parts 2 and 3 to his new employer. The new employer uses part 2 to open a deduction working sheet for the employee and so maintain tax deductions on a cumulative basis. The new employer forwards part 3 to his tax office.

A summary of the employee's deduction working sheet, form P14, is sent with the employer's certificate, form P35, to the Inland Revenue by May 19 following the end of the tax year.

NB: Candidates do not need to refer to form P46 as the question is only concerned with changes of employer.

73   (Answer 7 of examination)

Examiner's comments and marking guide

The question was in two parts, the first part on furnished holiday accommodation and the second part a Schedule A computation.

This was the most popular of the optional questions.

(a)   The majority of candidates were able to correctly state why the letting qualified as a commercial letting of holiday accommodation. Only a few candidates correctly calculated the deduction for insurance.

(b)   The rent receivable figures were mostly shown incorrectly and the premium on the lease figure was often shown as £160 and not £1,840. The deductions for insurance and repairs were wrongly calculated by most candidates.

			Marks
(a)	(i)	70 days	1
		140 days	1
		31 day rule	1
	(ii)	Insurance	1
		Private use restriction	1
		Advertising/Accountancy	1
(b)		Rent on Flat 1	1
		Rent on Flat 2	1
		Premium on Flat 2	1
		Insurance on Flat 1	1
		Repairs and decorating on Flat 1	1
Total			11

Step by step answer plan

Overview

This is really two separate questions albeit concerning the same taxpayer and involving her Schedule A income (see Tutorial Note 2 for why the taxpayer has two separate Schedule A amounts).

Step 1   In part (a) (i) there are some easy marks for applying the definition of furnished holiday accommodation.

Step 2   For part (a) (ii), the rent is compared to the expenses calculated on an accruals basis distinguishing those expenses which have to be apportioned for private use and those that are allowed in full.

Step 3   In part (b) you should produce a combined calculation of net rents for the two flats.

The examiner's answer

Jocelyn

(a)   (i)   The letting qualifies as a 'commercial letting of furnished holiday accommodation' because it was let for over 70 days and was available for letting for not less than 140 days. Furthermore the property was not in the same occupation for more than 31 days.

Did you answer the question?

Note that the examiner did not ask for a list of the tax advantages of the furnished holiday letting (FHL) status over ordinary furnished commercial letting.

    (ii)   Cottage - Schedule A income 1998-99.

	£	£
Rent		4,900
Insurance $\dfrac{500+450}{2}$	475	
Repairs and decorating	700	
Water rates	250	
Cleaning	300	
Loan interest	1,200	
Capital allowances	400	
	3,325	
Less private use (1/12)	277	3,048
		1,852
Accountancy	100	
Advertising	300	400
Assessable		1,452

(b)

Flats - Schedule A income 1998-99

			£		£
Rent receivable		- Flat 1			3,750*
Rent receivable		- Flat 2			2,400**
Premium on lease		- Flat 2			1,840***
					7,990
Insurance	- Flat 1		250****		
Insurance	- Flat 2		400		
Repairs	- Flat 1		4,200		
Repairs	- Flat 2		1,500		
Accountancy	- Flat 1		50		
Accountancy	- Flat 2		60		6,460
					1,530

Did you answer the question?

The current income tax Schedule A rules applying for 1995/96 onwards, unlike the previous rules, take no account of actual paydays, whether payment is due in advance or arrears, who is responsible for the repairs, and the treatment of expenditure incurred in a 'void' period. Such aspects of the question should therefore be ignored.

			£
*	9/12 × £5,000	=	3,750
**	3/12 × £3,600	=	900
	6/12 × £3,000	=	1,500
			2,400

***

Premium		2,000
less (5 - 1) × 2%		(160)
		1,840

****

10/12 × £300		=	250

Tutorial notes

1   The normal rule is to treat all property letting by the same landlord as if it was a single business (es, net rents on flats 1 and 2 are computed in a composite calculation) under Schedule A. Similarly all FHL net rents are treated as arising from a single Schedule A business. However, where there is both FHL and non-FHL lettings they must be kept separate. Thus parts (a) and (b) of the question concern two notionally separate Schedule A businesses and do not require to be combined.

---

74   (Answer 8 of examination)

(Examiner's comments and marking guide)

This is a question requiring the calculation of benefits-in-kind.

The question was very poorly answered with very little thought being given to the majority of answers. Even though the question stated that the tax-payer was required to live in the company-owned house and that the accommodation was job-related many candidates included the £4,000 annual value. This error then followed down to the 10% restriction which only applied where the annual value was not assessed. The two items most wrongly calculated were the benefit on the purchase of the furniture and the re-location benefit.

		Marks
Superannuation		
Working 1		1
Working 2		1
(a)	1	
(b)	1	
Choice	1	
	—	3
Working 3		1
Working 4		1
Restriction of amount assessable as ancillary services		2
Contribution		1
No council tax assessment		1
		—
Total		11

(Step by step answer plan)

Overview

This is clearly a question on Schedule E benefits. However, even after a brief reading of the question you should realise that, living in job related accommodation, the employee is only assessable on 'ancillary services' to a limit of 10% of his emoluments including other benefits. This will dictate the order of the computational layout. In other words don't slot in the ancillary services until after listing the rest of his emoluments.

Step 1   Head up your main answer sheet and slot in the salary.

Step 2 As superannuation is only based on basic salary deal with that next.

Step 3 The benefits (other than ancillary services) can then be calculated on the face of your main answer or relegated to working notes. For example, the annual furniture benefit calculation is simple enough not to need a working but the benefit of transferring the furniture, being quite lengthy, deserves a working note.

Step 4 Next list out the ancillary services and restrict the chargeable amount to 10% of the total of emoluments and benefits calculated so far. The employee's contribution then comes off this restricted amount. Step 3 could be dealt with in a working note but the examiner chose not to. Whether or not you use a working note is fairly subjective, but if you use a working it must be numbered and cross-referenced to the answer proper.

Step 5 Consider what comments should be made regarding the 'red herrings'. The examiner explains why council tax is excluded - and allocates a mark therefor - but makes no mention of the reason for excluding the annual value of the accommodation. As a general answering technique, if you have time, make a brief list of items correctly excluded and give reasons. It is possible that marks are available for one or more item. You will not be penalised for mentioning non-mark bearing items.

The examiner's answer

Rainier
Schedule E assessment 1998-99

		£	£
Salary		40,000	
Superannuation (6%)		2,400	37,600
Annual furniture benefit	(W1)		3,000
Benefit on purchase of furniture	(W2)		4,500
Loan benefit	(W3)		1,500
Re-location benefit	(W4)		2,000
			48,600
Ancillary services:			
Electricity		400	
Gas		800	
Water		300	
Decorating		4,200	
		5,700	
Restricted to 10% of £48,600		4,860	
Contribution		(1,000)	3,860
			52,460

The council tax is not assessable as the relevant accommodation is representative accommodation and therefore is not taxable.

WORKING 1

		£
Annual furniture benefit		
20% × £15,000	=	3,000

WORKING 2
Benefit on purchase of furniture

(a)   Market value   10,000
                  Paid   (7,500)

                  Excess   2,500

(b)   Cost   15,000
                  1998-99 benefit   (3,000)

                                 12,000
                  Paid   (7,500)

                  Excess   4,500

       (b)   £4,500 is the greater

WORKING 3
Loan benefit
£30,000 × (10% - 5%)   =   1,500

WORKING 4
£10,000 - exemption limit (£8,000)   =   2,000

Did you answer the question?

The examiner required no mention of the fact that the £8,000 exemption only applies to certain categories of relocation expenses. You clearly have to take such information at its face value and leave it at that.

DECEMBER 1997 QUESTIONS

Section A – ALL THREE questions are compulsory and MUST be attempted

75   (Question 1 of examination)

Uncut Undergrowth Limited (UUL) is a United Kingdom resident company which has been manufacturing garden machinery since 1990. It has no associated companies. The company results are summarised as follows:

	Year ended 30.6.97	6 months to 31.12.97	Year ended 31.12.98	Year ended 31.12.99 (forecast)
	£	£	£	£
Schedule D1 Profit/(Loss)	35,000	(45,000)	(350,000)	100,000
Non-trade loan interest received (gross amount)	-	15,000	22,000	-
Bank interest received	-	-	-	10,000
Schedule A	25,000	-	-	-
Chargeable gains	-	-	30,000	-
Patent royalties paid (gross amount)	10,000	6,000	12,500	13,000
Deed of covenant to charity (gross amount)	1,000	1,000	1,000	1,000

Notes:

1.   The loan interest received, patent royalties paid and deed of covenant payments were subject to deduction of income tax at source.

2.   On 1 July 1996 there was no trading losses brought forward but £40,000 of capital losses were available.

3.   Loan interest was received on the following dates:

	£
31.12.97	15,000
31.12.98	22,000

4.   Patent royalties were paid on the following dates:

	£
31.12.96	10,000
31.12.97	6,000
31.12.98	12,500
31.12.99 (forecast)	13,000

5.   Deed of covenant payments were made on the following dates:

	£
31.12.96	1,000
31.12.97	1,000
31.12.98	1,000
31.12.99 (forecast)	1,000

You are required:

(a)   to calculate the corporation tax liabilities for all years in the question after giving maximum relief at the earliest time for the trading losses sustained and any other reliefs,   **(11 marks)**

(b)   to show any balances carried forward, and   **(5 marks)**

(c)   to calculate any payments and repayments of income tax for the *final* three chargeable accounting periods.

   N.B. These calculations are NOT required for the first chargeable accounting period.

(5 marks)
(Total: 21 marks)

   N.B. All apportionments may be made to the nearest month.

---

76   (Question 2 of examination)

Elizabeth, who is 29 and unmarried, is employed as a health visitor at an annual salary of £22,880. She is provided with a company car by her employer. Until 5 October 1998 the car provided was a 1300cc petrol driven car which was first registered on 1 August 1994 and which then had a list price of £10,000. The car was changed on 6 October 1998 for a 1900cc new diesel car which had a list price of £12,500. Fuel for both business and private use was provided by the employer.

Car mileages are as follows:

6.4.98 - 5.10.98 2,000 private and 8,000 business
6.10.98 - 5.4.99 (estimated) 3,000 private and 10,000 business.

Elizabeth has a loan of £10,000 from her employer with interest being paid at 3% per annum. The loan is being used to purchase her house. She has no other mortgage on the property.

Elizabeth is in a not contracted-out occupational pension scheme into which she pays 6% of her salary. In addition she pays 9% of her salary as additional voluntary contributions into a separate scheme operated by an insurance company.

You are required to calculate:

(a)   Elizabeth's income tax liability for the year 1998–99 and   **(13 marks)**

(b)   the National Insurance contributions payable for 1998–99 by Elizabeth and her employer in respect of Elizabeth's employment.   **(4 marks)**
(Total: 17 marks)

   N.B. All apportionments may be made to the nearest month.

---

77   (Question 3 of examination)

(a)   Olivia purchased her house on 1 March 1975 for £20,000 and sold it on 31 August 1998 for £180,000. An extension had been added in July 1984 costing £8,000.

   From 1 January 1989 until 30 April 1992 one half of the house had been let for residential purposes. On 1 May 1992 Olivia went to live with her daughter and let the whole of the house for residential purposes until it was sold.

   The value of the house on 31 March 1982 was £50,000.

   You are required to calculate Olivia's capital gain for 1998–99. No election has been made to 're-base' the cost of all assets held on 31 March 1982 at their value on that date.   **(10 marks)**

(b)   Gaynor purchased an antique wardrobe for £3,000 in July 1984 and sold it at auction for £7,500 in September 1993. She paid the auctioneer 10% of the sale proceeds of £7,500.

   You are required to calculate Gaynor's capital gain for 1998–99.   **(4 marks)**

(c)   Howe Limited sold one of its factories in September 1998 for £1,500,000. The factory had been purchased in June 1991 for £1,000,000. In December 1997 the company had purchased another factory for £1,100,000 and claimed roll-over relief on the gain on the factory sold in September 1998.

You are required to calculate the capital gain on the sale of the first factory and state the amount of any roll-over relief available. **(3 marks)**

(d)   **You are required** to describe the capital gains tax consequences where a taxpayer claims that an asset has become of negligible value. **(4 marks)**

(Total: 21 marks)

N.B. All apportionments may be made to the nearest month.

Section B – THREE questions ONLY to be attempted.

---

78   (Question 4 of examination)

A client, Mr Edwards, has made an appointment to discuss his VAT position with you on Wednesday, 10 December 1998. He started in business making hand-made ladies' shoes on 1 April 1998. His monthly turnover figures to date are:

	£
April	5,694
May	5,326
June	7,295
July	7,314
August	8,405
September	9,792
October	10,977
November	11,291

Turnover is expected to continue to increase. Mr Edwards is concerned that he should now be charging customers VAT and is seeking your advice about registration.

He has heard that if he has to register for VAT he can submit an annual return to cut down on administration.

He would welcome your advice on **both** these matters.

You are required to prepare notes for your meeting with Mr Edwards. **(11 marks)**

---

79   (Question 5 of examination)

Lucifer commenced trading as a second-hand car dealer on 6 April 1996. He had had no taxable income prior to 1996-97.

His trading results, adjusted for income tax and capital allowances, were:

		£
Period ended	30.9.96	(20,000) loss
Year ended	30.9.97	(10,000) loss
Year ended	30.9.98	10,000 profit

He received dividend income as follows:

1996–97	3,000 net
1997–98	2,500 net
1998–99	1,500 net

In 1996–97 he had also realised a capital gain, after indexation but before annual exemption, of £15,000.

You are required:

(a)   to state in what ways the trading losses may be relieved, and **(3 marks)**

(b)   to show how the trading losses can be utilised most effectively by Lucifer, giving your reasoning.

(8 marks)

(Total: 11 marks)

N.B. Apportionments should be made in days.

80   (Question 6 of examination)

Roger and Brigitte commenced in business on 1 October 1995 as hotel proprietors, sharing profits equally.

On 1 October 1997 their son Xavier joined the partnership and from that date each of the partners was entitled to one-third of the profits.

The profits of the partnership adjusted for income tax, are:

			£
Period ended	30 June 1996		30,000
Year ended	30 June 1997		45,000
Year ended	30 June 1998		50,000
Year ended	30 June 1999		60,000

You are required to calculate:

(a)   the assessable profits on each of the partners for all relevant years from 1995–96 to 1999–2000 and

(7 marks)

(b)   the overlap profits for each of the partners.

(4 marks)

(Total: 11 marks)

N.B. Apportionments should be made in days.

81   (Question 7 of examination)

(a)   **You are required** to state the conditions under which the following income tax reliefs are available:

(i)   personal allowance for taxpayers aged 65 and over and   **(2 marks)**

(ii)   additional relief for widows and others in respect of the children (ignoring apportionment of the relief).   **(2 marks)**

(b)   Hubert, aged 68, married Winifred, aged 41, on 9 September 1998. Neither had been married previously. Hubert's income for 1998–99 is £19,600.

You are required to calculate the personal allowance to which Hubert is entitled in 1998–99 and also the married couple's allowance for 1998–99.   **(5 marks)**

(c)   **You are required** to state the circumstances under which it might it might be appropriate for a married man to disclaim the married couple's allowance.   **(2 marks)**

(Total: 11 marks)

82   (Question 8 of examination)

'Self-assessment' of income tax was introduced on 6 April 1996.

(a)   **You are required** to state the latest date by which the taxpayer should submit the tax return if:

(i)   he wishes the Inland Revenue to calculate his income tax liability, and

(ii)   he wishes to calculate his own liability.   **(2 marks)**

(b)   **You are required** to state:

(i)   The normal dates of payment of Schedule D1 and II income tax for a sole trader in respect of the fiscal year 1998–99 and

(ii)   how the amounts of these payments are arrived at.   **(5 marks)**

(c)   **You are required** to state:

(i)   the fixed penalties for late submission of tax returns and when they apply.

(ii)   the circumstances under which the penalties will be reduced and

(iii)   the further penalties which may be imposed when the Inland Revenue believe that the fixed penalties will not result in the submission of the return.   **(4 marks)**

(Total: 11 marks)

ANSWERS TO DECEMBER 1997 EXAMINATION

75   (Answer 1 of examination)

Examiner's comments and marking guide

A corporation tax question testing:

(a)   the treatment of trading losses sustained in consecutive accounting periods with consequential treatment of trade and non-trade charges and

(b)   the treatment of income tax withheld on payment of patent royalties and deed of covenant payments and income tax suffered on receipt of loan interest.

The performance of candidates on this question was disappointing. Many candidates failed to apply the basic loss relief rules. Such weaknesses in the treatment of losses is concerning as it is consistent with candidates' performance in this area on previous occasions.

Specific errors were as follows:

(a)   Many candidates had little idea of whether losses were to be set off before or after charges.

(b)   Similarly, many candidates failed to make any distinction between trade and non-trade charges for the purpose of off-setting losses.

(c)   Perhaps the major problem with many weaker candidates was the lack of a systematic approach for dealing with multi-period losses. Most obviously, many candidates failed to use a columnar approach, as in the question, preferring instead to set out each year on a separate page. This appeared both to create errors and results in a loss of candidates' time through repetition of the narrative descriptions.

(d)   Frequently the wrong rates were used for income despite these being given in the rubic.

(e)   Many of the weaker candidates spent considerable time explaining the nature of the loss relief rules in broad descriptive terms, rather than getting on which applying them to the circumstances of the question.

On a more positive note most candidates correctly dealt with the set-off of the capital loss brought forward.

			Marks
(a)	CAP to 31.12.99		
	Loss b/f s.393(1)	£100,000	1
	Bank interest		1
	Charges on income		
	CAP to 30.6.97–		
	'Trade'		1
	'non-trade'		1
	CAP to 31.12.99 –		
	'Trade'		
	'non-trade'		1
	Working 1(a) – (Loss to 31.12.97)		
	CAP to 31.12.97	£15,000	1
	CAP to 30.6.97	£30,000	1
	Working 1(b) – (Loss to 31.12.98)		
	CAP to 31.12.98	£22,000	1
	CAP to 30.6.97	£15,000	1
	C.T. liability		1
			— 11

(b)	(i)	Capital losses carried forward	1	
	(ii)	Working 2		
		Unrelieved trade charges –		
		CAP to 31.12.97	1	
		CAP to 31.12.98	1	
		CAP to 31.12.99	1	
		Unrelieved trade losses carried forward	1	
			—	5
(c)		CAP to 31.12.97	2	
		CAP to 31.12.98	2	
		CAP to 31.12.99	1	
			—	5
				21
				—

(Step by step answer plan)

Overview

This is clearly a corporation tax loss question with the minor complication of having two loss making periods. When the question was originally set, trading losses could be carried back 36 months and not just 12 months. Two more earlier periods were therefore shown but these have been 'updated away'. as they are no longer needed to show the correct use of the losses. Furthermore, as ACT is no longer examinable we have been able to exclude the problems of calculating ACT payments and relieving ACT where it interacts with loss relief. The updated version of this question has thus lost a lot of its bite and the marks available have therefore been reduced from 29 to 21. What remains is still a useful exercise.

Step 1   Prepare a columnar PCTCT layout dealing with the 4 periods side by side with suitable gaps for slotting in losses. There is clearly a likelihood of losses remaining to be carried forward so leave space just under the Schedule DI line for losses relieved under s.393(1).

Step 2   Slot the figures in for the various sources of income and charges. The examiner's layout deals with both forms of charges *after* losses relieved by carry back under s.393A(1). It is arguably better practice to show trade charges deducted *before* loss carry back but this can make the layout unwieldy. The examiner's approach is fine as long as you remember to leave sufficient profits after loss carry back to cover trade charges.

Step 3   The key working is the Loss Memorandum. Always deal with earlier losses before later losses. This is logical and easy to remember but to forget is to invite disaster! Set off the first loss against current 'total profits' then against total profits of the previous 12 months. Remember in the first instance 'profit' is before charges but in the second instance 'profit' is after trade charges. Then follow the same technique with the second loss. To carry it back only 12 months, only half of the remaining profits of the year to 30.6.97 can be used. All entries in the main layout must also appear in the loss memo to keep track of any loss remaining.

Step 4   After using s.393A(1) relief as far as possible, scoop up the remaining unrelieved trade charges into the loss memo and carry the loss and charges forward against future profits of the same trade.

Step 5   Total off the main layout to give PCTCT for every year and show the balance remaining on the loss memo.

Step 6   Calculate the CT payable where any PCTCT remains and show the usual peripheral information. For example, where losses are concerned this usually includes a note on the fate of unrelieved non-trade charges.

Step 7   Part (b) requires a clear statement of the capital losses and other losses remaining even where this information is already buried in working notes.

Step 8   Finally in part (c) there are an easy 5 marks for summarising the income tax year end quarterly accounting position for three of the years.

The examiner's answer

(a)

Uncut Undergrowth Ltd

	Year ended 30.6.97 £	6 months ended 31.12.97 £	Year ended 31.12.98 £	Year ended 31.12.99 £
Schedule D1	35,000	-	-	100,000
Losses b/f (s.393(1))				(100,000)
				————
Non-trade loan interest	-	15,000	22,000	-
Bank interest	-	-	-	10,000
Schedule A	25,000	-	-	-
Chargeable gains	-	-	-	-
	————	————	————	————
Total profits	60,000	15,000	22,000	10,000
Loss reliefs–				
CAP to 31.12.97				
(s.393A(1))	(30,000)	(15,000)	-	-
CAP to 31.12.98				
(s.393A(1))	(15,000)	-	(22,000)	-
	————	————	————	————
	15,000	-	-	10,000
Charges on income–				
Trade	(10,000)	-	-	(9,000)
Non-trade	(1,000)	-	-	(1,000)
	————	————	————	————
Profits chargeable	4,000	-	-	-
	————	————	————	————

Corporation Tax

$4,000 \times {}^{9}/_{12} \times 24\%$	720
$4,000 \times {}^{3}/_{12} \times 21\%$	210
	———
	930
	———

(b)   (i)   Capital Losses carried forward

	£
Loss brought forward 1.7.96	40,000
Utilised in CAP to 31.12.98	(30,000)
	————
Carried forward	10,000
	————

(ii)   Trading losses carried forward (s.393(1))

Trading losses and unrelieved trade charges (W2) £235,500

(c)   Income tax repayable/payable

		Income tax withheld on payment £		Income tax suffered on receipt of Loan interest £		Income tax repayable/ payable £
31.12.97	(A)	1,380	(6,000 at 25%)	3,000	(15,000 at 20%)	1,390
	(B)	230	(1,000 at 25%)			repayable
		1,610				
31.12.98	(A)	2,875	(12,500 at 24%)	4,400	(22,000 at 20%)	1,295
	(B)	230	(1,000 at 24%)			repayable
		3,105				
31.12.99	(A)	2,990	(13,000 at 23%)			3,220
	(B)	230	(1,000 at 23%)			payable
		3,220				

(A) Patent royalties
(B) Deed of covenant

Did you answer the question?

You were not required to show how much corporation tax would be repaid for the year to 30 June 1997 resulting from the loss carry backs.

Workings

W1. Loss memoranda

(a)	6 months 31.12.97	£
	Loss	45,000
	CAP to 31.12.97 (s.393A(1)(a))	(15,000)
		30,000
	CAP to 30.6.97 (s.393A(1)(b))	(30,000)
		-

(b)	Year ended 31.12.98	£
	Loss	350,000
	CAP to 31.12.98 (s.393A(1)(a))	(22,000)
		328,000
	CAP to 30.6.97 (s.393A(1)(b)) (restricted to half of profits, before all charges, but after earlier loss relief of CAP)	(15,000)
		313,000
	CAP to 31.12.99 (s.393(1))	(100,000)
	Carried forward to Working 2	213,000

		£	£
W2.	**brought forward from Working 1**		213,000
	Unrelieved trade charges (s.393(9))		
	CAP to 31.12.97	6,000	
	CAP to 31.12.98	12,500	
	CAP to 31.12.99 (13,000 − 9,000)	4,000	
			22,500
	Carried forward (s.393(1))		235,500
	Unrelieved non-trade charges		
			£
	CAP to 31.12.97		1,000
	CAP to 31.12.98		1,000

Tutorial notes

1   The examiner is able to avoid the clash between the received/paid basis and the accruals basis in the treatment of interest by having interest paid or received on the last day of the accounting period. It is then presumed that the year end accrual is nil.

2   Where losses are carried back to only part of a period (as above) the results of that period have to be time apportioned. As an earlier loss takes priority (as above) it has to be assumed that the profits to apportion are after reduction by the earlier loss carried back.

---

76   (Answer 2 of examination)

(**Examiner's comments and marking guide**)

A personal tax question testing the calculation of car and fuel benefits, a beneficial loan from employer, the treatment of loan interest on property outside the MIRAS scheme, payment of superannuation contributions and free-standing additional voluntary contributions, calculation of income tax liability and calculation of primary and secondary NICs.

Part (a)

Superannuation and FSAVC: In general, candidates handled the pension calculation (both basic and AVC) well. However, the adjustment to the income tax liability for tax deducted from the FSAVC was either overlooked or incorrectly treated by most candidates. Some candidates allowed a total deduction of 17½% when only 15% overall is permitted under the occupational pension provisions.

Car and fuel benefits: Most candidates gained good marks in this area, although a significant percentage had problems dealing with the mileage, age and time reductions in respect of both cars. Despite remarks in the June 1996 Examiners Report many candidates still insist on time-apportioning the benefits using days, which though more accurate is also more time consuming and not essential in this instance. It is quite acceptable and normal practice in examinations to time-apportion the car and fuel benefits to the nearest month.

Calculation of income tax liability: Some candidates, surprisingly, treated the loan benefit (£700) as savings income, taxed (incorrectly) at 20%. Only a few candidates remembered to adjust the income tax liability for loan interest and FSAVC (pension) deductions at source. Where attempted the FSAVC adjustment, in particular, was badly done. Most candidates were unaware that the deduction of basic rate tax at source applied only to the additional pension contribution (£2,059).

Part (b)

National insurance contributions (NICs): Compared to part (a) performance in this part of the question was disappointing. The most common errors were:

- application of incorrect rate(s);

- inclusion of car and fuel benefits when calculating Class 1 primary and secondary contributions;

- ignoring the tax on the first £64 when calculating Class 1 primary contribution payable by Elizabeth;

- basing the Class 1 secondary contribution (employer) on the amount after deducting £64, including the beneficial loan charge (£700) when calculating the Class 1A contribution;

- calculating the correct charge on the car and fuel benefits but not distinguishing it as Class 1A contribution;

- simply ignoring the Class 1A contribution (this was the case in the majority of the scripts marked).

		Marks
(a)	Superannuation	½
	Additional contributions	½
	Beneficial loan assessment	1
	Personal allowance	½
	Correct income tax rates	½
	Addition of income tax deducted from AVC	1
	Relief on loan interest	1
	Working	
	Car 1	
	35%	½
	Mileage reduction	1
	Age reduction	1
	Time reduction	1
	Car 2	
	35%	½
	Mileage reduction	1
	Time reduction	1
	Fuel benefit	
	Car 1	1
	Car 2	1
		13
(b)	Class 1A	1
	Class 1 – employer	1
	Class 1 – employee	2
		4
		17

Step by step answer plan

Overview

Part (a) is a straightforward Schedule E benefits question coupled with a standard Taxable Income/Income Tax Liability computation. There is the slight complication of additional voluntary contributions (AVCs) to a free standing pension scheme. Part (b) offers some easy marks for some basic NIC calculations.

Step 1 The main difficulty in doing Part (a) is making all the necessary adjustments to the car and fuel benefits. This requires a separate working.

Step 2 Next prepare the main layout generating the figure for Taxable Income. It is such a short question that it must be difficult to overlook any of the elements. As long you realise that the superannuation and AVC payments are deducted from the salary you should find the right taxable income amount.

Step 3 Finally construct a standard IT liability layout not forgetting relief for the loan interest and the add-back for relief already achieved on the AVC by paying net.

Step 4 Part (b) merely requires a separate computation for each of the three NIC amounts.

The examiner's answer

(a)

Elizabeth
Income tax computation 1998–99

	£	£
Salary		22,880
Superannuation (6%)	1,373	
Additional pension contributions (9%)	2,059	
		(3,432)
		19,448
Benefits-in-kind		
Car and Car fuel (W)		2,651
Beneficial loan (£10,000 × (10% - 3%))		700
		22,799
Personal allowance		(4,195)
Taxable income		18,604
4,300 at 20%		860
14,304 at 23%		3,290
18,604		4,150
Relief for loan interest £1,000 (£10,000 × 10%) at 10%		(100)
		4,050
Income tax deducted from additional pension contribution (2,059 at 23%)		474
Income tax liability		4,524

Working – Car and car fuel benefit	£	£
Car 1		
35% × £10,000	3,500	
Mileage reductions (equivalent of more than 2,500 but less than 18,000 pa)	(1,167) (1/3)	
	2,333	
Age reduction (over 4 years old on 5.4.99)	(778) (1/3)	
	1,555	
Time reduction (6/12)	(778)	
		777
Car 2		
35% × £12,500	4,375	
Mileage reduction (equivalent of more than 18,000 pa)	(2,917) (2/3)	
	1,458	
Time reduction (6/12)	(729)	
		729
Fuel – Car 1		
less than 1400cc (petrol)	1,010	
Time reduction	(505)	
		505
Fuel – Car 2		
1400cc to 2000cc (diesel)	1,280	
Time reduction	(640)	
		640
		2,651

(b)   National Insurance Computations 1998–99

      (i)   Class 1A – payable by employer only
                   Benefit in kind on cars and car fuel
                   £2,651 at 10% = £265.10

      (ii)   Class 1 – payable by employer
                   £22,880 at 10% = £2,288.00

      (iii)   Class 1 – payable by Elizabeth

				£
£64 × 52	=	3,328 at 2%	=	66.56
£376 × 52	=	19,552 at 10%	=	1,955.20
£440 × 52		22,880		2,021.76

Did you answer the question?

You were not asked for the paydays for any of the tax or NIC nor asked to describe how the benefits would impact on the PAYE code.

Tutorial notes

1   Whenever the examiner tests car and fuel benefits in detail he expects a working which explains each step in the adjustments. It would be possible to reduce the workings - for example, the figure of £777 could be derived as £10,000 x 35% x 2/3 x 2/3 x 6/12 - but if a slip is made it would be more difficult to give credit for a partly right working. Don't forget monthly rather than daily apportionment is quite acceptable for any Schedule E topic so don't waste time on apportioning to the nearest day!

2   The AVC is paid net of basic rate tax, the gross value is deducted from salary and the withheld tax has to be added into the final income tax liability (or else relief at the basic rate would be achieved twice over).

3   The loan interest paid on the qualifying loan and the loan interest taxed thereon as a benefit are both allowed as a tax reducer (at 10%).

4   For Class 1 purposes 'earnings' excludes benefits but no reduction is allowed for pension contributions or the personal allowance.

---

77   (Answer 3 of examination)

Examiner's comments and marking guide

A capital gains tax question testing:

(a)   the calculation of a gain on a principal private residence which had been partially let for residential purposes.
(b)   the calculation of a gain on the sale of a chattel sold for more than £6,000,
(c)   the capital gains position on the sale and replacement of a factory, and
(d)   the consequences of a taxpayer claiming an asset has become of negligible value.

The question was done very badly.

(a)   Many candidates overlooked PRR altogether but of those who did calculate PPR most went on to correctly calculate the letting relief and identify the three options.

(b)   Most candidates obtained the first two marks but failed to compare the result with marginal chattels relief. In many cases candidates stated the larger gain was taken.

(c)   Many candidates calculated the gain correctly but few then went on to recognise that roll-over relief was not available. Some candidates who recognised that the whole proceeds were not reinvested tried to apportion the gain between proceeds re-invested and proceeds not reinvested.

(d)   Few candidates displayed any knowledge of negligible value claims and many wrote about chattel relief and balancing allowances.

		Marks	
(a)	Unindexed gains - £152,000 and £122,000	2	
	Indexation on 31.3.82 value	1	
	Indexation on enhancement expenditure	1	
	Full exemption	2	
	Partial exemption	2	
	Letting relief	2	
		—	10
(b)	Unindexed gain	1	
	Indexation allowance	1	
	Maximum gain	1	
	Lower figure	1	
		—	4
(c)	Indexed gain	1	
	Conclusion	2	
		—	3
	Has become negligible in value	1	
	Treated as having sold and re-acquired at the negligible value	1	
	Date of claim	1	
	Negligible value figure will be treated as new cost	1	
		—	4
			21

Step by step answer plan

Overview

Question 3 is always on CGT and is usually split into 2, 3 or 4 quite separate mini-questions - here it is 4. Almost half the marks are for part (a) so you can expect it to take longer than the other parts. Taper relief was not around when the question was set but it is now! When faced with any CGT question involving an individual you should try to spot whether taper relief applies - for 1998/99 it can only relieve gains on 'business assets' - and annotate the question accordingly to reduce your chance of overlooking it. In fact it could only apply in parts (a) or (b) and clearly in neither case are we dealing with a business asset so the point does not arise. Nevertheless, get into the habit of thinking 'taper relief' where CGT questions appear.

Step 1   For part (a) prepare the standard double computation (re-basing election was not made) taking care to index each item separately and indexing only to April 1998.

Step 2   Then address the problem of non-occupation of a PPR. The examiner's answer takes a shorthand approach to identifying the various periods but it may be safer to produce a separate working to analyse periods between occupation and non-occupation. In a working you would have more room to note any reasons for deeming occupation.

Step 3   Finally for part (a), take the gain and show how it is reduced by PPR relief and PPR letting relief.

Step 4   For part (b) produce the standard indexed gain computation, the marginal chattel relief limit and a statement of which answer applies.

Step 5   For part (c) compute the gain not forgetting that there is no April 1998 restriction on the indexation allowance for gains by companies. Then comment on the roll-over treatment where there is only partial reinvestment.

Step 6   Part (d) requires a little thought as it involves a written answer. A careful rehash of your study notes on this point should yield all the marks on offer.

The examiner's answer

(a)   **Olivia**

	On cost £	On 31.3.82 value £
Sale proceeds	180,000	180,000
Cost	(20,000)	
Market value at 31.3.82		(50,000)
Enhancement expenditure	(8,000)	(8,000)
Unindexed gains	152,000	122,000

Indexation allowance – on M.V. at 31.3.82

$$\frac{161.2 - 79.44}{79.44} (1.029) \times £50,000$$

	On cost	On 31.3.82 value
	(51,450)	(51,450)

- on enhancement

$$\frac{161.2 - 89.10}{89.10} (.809) \times £8,000$$

	On cost	On 31.3.82 value
	(6,472)	(6,472)
	94,078	64,078

Lower indexed gain is   £64,078

less: principal private residence exemption

(i)   Full exemption
        1.4.82 – 31.12.88 + final 36 months (117 months)

$$\frac{117}{*197} \times £64,078$$

(38,056)

                                                                              26,022

        *Period 1.4.82 to 31.8.98

(ii)   Partial exemption (half let) 1.1.89–30.4.92 (40 months)

$$\frac{40}{*197} \times £64,078 \div 2$$

(6,505)

                                                                              £19,517

Letting relief, lowest of:

(i)   principal private residence exemption
         £44,561 (£38,056 + £6,505)

(ii)   £40,000

(iii)   amount chargeable, £19,517   19,517

         Chargeable gain   Nil

Tutorial note

The original question uses a value of 79.4 as the RPI for March 1982. We use a value of 79.44 in line with our policy throughout this book to use RPIs at their proper published value.

(b)   *Gaynor*
                                                                              £

Sale proceeds	7,500
Auctioneer's commission	750
	6,750
Cost	3,000
Unindexed gain	3,750

Indexation allowance

$$\frac{161.2 - 89.10}{89.10} = .809 \times £3,000$$

2,427
_____

Indexed gain

1,323
_____

The maximum gain is $5/3 \times (£7,500 - £6,000) = £2,500$
The gain chargeable is £1,323 being the lower figure.

(c)   *Howe Limited*
                                                                            £

Sale proceeds	1,500,000
Cost	1,000,000
	_____
Unindexed gain	500,000
Indexation allowance	
$\frac{163.3 - 134.1}{134.1} = 0.218$	218,000
	_____
	282,000
	_____

The amount of the sale proceeds from the first factory which are not re-invested is £400,000 (£1,500,000– £1,100,000). As this exceeds the amount of the gain on the first factory, £282,000, none of the gain can be rolled-over against the cost of the replacement factory.

Did you answer the question?

You were not required to comment on the time limit for reinvesting nor the consequence if further investments could be made.

(d)   Where the owner of an asset which has become of negligible value makes a claim to that effect he is treated as having *sold and immediately re-acquired* the asset at that negligible value. The date of disposal is normally the *date of* the taxpayer's *claim*. When the asset is ultimately disposed of the *negligible value* figure will be *treated as 'cost'*.

Tutorial notes

1   The original answer in part (d) mentioned the old pre-self assessment rule that the Inspector had to be satisfied of an assets negligible value before a claim would be allowed. This has been updated for self-assessment to show that it is now at the owner's option. This change is at the heart of self-assessment in that taxpayers have to take responsibility for their tax liability subject to the risk that their returns may be the subject of a Revenue enquiry and penalties could result if claims have been made erroneously.

2   Oddly the examiner's answer overlooked the rather obvious point that the 'consequence' chiefly sought by such a claim is the establishment of a loss for use against realised gains! This highlights the recurring problem in written questions of understanding exactly what points are expected. It is usually better therefore to make a lot of individual points in outline taking care not to waste time on areas which are clearly irrelevant.

---

78   (Answer 4 of examination)

Examiner's comments and marking guide

A VAT question testing candidates' knowledge of registration limits and annual accounting procedures. Although the question was in mini case study format many candidates gave rambling answers rather than focus on what advice they were going to give the client the next day. Candidates often confused the Customs and Excise with the Inland Revenue. Very few candidates gave any details at all about annual accounting. Many wrote about cash accounting and 'all I know about VAT in 20 minutes.'

Marks

(a)   Registration
1.   Turnover limit passed in October 1998   1
2.   Immediate registration is due (effective date 1 December 1998)   1
3.   Liability to VAT from 1 December 1998   1
4.   VAT to be charged immediately and invoices later   1
5.   5% penalty   1
                                                                                                                    — 5

(b)   Annual accounting
1.   Turnover limit   1
2.   12 month rule   1
3.   One return and due date   1
4.   (a)   Monthly payments on account   1
        (b)   Quarterly payments on account   1
        (c)   No payment on account   1
                                                                                                                    — 6
                                                                                                                         11

(Step by step answer plan)

Overview

As expected question 4 concerns VAT. The question makes it clear that there are two points to address - viz, (1) liability to register based on the turnover figures provided and (2) the facility for annual as opposed to quarterly returns. When figures are given in a question there is a temptation to incorporate them into elaborate workings. However, such efforts are not required here - you only need to cumulate them in a calculator to identify where the £50,000 turnover limit is exceeded. Most of the marks are instead given for discussing the outcome of exceeding the limit.

Step 1   Ascertain whether and when he should have registered. As he has already become liable you should jot down in rough the points that stem from that finding.

Step 2   Construct your answer on the registration liability in note form as required by the question.

Step 3   Now note down the 'study text' details of annual accounting.

Step 4   Re-read the question to ensure you have covered all the points which the client would expect to see. For example, have you mentioned the penalty for late registration?

(The examiner's answer)

(a)   Registration.

1.   Turnover exceed the registration limit of £50,000 by 31 October 1998 and registration was therefore necessary by 1 December 1998.

2.   Immediate registration is therefore necessary.

3.   There will be a liability for VAT from 1 December 1998 on any sales made since that date.

4.   VAT should be charged forthwith and customers advised that VAT invoices will be issued when the VAT registration number is known.

5.   Customs and Excise may charge a penalty for late registration of 5% of the VAT due from 1 December 1998 until the actual date of registration. This percentage increases if the registration is more than nine months late. The minimum penalty is £50.

(b)   Annual accounting.

1.   Annual turnover must be below £300,000.

2.   Business must have been VAT registered for at least 12 months.

3.   Only one return per annum is required and is due within two months of the accounting date.

4.   Payments on account must be made as follows:

(a)   equal amounts on a monthly basis from month four to month twelve based on 90% of the previous year's net payments. Any balance is due within two months of the accounting date.

(b)   if the annual turnover of the business is less than £100,000, four quarterly payments may be made, each of 20% of the previous year's net payments.

(c)   if the annual turnover is below £100,000 and net payments to Customs and Excise in the previous year were below £2,000, no payments on account are necessary and the liability for the year is due within two months of the accounting date.

Did you answer the question?

You were not required to discuss whether the business was making taxable supplies.

There is exemption from registration where a business exceeds the turnover threshold exceptionally but will fall below the limit in the future. This was clearly irrelevant as 'turnover is expected to increase'.

Tutorial notes

On registration, input tax is allowed on purchases of services in the previous six months and on purchases of goods still on hand at registration. This could have been mentioned for its relevance in calculating any penalty for late registration and just as a general point a trader would expect to be told in the circumstances.

---

79   (Answer 5 of examination)

Examiner's comments and marking guide

A question testing the ability of candidates to utilise trading losses to the taxpayer's best advantage against capital gains, dividend income and future trading income.

(a)   In this part of the question most candidates mentioned Section 381 as a matter of course although the question stated there was no taxable income prior to the tax year in which the first loss was sustained. Just as income tax loss relief section numbers were quoted in question 1 so corporation tax section numbers were mentioned here. Although this is not penalised *per se*, candidates should be aware that the easiest way to learn about losses, (both income tax and corporation tax), is to learn the correct section numbers. Very few candidates, for example, were aware of Section 72 relief.

(b)   Errors committed by candidates included the following:

(1)   There was no calculation of the loss relief. Most candidates simply utilised £20,000 and £10,000 rather than allocate the losses to the relevant tax years.

(2)   In most cases relief against capital gains was made after annual exemption.

(3)   Section 385 relief was wrongly set against dividend income in 1998-99.

(4)   Many candidates simply referred to accounting periods rather than fiscal years throughout the question.

(5)   Losses were frequently restricted to income remaining after personal allowances.

(6)   As in question 1 many candidates gave rambling answers rather than utilising the loss relief as required by the question.

(7)   Few candidates considered the maximisation of cash-flow in the allocation of the losses.

Marks

(a)   Section 380   1
       Section 385   1
       Section 72, FA 1991   1
                                           — 3

(b)   Loss calculation –
       1996-97   1
       1998-99   1
       Loss utilisation –
       1996-97 Section 380   1
       1996-97 Section 72, FA 1991   1
       1998-99(1)   Section 385   1
       1998-99(2)   Section 385   1
       1999-2000   Section 385   1
       Rationale   1
                                           — 8

                                           11

Step by step answer plan

Overview

This is clearly a question on the best use of opening period trading losses but without the complication of s.381 relief (three year carry back) since there was no income in the years prior to the year the trade commenced. The examiner knows that candidates have difficulty in juggling with loss options so the question, as here, will normally be kept as simple as possible. The approach is to identify what amounts of loss are available and what income (and gains) could be relieved in each of the years concerned.

Step 1   For part (a) list out the basic options available under s.380, s.385 and s72. This is one of the few areas of taxation where familiarity with section numbers is really worthwhile even though not mandatory.

Step 2   For part (b) start by calculating the loss of 1996/97 and the loss of 1997/98 not forgetting that for Sch D I income tax the examiner expects apportionment to be made to the nearest day.

Step 3   As you have to show the best use of the losses a rough working of the STI and gains for 1996/97, 1997/98 and 1998/99 will help you to decide. (1995/96 could be a target year but it can be ignored as STI and gains are nil).

Step 4   Clearly the gain in 1996/97 needs relieving but this means first using s.380 relief in the same year. Your rough working should also make it obvious that 1997/98 STI needs no loss relief being covered already by PA. Once past 1997/98, losses are being carried forward and must be used under s.385 as soon as future trading profits become assessable.

Step 5   Show the effect of these decisions in your formal answer and tie it in with a loss memoranda.

Step 6   The question asks for your reasoning so don't forget to explain your choices.

The examiner's answer

(a)   The loss may be relieved in three ways:

   (i)   Section 380(1)(a) and (b). The relief may be allowed against income of the year of the loss and/or against income of the preceding year.

   (ii)   Section 385. The relief may be carried forward against trading profits of the same trade.

   (iii)   Section 72, FA 1991. Where the loss exceeds the income for the year of claim the relief may be allowed against capital gains of the year.

(b)   (i)   Calculation of loss
1996–97
Period ended 30.9.96

	£
	20,000

Year ended 30.9.97 (1.10.96–5.4.97) 187 ie, $\frac{187}{365} \times £10,000$ 5,123

25,123

1997–98
Year ended 30.9.97   10,000
less period 1.10.96–5.4.97   (5,123)

4,877

(ii)   Calculation of loss relief

	1996–97 £	1998–99 £
Schedule D1	-	10,000
Loss (s.385)		(6,373) (1)
Loss (s.385)		(3,627) (2)
		-
Dividends	3,750	1,875
Loss s.380(1)(a)	(3,750)	-
	-	1,875
Capital gain	15,000	
Loss (s.72, FA 1991)	(15,000)	
	-	

(iii)   Loss memoranda

1996–97

	£
Loss	
1996–97 (s.380(1)(a))	25,123
	(3,750)
	21,373
1996–97 (s.72, FA 1991)	(15,000)
	6,373
1998–99 (s.385)	(6,373)
	-

1997–98

	£
Loss	4,877
1998–99 (s.385)	(3,627)
1999–2000 (s.385)	(1,250)
	-

Although the method of loss utilisation chosen entails a loss of personal allowances for 1996–97 it is considered the best of the many options available.

There is rarely a guarantee of future profits and in view of the poor trading results it is thought the maximisation of cash-flow is the critical factor.

Did you answer the question?

You were not expected to discuss s.381 relief (three year carry back).

Tutorial notes

1   Loss questions can be answered successfully by following a few simple rules. Firstly, identify the loss of the fiscal year. Normally this is the loss of the accounting period ending in the fiscal year but in the opening periods losses follow the same rules as profits. However, we cannot create 'overlap losses'. Instead losses entering into the calculation for more than one fiscal year (see the £5,123 amount above) are only counted in the first such fiscal year.

2   Secondly, each loss so identified has to be dealt with separately. The choice is usually to relieve STI in the fiscal year of loss and/or the previous year. These two claims are independent of each other and are at the taxpayer's choice but cannot be restricted to preserve income to cover the PA. Any loss remaining must be carried forward under s.385.

3   An occasional complication (as here) is the presence of a capital gain. Unless the gain is wholly or substantially covered by the annual exemption it can be worthwhile making a s.72 FA 1991 claim but this can only be done if STI has been fully relieved by a s.380 claim for the same year.

---

80   (Answer 6 of examination)

Examiner's comments and marking guide

A partnership question in which candidates had to (a) apportion profits initially between 2 and later 3 partners and (b) calculate overlap profits for each of the partners.

Many candidates scored full marks on this question and many more only lost marks in calculating Xavier's overlap profits. Candidates who had not prepared fully scored badly because they had difficulty in allocating basis periods to fiscal years.

		Marks	
Assessable profits –			
Roger and Brigitte			
1995-96		1	
1996-97		1	
1997-98		1	
1998-99		1	
Xavier			
1997-98		1	
1998-99		1	
Combined			
1999-00		1	
			7
Overlap profits			
Roger and Brigitte			
1996-97		1	
1997-98		1	
Xavier			
1998-99		1	
1999-00		1	
			4
			11

Step by step answer plan

Overview

This is clearly a partnership question but with not all the partners starting at the same time. Although there are a lot of calculations to get right (and the requirement for daily apportionment is no help!) the principles are straightforward. First, divide the profits for each period between the partners in accordance with their profit sharing agreement(s) in force for the period. Then treat each partner as if he was a soletrader in respect of his share of profit. Thus R & B are both assessable under the opening year rules with 1995/96 as their first year (on an actual basis). X joins in 1997/98 so that is his first year. The overlap profit calculations also follow the 'soletrader' rules and should present no problem.

Step 1   Prepare a working to show the division of the four amounts of profits between the partners. The examiner's answer just shows the key figures (workings 1 - 5) but a fuller working would be more helpful.

Step 2   For each partner (R & B can share the same answer) for all the tax years concerned show the basis periods and the assessable profits. The examiner has approached this in a more compact way by listing out the basis periods in a table then listing out the profits assessable year by year in a tabular layout.

Step 3   Do not overlook part (b) for a relatively easy 4 marks. Unfortunately part (b) may be difficult to satisfy if you have come unstuck in part (a).

The examiner's answer

(a)   The basis periods will be:

	Roger & Brigitte	*Xavier*
1995–96	1.10.95—5.4.96	-
1996–97	1.10.95–30.9.96	-
1997–98	1.7.96–30.6.97	1.10.97–5.4.98
1998–99	1.7.97–30.6.98	1.10.97–30.9.98
1999–00	1.7.98–30.6.99	1.7.98–30.6.99

The profits assessable will be:

	Roger £	*Brigitte* £	*Xavier* £
1995–96	10,274 (W1)	10,275 (W1)	-
1996–97	20,671 (W2)	20,671 (W2)	-
1997–98	22,500	22,500	8,539 (W3)
1998–99	18,767 (W4)	18,767 (W4)	17,507 (W5)
1999–00	20,000	20,000	20,000

Workings:

1. $187/273 \times £30,000 \div 2$
2. $[£30,000 + (92/365 \times £45,000)] \div 2$
3. $187/365 \times £50,000 \div 3$
4. $(92/365 \times £50,000 \div 2) + (273/365 \times £50,000 \div 3)$
5. $(273/365 \times £50,000 \div 3) + (92/365 \times £60,000 \div 3)$

(b)   Overlap relief

	Roger £	*Brigitte* £
1996–97 (1.10.95–5.4.96)	10,274	10,275
1997–98 (1.7.96–30.9.96)	5,671 (W6)	5,671 (W6)
	15,945	15,946

	Xavier
	£
1998–99 (1.10.97–5.4.98)	8,539
1999–00 (1.7.98–30.9.98)	5,041 (W7)
	13,580

Workings:

6. $92/365 \times £45,000 \div 2$

7. $92/365 \times £60,000 \div 3$

Did you answer the question?

You were not required to explain how relief would be given for overlap profits.

---

81   (Answer 7 of examination)

Examiner's comments and marking guide

A question on personal reliefs in which candidates had to

(a)   explain age relief and additional personal relief
(b)   calculate allowances from given data, and
(c)   explain when married couple's allowance should be disclaimed.

A minority of candidates gave the wrong figure for the income limit even though it was provided on the question paper. Most candidates wrote about widows bereavement allowance which was not asked for. Only a few candidates mentioned individuals whose spouses were incapacitated. Few candidates stated that entitlement to the married couple's allowance was a bar to claiming additional personal allowance. Most candidates assumed that the question only concerned widows and single women.

In part (b) most candidates correctly calculated the personal allowance but there were very few correct answers to the married couple's allowance. Most candidates ignored the reduction in the personal allowance of £1,215 which had already been made.

In part (c) only a few candidates realised that married couple's allowance could be less than additional personal allowance and therefore not claimed. Many candidates mentioned differential marginal rates of spouses which of course overlooks the fact that married couple's allowance is given as a standard tax reducer. Most candidates wrongly interpreted the word 'disclaim' as meaning 'transfer'.

			Marks	
(a)	(i)	65 or over in year of assessment	1	
		restriction of relief where income over £16,200	1	
	(ii)	not entitled to MCA	1	
		at least once qualifying child resident	1	
				4
(b)	(i)	reduced allowance calculation	1	
		restriction of reduction	1	
	(ii)	married couple's allowance	1	
		excess calculation (£485)	1	
		test on 'normal' married couple's allowance	1	
				5
(c)		marriage after May 5	1	
		qualifying proviso	1	
				2
				11

Step by step answer plan

Overview

This requires some fairly basic knowledge of personal allowances. Effectively there are 4 separate questions which should each be given some care in answering especially where a written answer is required.

Step 1   Answer part (a) (i) being sure to mention the income restriction.

Step 2   For your answer to part (a)(ii) you have to use the term 'qualifying child'. Therefore it is appropriate to say what the term means. Note that as there is a maximum of 2 marks there is clearly no need to go into prolonged detail such as the restriction where a cohabiting couple each have a qualifying child.

Step 3   Part (b) may offer the most marks and the computations are fairly straightforward but it is still important to take care and perhaps to annotate clearly any steps taken. Note that the age related MCA is first restricted for the date of marriage and then restricted for income.

Step 4   It might be easy to overlook part (c) but that would waste 2 of the least difficult marks in the question. This concerns one of the few tax planning opportunities for personal allowances.

The examiner's answer

(a)   (i)   A taxpayer aged 65 or over at any time in the year of assessment is entitled to a higher rate of personal allowance: the rate increases again when the taxpayer is 75 or over in the year of assessment.

Where the income of the taxpayer exceeds £16,200 the relief is abated by 50% until the normal levels of personal allowance are reached.

(ii)   The relief is available to persons who are not entitled to the married couple's allowance and to any individual who is married to/and living with a spouse who is totally incapacitated throughout the year of assessment.

A taxpayer can claim the allowance if he has at least one qualifying child resident with him for the whole or part of the year.

A qualifying child is one who is born in, or is under 16 on 6 April in, the year of assessment. If over 16 the child must be receiving full-time education or vocational training. The qualifying child must also be a child of the claimant, or if not is born in, or is under 18 on 6 April in, the year of assessment and maintained by the claimant for the whole or part of the year.

(b)   (i)

Personal allowance	£
Total income	19,600
Allowance limit	16,200
Excess	3,400
Higher personal allowance	5,410
50% of excess	1,700
	3,710

As this reduction takes the level of personal allowance below £4,195, it will be restricted to an amount (£1,215) to leave the allowance at £4,195, the basic personal allowance.

(ii)   Married couple's allowance

The reduction of £1,215 in the personal allowance will be taken into consideration.

		£	£
Married couple's allowance			1,928*
50% of excess (as above)		1,700	
reduction in personal allowance		1,215	
			485
			1,443**

* £3,305 × 7/12
** This is in excess of the basic married couple's allowance (£1,900 × 7/12 = £1,108) and no further adjustment is necessary.

(c)   Where a man has a qualifying child living with him during a year of assessment in which he marries after May 5 it would be beneficial for him to continue to claim additional personal allowance for that year and not to claim the reduced married couple's allowance.

The disclaimer of the married couple's allowance would only be beneficial if he was paying sufficient income tax to absorb the tax relief on the additional personal allowance. Otherwise it would be appropriate to claim the married couple's allowance and transfer the unused relief to his wife.

Did you answer the question?

For part (a) (ii) you were not required to discuss the APA rules in non-standard situations such as marriage breakdown.

---

82   (Answer 8 of examination)

Examiner's comments and marking guide

A factual question and topical question about the introduction of self-assessment into the UK tax system. Parts (a) and (b) were reasonably well answered although traces of fanciful imagination were portrayed in answers to (c) (i) and (ii). A wide range of incorrect excuses and reasons were provided as grounds for penalty reduction but relatively few candidates were aware of penalty limitation being restricted to the amount of the liability.

				Marks	
(a)	(i)			1	
	(ii)			1	
				—	2
(b)	(i)	1.	31 January	1	
		2.	31 July	1	
		3.	31 January	1	
	(ii)	Payments one and two		1	
		Payment three		1	
				—	5
(c)	(i)	1.		1	
		2.		1	
	(ii)			1	
	(iii)			1	
				—	4
					11

Step by step answer plan

Overview

This is a straightforward question on the basics of self-assessment. In both parts (a) and (c) it is clear that marks are limited and your answer should therefore be strictly confined to the point. For example, it is unlikely that any marks are available for rambling on about the extension of deadlines where returns arrive from the Revenue late through no fault of the taxpayer.

| Step 1 | Write down the dates required in part (a) making clear which '30 September' and '31 January' you mean. |

| Step 2 | Answer part (b) as briefly as possible making clear how the out turn for the previous year determines the interim payments. |

| Step 3 | Part (c) requires yet more basic knowledge of self-assessment. |

The examiner's answer

(a)   (i)   30 September following the tax year to which the return relates.

(ii)   31 January following the tax year to which the return relates.

(b)   (i)   1.   31 January in the tax year.
            2.   31 July following the tax year.
            3.   31 January following the tax year.

(ii)   Payments one and two are equal amounts each amounting to half the Schedule DI or II income tax liability in respect of the preceding income tax year.
Payment three is the balancing figure, ie, it is the amount of the final Case I or II liability for the year less payments one and two.

(c)   (i)   1.   £100 if the return is outstanding after 31 January following the tax year.
            2.   A further £100 if the return is still outstanding after 31 July following 31 January following the tax year.

(ii)   Where a fixed penalty has been imposed for late submission of a return but the amount of the income tax liability is less than the penalty, the penalty will be reduced to the amount of the liability.

(iii)   Where the Inland Revenue are of the opinion that the fixed penalties imposed will not result in the return being submitted they may ask the Commissioners to apply further penalties of up to £60 a day until the return is submitted.

Did you answer the question?

You were not expected to comment on the payment of Class 4 NIC or CGT under self-assessment.

Tutorial note

Under self-assessment the payments on account and the final liability concern the taxpayer's total liability regardless of source. The examiner's answer to part (b) (ii) infers that the sole trader has no other sources of income received gross.

JUNE 1998 QUESTIONS

Section A – ALL THREE questions are compulsory and MUST be attempted

---

83   (Question 1 of examination)

Unforeseen Upsets Limited (UUL) is a United Kingdom resident company which has been manufacturing lifeboats for many years. It has no associated companies. The company has previously made up accounts to 31 December but has now changed its accounting date to 31 March.

The company's results for the 15-month period to 31 March 1999 are as follows:

	£
Trading profits (as adjusted for taxation but before capital allowances)	1,125,000
Bank interest receivable (Note 4)	20,000
Debenture interest receivable (Note 5)	17,500
Chargeable gain (Notes 6 and 7)	30,000
Patent royalties paid (Note 8)	20,000
Dividends received from UK companies (Note 9)	33,600

Note 1.
UUL is a medium-sized company with a turnover in the period of account ended 31 March 1999 of £5,000,000.

The average number of employees for the period of account was 150.

Note 2
Capital allowances – Plant and Machinery

On 1 January 1998 the tax written-down values of plant and machinery were:

	£
Pool	95,000
Car pool	47,000

Sales during the accounting period were:

		£
31.7.98	3 cars	15,000
30.9.98	Plant and machinery	12,000

Additions during the accounting period were:

		£
1.6.98	1 car	14,000
1.8.98	3 cars (£8,000 each)	24,000
30.11.98	Plant and machinery	92,000
28.2.99	Plant and machinery	6,000

Note 3
On 1 January 1998 the company had trading losses brought forward of £609,200.

Note 4

Bank interest receivable	£
31.3.98 received	3,000
30.6.98 received	4,000
30.9.98 received	5,000
31.12.98 received	6,000
31.3.99 received	2,000
	20,000

Note 5

Debenture interest receivable (gross amounts)	£
31.3.98 received	3,500
30.9.98 received	7,000
31.3.99 received	7,000
	17,500

a.   The loan was made on 1 January 1998.
b.   £3,500 was accrued at 31 December 1998.
c.   Income tax has been deducted at source.
d.   The interest was non-trading income.

Note 6
Chargeable gain
The chargeable gain was realised on 1 July 1998.

Note 7
On 1 January 1998 the company had capital losses brought forward of £50,000.

Note 8

Patent royalties paid (gross amounts)	£
28.2.98	7,000
31.5.98	4,000
28.2.99	9,000
	20,000

Income tax has been deducted at source.

Note 9

Dividends received	
28.2.98	16,000
31.7.98	12,000
28.2.99	5,600
	33,600

You are required:

(a)   to prepare entries relating to income tax as they would appear on forms CT61 to be submitted to the Collector of Taxes for the five quarterly periods to 31 March 1999.

(4 marks)

(b)   to calculate the corporation tax payable for the fifteen month period of account and

(18 marks)

(c)   to state what unrelieved amounts are carried forward at 31 March 1999.   **(1 mark)**
(Total: 23 marks)

NB All apportionments should be made to the nearest month.

---

84   (Question 2 of examination)

Austin, who is 40, is married to Jane, age 39.

Austin opened a book shop on 1 September 1995. The profits, as adjusted for income tax, but before capital allowances, were as follows:

	£
1.9.95 – 31.8.96	15,000
1.9.96 – 31.8.97	25,000
1.9.97 – 30.6.98	22,500

Capital additions were:

	£
1.9.95 – Second-hand car	8,800
- Computer	1,500
- Shelving and furniture	2,500

No claim is to be made to treat any of the assets as 'short life' assets.

Private use of the car was 50%.

On 30 June 1998 Austin sold the business to a national chain of booksellers and continued to work for them as branch manager. The capital gain on the sale of the business was £30,000 (after indexation but before taper relief). Sales proceeds at 30 June 1998 of assets qualifying for capital allowances were:

	£
Car	5,000
Computer	500
Shelving and furniture	1,500

From 1 July 1998 Austin was provided by his new employer with the car he had previously owned. Fuel for both business and private motoring was also provided. The car had first been registered on 1 August 1994 and had cost £12,000 when new. It was petrol-driven with a cylinder capacity of 1600cc. The 1998-99 mileage figures, from 1 July 1998, were 2,000 for business and 8,000 for private use.

In addition to the above Austin had the following income in 1998-99:

	£
Branch Manager – salary	22,500 (gross)
Interest on National Savings Bank ordinary account	100
Interest on Midland Bank deposit account (net)	250
Dividends	3,000

PAYE of £5,175 was deducted from the salary of £22,500. Austin paid the maximum personal pension contribution for 1998-99 as an employee. He had decided not to pay any contributions in respect of the period of self-employment.

Austin had borrowed £20,000 from his father to pay for the marital home.

The interest on this loan in 1998-99 was £1,000. There were no other loans on the property.

You are required to calculate:

(a) the amounts assessable to income tax under Schedule D Case I on Austin for the years 1995-96, 1996-97, 1997-98 and 1998-99. **(10 marks)**

(b) the income tax and capital gains tax still to be paid by Austin for the year 1998-99. **(15 marks)**
(Total: 25 marks)

(*Note:* The pension relief limit for a taxpayer aged 36 to 46 is 20%).

NB All apportionments in part (a) should be made in days.

---

85   (Question 3 of examination)

(a)   In September 1987 Fred purchased a flat, not his principal private residence, for £50,000. In May 1990, when its value was £120,000 he gave the flat to his wife Freda. In May 1998 Freda sold the flat for £170,000. Fred and Freda were living together throughout the period.

You are required to calculate the amount of any capital gains arising on these transactions.   **(3 marks)**

(b)   Nelson had been a full-time working director of Trafalgar Limited since 30 April 1993 when he acquired 20% of the company's ordinary shares. He retired from the company on 30 April 1998 on his 60th birthday when he gave all his shares in the company, valued at £600,000, to his son Hardy. The capital gain arising on the gift was £350,000 after indexation allowance but before any other reliefs. Nelson and Hardy have jointly elected to have the gain deferred.

The following values were extracted from the balance sheet of Trafalgar Limited on 30 April 1998:

	£
Buildings	350,000
Goodwill	200,000
Plant (all items costing more than £6,000)	100,000
Motor cars	75,000
Investments	60,000

You are required to calculate Nelson's capital gain, after all reliefs have been claimed, and Hardy's base acquisition costs.   **(8 marks)**

(Total: 11 marks)

Section B – THREE questions ONLY to be attempted.

---

86   (Question 4 of examination)

(a)   You are a recently qualified chartered certified accountant and have decided to start in practice. In your first year your turnover is below the VAT registration threshold but you are considering voluntary registration.

You are required to state what factors you would take into consideration before applying for registration.
(4 marks)

(b)   You are provided with the following information for the quarter ended 31 March 1999 relating to your client Marlyse:

	£
Supplies (all VAT – exclusive)	
Standard-rated supplies	190,000
Zero-rated supplies	50,000
Exempt supplies	10,000
Input tax	
Taxable supplies	16,000
Exempt supplies	9,000
Non-attributable	2,000

Bad debts of £1,000 (exclusive of VAT) were written off in March 1999 in respect of goods supplied in November 1998, payment for which was due in December 1998.

Marlyse ran a car on the business with an engine capacity of 1600cc. Petrol for both private and business mileage was paid for by the business. The quarterly scale charge figure is £268 (inclusive of VAT).

You are required to calculate the VAT payable for the quarter ended 31 March 1999 and to state when this will be payable to Customs and Excise.   **(7 marks)**

(Total: 11 marks)

87   (Question 5 of examination)

Benny has owned and operated a hotel in the English Lake District for many years. The hotel is open all year for the convenience of tourists. It has 12 bedrooms. Accounts are prepared annually to 31 March. On 1 August 1998 work started on an extension consisting of an extra four bedrooms and entrance hall: it was brought into use on 1 January 1999.

The extension cost £75,000, of which £5,000 was attributable to the cost of land, and included the following items:

1.	Fire proof doors to comply with fire-safety regulations	£6,000
2.	Laying special tiles in the entrance hall depicting the hotel crest.	£2,000

You are required:

(a)   to state the requirements for a hotel to be treated as a 'qualifying hotel' for tax purposes and   **(6 marks)**

(b)   to calculate the maximum capital allowances due on the extension for the year ended 31 March 1999 assuming the hotel fulfils these requirements.   **(5 marks)**

(Total: 11 marks)

88   (Question 6 of examination)

Capital gains tax payable by individuals can be paid by instalments in the following circumstances:

(a)   where there is little or no consideration and

(b)   where consideration is delayed.

You are required to state the conditions that apply in these circumstances and the rules concerning payment of interest on delayed capital gains tax in each situation.   **(11 marks)**

89   (Question 7 of examination)

Madelaine has for many years been in business as a furniture and carpet retailer. Her trading and profit and loss account for the year ended 31 March 1999 is as follows:

	£	£
Sales		89,323
Opening stock	26,544	
Purchases	23,338	
	49,882	
Closing stock	24,628	25,254
Gross profit		64,069
Wages and national insurance	12,197	
Repairs and renewals	491	
Rent and rates	13,984	
General expenses	719	
Bad debts	955	
Depreciation of fixtures and fittings	415	
Interest	1,780	
Motor vehicle running costs	1,404	
Premium on lease	3,000	
Lighting and heating	2,954	
Relocation expenses	741	
Professional fees	645	

Subscriptions and donations	194	39,479
Net profit		24,590

You are required to state what additional information you would need in order to calculate Madelaine's tax adjusted Schedule D Case I profit for the year ended 31 March 1999 and to explain why you need it.   **(11 marks)**

---

90   (Question 8 of examination)

(a)   Agnes rents out a room in her house. In 1998-99 she received rent of £4,900 and paid allowable expenses of £2,000.

You are required to calculate the amount of Agnes' Schedule A assessment for 1998-99 assuming any necessary election is made. (*Note*: The rent-a-room relief figure for 1998/99 is £4,250).   **(2 marks)**

(b)   Harry owns three flats which he lets out.

Flat 1. The flat was purchased on 6 September 1998 and let unfurnished on a landlord's repairing lease, from 29 September 1998. The new seven-year lease was at an annual rental of £3,500 payable on the usual quarter days. The incoming tenant was required to pay a premium of £5,000.

Flat 2. The flat was let unfurnished at an annual rental of £4,000 on a tenant's repairing lease which expired on 23 June 1998, the rent having been paid on the usual quarter days.   The property was re-let on 29 September 1998 on the same conditions at an annual rent of £6,000.

Flat 3. The flat was let furnished for the full year on a weekly rental of £120. The usual quarter days are 25 March, 24 June, 29 September and 25 December.

Details of expenditure in the year ended 5 April 1999 were:

	Flat 1 £	Flat 2 £	Flat 3 £
Insurance	400 (note 1)	200	600
Repairs	4,500 (note 2)	600	350
Water rates	-	-	400
Council tax	-	-	800

Notes

1.   The amount of £400 was an annual premium

2.   £4,000 was spent on UPVC double glazing in September 1998 replacing the leaking wooden window frames. To have replaced with wooden frames would have cost £1,200.

You are required to calculate Harry's Schedule A profit for 1998-99.   **(8 marks)**

NB Calculations may be made to the nearest month.

(c)   **You are required** to state how Schedule A loss relief is given where the loss is in respect of property let unfurnished.
      (1 mark)
      (Total: 11 marks)

ANSWERS TO JUNE 1998 EXAMINATION

83   (Answer 1 of examination)

Examiner's comments and marking guide

A corporation tax question testing:

(a)   the preparation of entries in relation to income tax as they would appear on forms CT61.

(b)   the apportionment of a 15-month accounting period into 12-month and three-month chargeable accounting periods.

(c)   the treatment of trading and capital losses brought forward.

(d)   the calculation of corporation tax at the small company rate, and

(e)   the calculation of corporation tax payable for a three-month chargeable accounting period at the marginal rate.

Candidates demonstrated a reasonable knowledge of the basic rules and layout but in many cases were unable to deal with a number of issues raised by the question, specifically:

(a)   Many candidates used the wrong tax rates in their CT61 computation with respect to income tax and many candidates failed to make clear whether amounts were actually paid/repaid in each quarter or carried forward.

(b)   The calculation of profits for the purpose of tapering relief frequently failed to split the period into two.

(c)   Many candidates either failed to split the 15 month accounting period at all or did so incorrectly eg, 3 months and 12 months.

(d)   Many candidates used the small company rate of corporation tax when applying tapering relief.

(e)   Many candidates failed to apportion the capital allowances into two chargeable accounting periods.

(f)   The trading loss brought forward was dealt with incorrectly by many candidates.

(g)   Many candidates thought that because the company was 'medium-sized' the normal rules of rate determination did not apply.

		Marks	
(a)	Income tax –		
	Quarter to 31.3.98 - £910	1	
	Quarter to 30.6.98 - £920	1	
	Quarter to 30.9.98 - £(1,400)	1	
	Quarter to 31.3.99 - £670	1	4
(b)	Division of trading profit	1	
	Trading losses brought forward	1	
	Bank interest	1	
	Debenture interest	1	
	Charges on income – Patent royalties	1	
	Working 1 – Capital allowances		
	CAP to 31.12.98		
	Sales and additions	1	
	WDA	1	
	FYA	1	
	CAP to 31.3.99		
	WDA	1	
	FYA	1	
	Working 3 –		

CAP to 31.12.98		
Calculation of 'P'	1	
Recognition of applicable rate	1	
CT calculation	1	
Working 4		
CAP to 31.3.99		
Calculation of 'P'	1	
Calculation of reduced limits	1	
Recognition of applicable rate	1	
Calculation of liability	2	
	—	18
		—
(c) Amounts carried forward		
Capital losses	1	1
	—	—
		23
		—

(Step by step answer plan)

Overview

By long standing tradition question 1 is the corporation tax question and usually carries the most marks for any one question on the paper. However, as ACT (advance corporation tax) is no longer an examinable topic the number of marks has been reduced from 31 to 23 on updating for FA 1998. It remains a worthwhile practice exercise as it still contains many of the standard elements of a paper 7 CT question.

Step 1   Read through the question carefully with an eye on the requirements noting where information will be needed. For example, Notes 1 and 2 are relevant to computing capital allowances to be slotted in for part (b) and Notes 5 and 8 are needed for the CT61 preparation in part (a).

Step 2   Prepare an income tax quarterly accounting layout for the 2 CAPs and fill in from Notes 5 & 8.

Step 3   For part (b), start with a Plant and Machinery capital allowances working for each of the two CAPs.

Step 4   Next prepare a PCTCT layout for the two CAPs side by side and fill in from the question apportioning or allocating as appropriate. The examiner includes 5 notes to explain the basis of allocating but this does not appear to be required in your answer. In any case, no marks are separately allocated for this in the marking scheme.

Step 5   Finally for part (b), compute the CT payable for each CAP. The examiner usually expects to see this done in a separate working or workings and you have to show you have considered the small company limits adjusted as appropriate.

Step 6   Don't overlook the final part even though it carries hardly any reward. That one mark could make all the difference! Although you might have netted off the capital gain with the loss brought forward without recourse to a working in part (b) you should preferably show the capital loss to carry forward in a working note as well as formally in the part (c) answer.

The examiner's answer

(a)

Unforeseen Upsets Limited
CT61 forms

	Income Tax	*Tax deducted on payment* £	*Tax suffered on receipt* £	*IT payable (re-payable)* £
(i)	CAP to 31.12.98			
	Period			
	1.1.98-31.3.98	1,610 *	700 **	910
	1.4.98-30.6.98	920 **		920
	1.7.98-30.9.98		1,400 ****	(1,400)
	1.10.98-31.12.98	No return		
		2,530	2,100	430
(ii)	CAP to 31.3.99			
	Period			
	1.1.99-31.3.99	2,070 *****	1,400 ****	670

*	£7,000 at 23%
**	£3,500 at 20%
***	£4,000 at 23%
****	£7,000 at 20%
*****	£9,000 at 23%

(b)   Corporation tax computations

	12 month CAP to 31.12.98 £	*3 month CAP to 31.3.99* £
Trading profit	900,000	225,000
Capital allowances-		
Plant and machinery	(74,550) (W1)	(13,054) (W1)
	825,450	211,946
Trading losses brought forward	(609,200)	-
	216,250	211,946
Bank interest	18,000	2,000
Debenture interest	14,000	3,500
Chargeable gain	Nil (W2)	Nil (W2)
Total profits	248,250	217,446
Charges on income –		
Patent royalties	(11,000)	(9,000)
Profits chargeable	237,250	208,446
Corporation tax payable	49,822 (W3)	60,759 (W4)

(c)   Amounts carried forward
           Capital losses   £20,000

Notes:

1.   Trading profit is apportioned on a time basis
2.   Debenture interest is allocated on the accruals basis.
3.   Bank interest is allocated according to the date of receipt.
4.   Chargeable gains are allocated according to the date of disposal of the chargeable asset.
5.   Patent royalty payments are allocated according to the date of payment.

Working 1

Capital allowances – Plant and Machinery

		Pool £	Expensive Car £	Car Pool £	Total £
WDV b/f		95,000	-	47,000	
CAP to 31.12.98					
Sales		(12,000)		(15,000)	
		83,000		32,000	
Additions			14,000	24,000	
				56,000	
WDA (25%)		20,750	3,000 (R)	14,000	37,750
		62,250	11,000	42,000	
Qualifying for					
FYA	92,000				
FYA (40%)	36,800	55,200	-	-	36,800
WDV at 31.12.98		117,450	11,000	42,000	
					74,550
CAP to 31.3.99					
WDA (25% × 3/12)		7,341	688	2,625	10,654
		110,109	10,312	39,375	
Qualifying for					
FYA	6,000				
FYA (40%)	2,400	3,600	-	-	2,400
WDV c/f		113,709	10,312	39,375	
					13,054

Did you answer the question?

You were not required to discuss why FYA was available even though the conditions were shown in Note 1 of the question to have been satisfied .

Working 2

Chargeable gains

CAP to 31.12.98

	£
Gain in period	30,000
Losses brought forward	50,000
Losses carried forward	20,000

Working 3

Corporation tax payable – CAP to 31.12.98

		£
'I' (Chargeable profits)	=	237,250
'P' (Chargeable profits + franked investment income*)	=	272,250

* FII = (16,000 + 12,000) = 28,000 × $^{100}/_{80}$ = £35,000.
'P' is below the lower limit and the small companies rate applies.

£

£237,250 × 21%   49,822

Working 4

Corporation tax payable –
CAP to 31.3.99

£

'I' (Chargeable profits)   =   208,446
'P' (Chargeable profits + franked investment income)   =   215,446
The reduced limits are:
Upper (3/12 × £1,500,000)   =   375,000
Lower (3/12 × £300,000)   =   75,000

'P' is between the reduced limits and the marginal rate of corporation tax applies.

£

£208,446 at 31%   64,618
Taper relief

$(375,000 - 215,446) \times \dfrac{208,446}{215,446} \times \dfrac{1}{40}$ =   (3,859)

                                                                 60,759

| **84** | **(Answer 2 of examination)** |

(Examiner's comments and marking guide)

An income tax question testing:

(a)   the calculation of income tax assessments, including capital allowances computations, for a short-lived business involving both commencement and cessation rules of assessment.

(b)   calculation of an income tax liability involving benefits-in-kind, savings income, personal pension premiums and non MIRAS loan interest.

In general, the answers to this question were satisfactory. The main problems encountered by candidates are itemised below.

(a)   **Assessments**

When calculating the assessments, many candidates either did not adjust for capital allowances or they deducted them, incorrectly, after first relating the profits to tax years (as under the old regime). Surprisingly, there were cases where the adjusted profits were not actually used in computing the assessments, instead the candidates insisted on using pre-capital allowances profits.

The 1995/96 and 1996/97 assessments presented problems to many candidates. Many candidates did not deduct the overlap profits from the final assessment. It was, however, pleasing to note that, unlike previous diets, most candidates used the calendar provided for apportionment purposes.

Capital allowances

Overall, this part was well attempted by most candidates. However, as in the past candidates did experience some difficulties with computing capital allowances for the first period 1.1.95 to 31.8.96 and computing the balancing adjustments. Although restriction for private use was applied when computing writing down allowances many candidates overlooked this when calculating the balancing adjustments. Further, on expensive cars the amount deducted from the qualifying expenditure should be the full amount of WDAs available (ie, before restriction for private use) when carrying forward the balance for future WDAS.

(b)   Austin's personal tax computation was handled competently and the car benefit, in particular, was well done. some candidates continue (despite comments in the previous Examiners' Reports) to time apportion the benefit using days which though more accurate is also more time consuming and not essential in this instance. It is quite acceptable and normal practice in examinations to time-apportion the car and fuel benefits to the nearest month. In many cases, although the time restriction was applied in respect of the car benefit, it was ignored when determining the fuel benefit.

A significant number of candidates excluded benefits-in-kind when calculating the personal pension premium. Although savings income was correctly computed, the majority of candidates appear to be ignorant of the fact that NSB interest is received gross.

Calculation of the income tax liability was well handled by the majority of candidates. The adjustments to the liability were also, in most cases, well performed except for the relief for loan interest, which was either ignored or incorrectly computed.

			Marks	
(a)	A	Capital allowances computation		
		WDA 1.9.95 – 31.8.96	1	
		WDA 1.9.96 – 31.8.97	1	
		Balancing allowance	1	
		Balancing charge	1	
	B	Profits for accounting periods	1	
	C	Assessments		
		1995-96	1	
		1996-97	1	
		1997-98	1	
		1998-99	1	
		Working 2	1	
				10
(b)		Personal pension premium	1	
		National Savings Bank	1	
		Midland Bank	1	
		Dividends	1	
		Personal allowance and income tax payable	1	
		Married couple's allowance	1	
		Income tax withheld on pension premium	1	
		Relief for loan interest	1	
		Income tax suffered	2	
		Capital gains tax	1	
		Car benefit	3	
		Fuel benefit	1	15
				25

(Step by step answer plan)

Overview

There is quite a lot to do in this husband and wife personal tax question but then there are 25 marks on offer. As this is a high mark compulsory question you have to try for every mark - you cannot afford to panic! Like all long questions it can be broken into sections. As you read the question those sections and their inter-relatedness should be noticed. For example, part (a) concerns the assessable income over the brief life of the business and the information for this is found in the first half of the question down to where the sale proceeds of the plant is given. Also, you are given the taxpayers' ages in the first line but it is not until almost the end when pension contributions are mentioned that the taxpayer's age has any relevance. Part (b) will take you longer than part (a) but you should be familiar with all the computational techniques required.

Step 1   Prepare a capital allowances computation covering the three periods of the business.

Step 2   State the adjusted profits for each period - ie, deduct capital allowances from the profit figures provided in the question.

Step 3 Compute the assessable profits for each of the four tax years covering the life of the business apportioning on a daily basis as required. Remember as there is a profit overlap at the start there will be overlap relief for the final tax year. Check that the total of profits earned equals the total of profits assessed over the life of the business.

Step 4 Move on to part (b) and start by deciding what needs to be done. Obviously income tax has to be computed in priority to CGT as CGT depends on the marginal IT rate. Also there is a fairly meaty working required on the car and fuel benefit so that is probably where to start.

Step 5 Construct a standard Taxable Income layout and fill it in from the question not forgetting to deduct the maximum pension contribution (20% of salary and benefits being aged between 36 and 45). There is no need for a layout that gives separate columns for savings and non-savings income as long as you can identify the savings income total.

Step 6 Convert the income figure into tax with all the necessary adjustments for MCA, tax added back on pension contributions paid net and relief (at 10%) on non-MIRAS loan interest. As savings income is all clearly taxed at 40% there is no need to show it taxed separately.

Step 7 Finally compute the CGT liability not forgetting the availability of taper relief.

The examiner's answer

(a) A.

Capital allowances claim

	Pool 25% £	Car (50% pte) 25% £	Claim £
1.9.95-31.8.96			
Additions	4,000	8,800	
WDA 25%	1,000	2,200 (1,100)	2,100
	3,000	6,600	
1.9.96-31.8.97			
WDA 25%	750	1,650 (825)	1,575
	2,250	4,950	
1.9.97-30.6.98			
Sales	2,000	5,000	
	250	50	
Balancing allowance	250		250
	-		
Balancing charge		50 (25)	(25)
	-	-	225

B.

Profits for accounting periods

			£
1.9.95-31.8.96 15,000 – CA's 2,100		=	12,900
1.9.96-31.8.97 25,000 – CA's 1,575		=	23,425
1.9.97-30.6.98 22,500 – CA's 225		=	22,275

C.

Tax year	Basis period	Amount assessable £
1995-96	1.9.95-5.4.96	7,669 (W1)
1996-97	1.9.95-31.8.96	12,900
1997-98	1.9.96-31.8.97	23,425
1998-99	1.9.97-30.6.98	14,606 (W2)

Working 1

$$£12,900 \times \frac{217}{365}$$

Working 2

£22,275 – overlap profit (D) £7,669 - £14,606

D.   Overlap profit

Period 1.9.95 to 5.4.96 = £7,669

(b)   (i)   **Income tax liability**
                                              1998-99

	£	£
Non-savings income		
Business profits	14,606	
Salary	22,500	
Benefit-in-kind (W3)	2,360	
	39,466	
Personal pension premium		
(20% × £24,860)	4,972	34,494
Savings income		
National Savings Bank		
(100 – 70 exempt)	30	
Midland Bank $\left(250 \times \dfrac{100}{80} \right)$	312	
Dividends $\left(3,000 \times \dfrac{100}{80} \right)$	3,750	4,092
Taxable income		38,586
Personal allowance		4,195
Taxable income		34,391

Income tax payable		£
£		
4,300 at 20%	=	860
22,800 at 23%	=	5,244
7,291 at 40%	=	2,916
34,391		9,020
Married couple's allowance		
£1,900 at 15%		(285)
		8,735
Basic rate tax withheld on pension premium (£4,972 at 23%)		1,144
		9,879
Relief for loan interest (£1,000 at 10%)		(100)
		9,779

Income tax suffered		
PAYE	5,175	
Bank interest (£312 at 20%)	62	
Dividends (£3,750 at 20%)	750	5,987
Income tax still to be paid		3,792

(ii)
Capital gains tax liability
1998-99

	£
Capital gain	30,000
Capital gain tapered to 92.5%	27,750
Annual exemption	6,800
	20,950
Capital gains tax payable	
£20,950 at 40% =	£8,380

Working 3

	£	£
Car and fuel benefits		
Car benefit		
35% × £12,000	4,200	
Mileage reduction for business use		
(equivalent of more than 2,500 pa)	(1,400) (1/3)	
	2,800	
Age reduction		
(over 4 years old on 5.4.99)	933 (1/3)	
	1,867	
Time reduction	467 (1/4)	1,400
Fuel benefit		
1400cc to 2000cc (petrol)	1,280	
Time reduction	(320)	960
		2,360

Did you answer the question?

You were not required to give the dates on which tax would be payable.

Tutorial notes

1   The examiner expects to see the above detailed form of working where the car and fuel benefit figures require adjustment.

2   The taxpayer in this situation is likely to have made payments on account of income tax for 1998/99 which should also be taken into account as a tax credit to determine his income tax payable. They were not mentioned in the question so they have to be ignored.

3   A commonly examined point is the add back of basic rate tax deducted on pension contributions made on the basis of Schedule E relevant earnings. If they are paid net but deducted gross in the taxable income computation relief is obtained twice over and an adjustment is obviously needed. Of course, we cannot ignore the contributions altogether as this would result in excluding the higher rate relief as in this case.

<table>
<tr><td>4</td><td>If you need the higher maximum percentages for pension contribution relief for older taxpayers these will be provided in the exam paper table of rates etc.</td></tr>
</table>

85   (Answer 3 of examination)

Examiner's comments and marking guide

A two-part capital gains tax question testing:

(a)   the transfer of property between spouses followed by sale by the transferee spouse to a third party, and

(b)   retirement relief on disposal of shares in a personal company, with restriction for non-business assets and calculation of gift relief, assessable gain and base acquisition cost of donee after joint election has been made for gift relief.

Capital gains tax remains a continuing weakness with answers betraying an absence of study in sufficient depth.

(a)   Few candidates stated that inter-spouse transfers are made on a no gain/no loss basis and simply did a computation comparing Freda's sale proceeds with Fred's purchase price plus indexation.

(b)   Most candidates recognised that retirement relief was in point and that it was restricted to 50%. Few however then went on to correctly calculate marginal relief. Most candidates correctly computed the restriction of the gain eligible for retirement relief. Some however seemed to think that motor cars are chargeable assets. Most candidates ignored computing the marginal relief maximum having already computed the gain eligible for retirement relief which is a lower figure. Of the few candidates who correctly identified the gain eligible for gift relief most then used the immediately chargeable gain to calculate Hardy's base cost.

			Marks	
(a)	(i)	Transfer to Freda - £61,600	1	
		No gain/no loss on transfer between husband/wife	1	
	(ii)	Gain on Freda £91,337	1	3
(b)		Retirement relief - first tranche	1	
		- second tranche	1	
		Assessable gain - £27,359	1	
		Hardy's base acquisition cost –		
		£502,289	1	
		Working 1 - £320,423	1	
		- Maximum test	1	
		Working 2	1	
		Working 3	1	8
				11

Step by step answer plan

Overview

In this paper the capital gains question (always number 3) has only 2 parts - the first concerns a husband and wife transaction and the second is a standard exercise in retirement relief and gift relief (and taper relief in the updated form of the question). It should be possible to obtain full marks quite easily.

Step 1   Part (a) requires two steps - viz, the calculation of the no gain/no loss price on the inter spouse transfer in 1990 and the calculation of the gain when the wife sells the asset in 1998. Both are standard layouts.

Step 2   For part (b) the key working is the analysis of the chargeable assets held by the company between business and non-business assets. This leads onto the apportioning of the gain on the shares between the part that qualifies for retirement relief and gift relief (in that order) and the non-qualifying part. The examiner splits this over 3 working notes but a more compact approach would be just as acceptable.

Step 3   Next your part (b) answer should show the full gain reduced by retirement relief and gift relief to leave the portion of gain qualifying for neither. As this is a gain on shares in a 'qualifying company' (for taper relief purposes) taper relief at business assets rates then applies.

Step 4   Finally, do not overlook the requirement to show the donee's base cost - ie, the market value of the shares as reduced by the gift relief.

The examiner's answer

(a)   (i)   **Fred**

		£
Cost		50,000
Indexation allowance to May 1990		
$\dfrac{126.2 - 102.4}{102.4}$		
$= .232 \times 50,000$		11,600
Transferred to Freda		61,600

There is a no gain/no loss position on transfers between husband and wife.

(ii)   **Freda**

		£
Sale proceeds		170,000
Deemed acquisition price		61,600
		108,400
Indexation allowance to April 1998		
$\dfrac{161.2 - 126.2}{126.2}$		
$= .277 \times 61,600$		17,063
		91,337

(a)   **Nelson**

		£
Gain on disposal of shares		350,000
Retirement relief		
First tranche		
$£250,000 \times \dfrac{5}{10}$	125,000	
Second tranche		
$\dfrac{£320,423 \ (\text{W1}) - £125,000}{2}$	97,712	222,712
Gain before gift relief		127,288
Gain attributable to business assets		320,423
less: retirement relief		222,712
Eligible for gift relief		97,711
Assessable gain (£127,288 - £97,711)		29,577
Tapered to 92.5%		27,359

Hardy

Base acquisition cost (£600,000 - £97,711)   502,289

Working 1

$$£350,000 \times \frac{£650,000 \quad (W2)}{£710,000 \quad (W3)} \qquad = \qquad £320,423$$

NB The second tranche maximum is

$$\frac{5 \text{ years}}{10 \text{ years}} \times £1,000,000 \qquad = \qquad £500,000$$

Working 2   Chargeable business assets

	£
Buildings	350,000
Goodwill	200,000
Plant	100,000
	650,000

Working 3   Chargeable assets

	£
Buildings	350,000
Goodwill	200,000
Plant	100,000
Investments	60,000
	710,000

Did you answer the question?

You were not required to give the time limit for the gift relief election nor any other information concerning the election.

Tutorial notes

1   An item of plant is a chargeable asset if it cost more that £6,000 or is valued above that amount.

2   Although retirement relief is being phased out with the limits of £250,000 and £1,000,000 reducing by £50,000 and £200,000 pa from 6 April 1999 onwards the examiner has said he will not test the phasing out rules for exam sittings in 1999.

3   Taper relief rules are unfair in roll-over situations - ie, where a gain is deducted from a base cost as opposed to merely being deferred (ie, put in suspense). For example, the taper relief entitlement on the £97,711 of gain held over by gift relief is lost for all time. The donee, Hardy, will only obtain taper relief based on his own period of ownership despite effectively taking over the liability on the earlier gain.

---

86   (Answer 4 of examination)

Examiner's comments and marking guide

A two-part VAT question testing:

(a)   the factors to be taken into account when considering voluntary registration and

(b)   a VAT calculation.

(a) Many candidates correctly stated the 4 main considerations but many more did not grasp the practicality of the question and gave the usual VAT answer for which no marks were given. Candidates must learn to apply their knowledge to the facts of the question.

(b) Many candidates did not read the question and did not realise the £16,000 was input tax. Many candidates wrongly dealt with the bad debt and the car fuel charge was frequently treated as input tax. Only a very few candidates were aware of the VAT payment date.

			Marks	
(a)	(i)		1	
	(ii)		1	
	(iii)		1	
	(iv)		1	4
(b)	Output tax on standard-rated supplies		1	
	Car fuel		1	
	Input tax –			
	Taxable supplies ⎱		1	
	Exempt supplies ⎰			
	Non-attributable supplies		2	
	Non inclusion of bad debt relief		1	
	Due and payable date		1	7
				11

Step by step answer plan

Overview

Question 4 always concerns VAT and seldom requires any information or skill which an averagely prepared candidate could not furnish. This is the case here. Part (a) requires a few brief lines on the merits and demerits of voluntary registration and part (b) is a standard partial exemption exercise not unknown in past paper 7 exams.

Step 1 For part (a) there is no particular requirement to list the relevant factors in any order of importance so planning your answer is almost unnecessary. Obviously, for each sentence you have to craft the words to convey your meaning but there is no risk of omitting a point you should have mentioned earlier - just add any afterthoughts to the list. There are only 4 marks so there is no need to go into detail. Width rather than depth is required.

Step 2 For part (b) the key working is finding the proportion of input tax on non-attributable purchases. This is done on the ratio of taxable supplies to total supplies using the VAT exclusive figures.

Step 3 Next prepare a 'VAT account' showing in memorandum form the output tax and input tax for the quarter. The examiner's answer explains why the output tax accounted for earlier on the bad debt is not yet recoverable and he allocates a mark for this in the marking guide even though explanations were not required in the question. It is probably wise practice therefore to give brief explanations for ignoring items thereby distinguishing yourself from less informed candidates!

Step 4 Do not waste an easy mark by omitting the date the VAT is payable.

The examiner's answer

(a) Voluntary registration will have the following consequences:

(i) input tax can be reclaimed including input tax on all car expenses even where the car is also used privately, subject to output tax on the fuel scale figures.

(ii) the impression of substantial business activity will be created.

(iii) there will be a need to maintain VAT records and meet compliance requirements and

(iv)   non-VAT registered clients will have to pay an extra 17.5% on their bills but clients registered for VAT will not be affected as they can set the input tax against their output tax.

(b)

Marlyse
VAT payable – quarter to 31 March 1999

	£	£
Output tax		
Standard-rated supplies - £190,000 at 17.5%		33,250
Car fuel charge £268 at $^7/_{47}$		40
		33,290
Input tax	16,000	
Non-attributable	1,920 *	17,920
VAT payable		15,370

Due and payable date is 30 April 1999

$$* \frac{190,000 + 50,000}{190,000 + 50,000 + 10,000}$$

$$= 96\% \times £2,000 = £1,920$$

NB No relief for bad debts was available as the debt was not over six months old.

Did you answer the question?

You were not required to mention other matters concerning partial exemption such as the £625 per month de minimis limit (not applicable here) or the annual adjustment or the option for alternative ways of calculating the recoverable part of the non-attributable input tax.

Tutorial notes

1   Up until 1997/98 the VAT fuel scale figures aligned with the corresponding values for Schedule E (and Class1A).   The FA 1998 increased the Schedule E fuel benefit values significantly above inflation to discourage employers from providing private use fuel. However, it would have been inappropriate to increase the VAT charge so dramatically and therefore separate lower VAT fuel scales apply for 1998/99 onwards. We have put the required figure into the question but it will be given in the exam in the table of rates etc. if it is needed.

---

87   (Answer 5 of examination)

Examiner's comments and marking guide

A question on the requirements for a hotel to be treated as a qualifying hotel and then requiring a calculation of the capital allowances on a qualifying hotel. This was a popular question and most candidates made a reasonable attempt at the definition but there were varying degrees of success at guessing the number of bedrooms and opening dates. Most candidates excluded the land cost from the computation. The annual allowance was often wrongly scale down to $^1/_4$. The fire doors were usually excluded, without explanation, but not made the subject of a plant and machinery claim. Similarly the cost of tiles was often excluded without explanation.

			Marks	
(a)	1.		1	
	2.		1	
	3.		1	
	4.		1	
	5.		1	
	6.		1	6

(b)   1.   1
         2.   1
         3.   1
         4.   - IBA   1
                 - P & M   1   5
                                                                                    ――   ――
                                                                                             11
                                                                                             ――

Step by step answer plan

Overview

This is a question applying some of the basic points on capital allowances - notably the qualifying hotel rules and the case law based distinction between 'plant' and 'premises'.

Step 1   Read the requirements of part (a) and then review the situation given in the question to assist your memory on the conditions for being a qualifying hotel. Then list out the points - pity you cannot photocopy your study text since that is all that is needed for the 6 marks!

Step 2   Part (b) only asks for a calculation but the examiners answer gives some narrative and reasons on the items concerned and this is reflected in the marking guide. Therefore it appears to be good practice to provide some narrative where as many as 5 marks are given for a relatively short calculation if only to explain briefly why you have taken the action you have.

The examiner's answer

(a)   (1)   The accommodation is in buildings of a permanent nature.

         (2)   The hotel is open for at least four months in the season (April to October).

         (3)   The hotel has at least ten letting bedrooms which are available to the public and are not normally occupied by the same person for more than one month.

         (4)   The hotel offers sleeping accommodation consisting wholly or mainly of letting bedrooms.

         (5)   The hotel provides services for guests including breakfast and evening meals, bed-making and the cleaning of rooms.

         (6)   The trade must have been carried on for the 12 months ending with the last day of the accounting period in question.

(b)   (1)   The cost of the land does not qualify for capital allowances.

         (2)   The fire doors will be treated as plant and machinery.

         (3)   The tiles, although contributing to the setting, are essentially part of the building.

         (4)

Allowances	£	£
IBA (Hotel)	64,000 at 4% (WDA)	2,560
P&M	6,000 at 40% (FYA)	2,400
	70,000	4,960

Did you answer the question?

You were not required to make reference to specific case law decisions.

88 (Answer 6 of examination)

Examiner's comments and marking guide

A capital gains tax question requiring a statement of the conditions necessary for the payment of capital gains tax by individuals in instalments. The question was attempted by very few candidates, all of whom displayed little or no knowledge of the conditions.

		Marks
(a)	Transfer to a connected person	1
	No gift relief available	1
	10 annual equal instalments	1
	Assets –	
	Land	1
	Controlling interest of shares	1
	Minority holding in unquoted company	1
	Sale within ten-year period	1
	Interest on outstanding tax	1
(b)	Instalment period exceeding 18 months	1
	Instalments of tax spread over same period up to eight years	1
	No interest on outstanding tax	1
		11

Step by step answer plan

Overview

You either know the details of this relatively fringe topic of CGT administration or you don't. For most candidates this is probably the obvious discard in the optional part of the paper.

Step 1 Choose another question/ rue the advice of a colleague to ignore revising VAT thereby putting the easy VAT question out of the frame.

Step 2 If you still have no other more attractive question to choose and you have more than your imagination with which to answer this question start by realising that there are two quite separate circumstances to deal with.

Step 3 Craft your answer to part (a). Keep to the points you actually know and don't create a bad impression by writing a work of fiction.

Step 4 For part (b) prepare your answer emphasising the maximum of eight years for delaying full payment of the CGT.

Step 5 Re-read the question. Have you dealt with the requirement concerning payment of interest?

The examiner's answer

(a) Where there is a CGT liability arising out of transfers of certain assets to a connected person and no gift relief is available the taxpayer may elect to pay the tax in ten equal annual instalments. These assets are land, a controlling interest of shares in a company or a minority holding of shares in an unquoted company. If the transferee sells the assets within the ten-year instalment period, all outstanding tax and interest will become due for immediate collection. Interest on overdue tax will be payable on the tax paid by instalments.

(b) The capital gains tax may be paid in instalments where the taxpayer receives the consideration for the sale in instalments over a period of 18 months or more. The instalments of tax may be spread over the period during which the instalments of consideration are receivable or eight years whichever is shorter. No interest on outstanding tax is payable if the CGT instalments are paid on the due dates, ie, 31 January each year.

89	(Answer 7 of examination)

Examiner's comments and marking guide

The question required a statement, with accompanying explanations, of the additional information required to prepare a profit adjustment statement from the trading and profit and loss account provided.

This was a hugely popular question with candidates queuing up to answer it. Most did a reasonable job going through the accounts and commenting on the various items. The non-practical candidates gave learned discussions on what to add-back and deduct without any reference whatsoever to the question and therefore to no avail. Some even extended their answers to cover personal allowances. For some inexplicable reason some candidates assumed the interest and lease premium were received rather than paid.

	Marks
1.	½
2.	½
3a.	½
3b.	½
3c.	½
4.	½
5.	1
6.	1
7.	1
8.	½
9.	1
10.	½
11a.	½
11b.	½
11c.	½
11d.	½
11e.	½
11f.	½
	11

Step by step answer plan

Overview

This is a relatively easy question where you have to review the various items in a P & L account and decide for each one whether you need more information to make an adjustment. Before choosing to answer this style of question in an exam see if you can count 11 items (the number of marks available) on which you can comment productively. If so you may be able to score well on this choice.

Step 1 Prepare a table with two major columns - one headed 'Information' and the other headed 'Reason needed'.

Step 2 Work through the account headings listing the further information needed and the reasons. The examiner's answer takes a slightly more thoughtful approach by linking together items which have a common treatment where appropriate - see item 11 in his answer. Unfortunately there is some time pressure in this question and it may be quicker to work through each individual item as it comes rather than spending too long on considering the best way of presentation.

The examiner's answer

The following information would be required.

	Information	Reason
1.	**Sales**	
	Were any goods taken for own consumption at less than selling price?	These should be included at selling price.
2.	**Stock**	
	Were any contingency reserves included in the stock valuations?	These should be disregarded for tax purposes.
3.	**Wages and National Insurance contributions**	
	(a) were Madelaine's NIC contributions included?	If so they should be disallowed.
	(b) Were any salary payments made to Madelaine?	If so they should be disallowed.
	(c) Were any payments made to Madelaine's family?	Payments should be reasonable for the work done.
4.	**Repairs and Renewals**	
	Was any capital expenditure included?	If so it should be disallowed.
5.	**General expenses**	
	Were any of these of a non-trading or capital nature?	If so they will be disallowed.
6.	**Bad Debts**	
	Were there any specific or general provisions made?	Only specific provisions are allowable.
7.	**Lease premium**	
	What was the length of the lease?	If it was a short lease, relief may be obtained over the duration of the lease.
8.	**Interest**	
	Did the charge include any interest on overdue tax?	If so it should be disallowed.
9.	**Relocation expenditure**	
	Was the move to large premises?	If so the expenditure will be disallowed.
10.	**Professional fees**	
	Did these include any costs in connection with the new lease or capital items?	If so they will be disallowed
11.	(a) Rent and Rates	
	(b) Interest	
	(c) Motor vehicle running costs	
	(d) Lighting and heating	

(e)   Professional fees
(f)   Subscriptions and donations

Was there any private element in any of the   If so, it should be disallowed.
above items?

Did you answer the question?

You were not required to produce any computations or formulae such as might be relevant for calculating the allowable
portion of a lease premium.

---

90   (Answer 8 of examination)

Examiner's comments and marking guide

Schedule A income tax question covering (a) Rent-a-Room relief, (b) income and expenditure on unfurnished and
furnished accommodation and (c) the treatment of losses.

Part (a) was surprisingly badly answered with many candidates attempting to combine expenses with rent a room relief
to give an overall loss. In part (b) far too many candidates calculated the rents incorrectly. The insurance figure was
only infrequently correctly calculated. The repairs deduction for flat one was not dealt with satisfactorily by most
candidates. Some candidates still persist in deducting the discount element of the lease premium (£600 rather than
£4,400). Very few candidates included a wear and tear allowance for flat three and even fewer arrived at the correct
deduction.

Part (c) was answered satisfactorily.

		Marks	
(a)	Ordinary basis	1	
	Alternative basis	1	2
(b)	Rent – Flat 1	1	
	Rent – Flat 2	1	
	Rent – Flat 3	1	
	Premium on lease – Flat 1	1	
	Insurance – Flat 11		
	Repairs – Flat 1	1	
	Wear and Tear – Flat 3	1	
	Water rates and council tax – Flat 3	1	8
(c)			1
			11

Step by step answer plan

Overview

This is a relatively straightforward three part question on Schedule A. You should be able to complete the main part
(part (b)) without losing any marks. As the Schedule A rules were substantially simplified in 1995/96 ahead of the
start of self-assessment, the computation is not difficult. The examiner, however, could not resist throwing in some
red herrings such as whether a lease is 'tenant repairing' or 'landlord repairing' - distinctions of no tax significance
under the current Schedule A rules. Essentially all letting is a single 'business' with income and expenses recognised
as under Schedule D Case I rules but without the opening and closing rules etc. Instead the 'business' is forced to
have a 5 April year end.

Step 1   For part (a) compute the income assessable on the normal basis and then the income assessable if the
alternative rent-a -room basis is used not forgetting to state your conclusion.

Step 2   Next construct your answer to part (b) using a simple layout showing rents etc receivable less expenses payable. You can use a series of working notes as per the examiner's answer but most items except perhaps the lease premium could be dealt with quite satisfactorily on the face of the main layout.

Step 3   Even though explanations are not actually asked for in the question, the examiner expected a comment on why the window frame repair is excluded and it is clearly good practice to comment on items ignored.

Step 4   Finally don't forget part (c).

The examiner's answer

(a)
                                          Agnes
      (i)   Ordinary basis   £

             Rent   4,900
             Expenses   2,000
                                                                       _____
                                                                        2,900
                                                                       _____

      (ii)   Alternative basis   £

             Rent   4,900
             'Rent a room' limit   4,250
                                                                       _____
                                                                          650
                                                                       _____

             Assessment (lower figure) £650

(b)   **Harry**
                              Schedule A Income 1998-99

                                                          £   £
             Rent receivable   - Flat 1   1,750 (W1)
                                     - Flat 2   4,000 (W2)
                                     - Flat 3   6,240
             Premium on lease   - Flat 1   4,400 (W3)
                                                                   _____
                                                                  16,390
             Insurance   - Flat 1   233 (W4)
                                     - Flats 2 & 3   800
             Repairs   - Flat 1   500 (W5)
                                     - Flats 2 & 3   950
             Wear and Tear
             Allowance   - Flat 3   504 (W6)
             Water rates and council tax - Flat 3   1,200   4,187
                                                    _____   _____
             Schedule A profit   12,203
                                                                 _____

   Working 1
        6/12 × £3,500   £1,750

   Working 2
             3/12 × £4,000   £1,000
             6/12 × £6,000   £3,000
                                                                 _____
                                                                 £4,000
                                                                 _____

Working 3

Premium	£5,000
less (7-1) × 2%	600
	£4,400

Working 4

7/12 × £400	£233

Working 5

As the replacement of the window frames was necessary before the flat could be let, the expenditure is deemed to be capital expenditure and not, therefore, allowable.

Working 6

The 'wear and tear' allowance is 10% of the rent less the items which are the tenant's responsibility, ie, water rates and council tax:
£6,240 – (400 + 800) = £5,040
10% - £504

(c) If the expenses of letting property in a tax year exceed the income from property, the excess is carried forward to be set against the first available Schedule A income in the future.

Tutorial notes

1   Although you should not find it difficult to remember the rent-a-room figure of £4,250, the examiner will include it in the table of rates etc. if it is needed and we have included it here in the question even though it arguably gives the game away!

2   Part (c) refers to relief for a loss on property let unfurnished. In fact it generally does not matter whether the property is furnished or unfurnished so it seems as if the examiner was throwing in another red herring. However, he might have been trying to pre-empt mention of loss relief for the special situation of furnished holiday letting. If that situation arises the 'furnished' loss is available in the same way as relief is given for a trading loss.

DECEMBER 1998 QUESTIONS

Section A – ALL THREE questions are compulsory and MUST be attempted

91   (Question 1 of examination)

Unashamedly Upmarket Limited (UUL) is a UK resident company which manufactures distinctive kitchen furniture and fittings. It has no associated companies and has always made accounts up to 31 January. The company's results excluding capital transactions for the year ended 31 January 1999 were as follows:

	£
Trading profits	
(as adjusted for taxation but before capital allowances)	390,000
Debenture interest receivable (note 2)	60,000
Patent royalties payable (note 3)	38,000
Dividends received from UK companies	10,000

Note 1

Unashamedly Upmarket Limited is a medium-sized company with a turnover in the year ended 31 January 1999 of £4,000,000. The average number of employees during the accounting period was 125.

Note 2

Debenture interest receivable (gross amounts)	£
30.6.98 received	18,000
31.12.98 received	36,000
31.1.99 accrued	6,000
	60,000

(a)   The loan was made on 1 April 1998

(b)   Income tax has been deducted at source.

(c)   The interest was non-trading income.

Note 3

Patent royalties payable (gross amounts)	£
31.3.98 paid	9,000
30.6.98 paid	7,000
30.9.98 paid	11,000
31.12.98 paid	8,000
31.1.99 accrued	3,000
	38,000

Income tax has been deducted at source from the amounts paid.

Note 4

Plant and machinery
On 1 February 1998 the tax written down values of plant and machinery were:

	£
Main pool	75,000
Car pool	23,000
Expensive car	11,000

In August 1998 machinery costing £100,000 was sold for £20,000 and replaced by new machinery costing £150,000. The new machinery is not to be treated either as a 'short-life' asset or a 'long-life' asset. In September 1998 one of the cars in the car pool was sold for £4,000 and replaced with one costing £11,000. In the same month the expensive car was sold for £9,000 and replaced with one costing £24,000.

Note 5

On I May 1985 company has purchased a new factory costing £200,000 and commenced manufacturing there immediately. The factory was rented out to a mail-order company during a period of recession between 1 August 1990 and 31 October 1992 after which manufacturing recommenced. On 30 November 1998 the company sold the factory for £400,000 and moved into rented premises. The company had claimed the maximum initial allowance of 25%. The factory was not situated in an enterprise zone.

Note 6

On 1 February 1998 the company had no trading losses brought forward and no capital losses brought forward.

You are required to calculate the corporation tax payable for the year ended 31 January 1999.

NB All apportionments should be made in months.

(Total: 22 marks)
(as amended)

---

92 **(Question 2 of examination)**

(a) Otto is a self-employed television engineer.

He commenced in business on 1 June 1995 and initially made up accounts to 30 November but has now changed his accounting date to 28 February.
His profits adjusted for income tax, are:

	£
1.6.95–30.11.95	7,000
1.12.95–30.11.96	16,000
1.12.96–30.11.97	19,000
1.12.97–28.2.99	25,000

You are required to calculate the amounts chargeable to income tax under Schedule D, Case I for the years 1995–96, 1996–97, 1997–98 and 1998-99.

NB All apportionments in part (a) should be made in days. **(6 marks)**

(b) Jeremy, who is married, is 77-years-old and receives a state retirement pension of £8,100 per annum. He also receives dividend income of £6,000 per annum (net). In 1997 Jeremy purchased a life annuity from which a monthly income of £325 (gross) is paid. The capital element of each payment was agreed with the Inland Revenue at £300. Income Tax is being deducted from the income element

Jeremy owns a furnished cottage which he rents to holidaymakers. In the tax year 1998–99 it was let for 20 weeks at a weekly rental of £250.

The following expenditure was incurred:

	£
Insurance (note I)	400
Water rates	200
Council tax	300

Note 1: The £400 was paid on 1 January 1999: the insurance paid on 1 January 1998 was £360.

You are required to calculate the Income Tax payable by Jeremy for the year 1998–99. **(14 marks)**
(Total: 20 marks)

16Y.   6m.

93   (Question 3 of examination)

2015

(a)   On 1 May 1985 Nigel acquired a 30-year lease for £20,000. On 1 November 1998 he assigned the lease for £75,000.

You are required to calculate Nigel's capital gain for 1998–99, before annual exemption.

NB All apportionments should be made in months.   **(4 marks)**

(b)   Kay purchased 20 acres of land in February 1993 for £40,000. In March 1999 she sold part of the land for £18,000 when the value of the remainder was £60,000. Kay had made no other capital disposals in 1998–99.

You are required to calculate the capital gains chargeable on Kay for 1998–99.   **(5 marks)**

(c)   Shirley had the following dealings in the shares of Wingfield Plc, a UK quoted company

	Number of shares	£
January 1981 – bought	4,000	16,000
March 1993 – rights issue 1 for 4	1,000	7,000
November 1995 – bought	3,000	24,000
January 1998 – bonus issue 1 for 2	4,000	–
March 1999 – sold	7,000	56,000

The adjusted 31 March 1982 value after the bonus issue is £8. No election has been made to 're-base' the cost of all assets held on 31 March 1982 at their value on that date.

You are required to calculate Shirley's capital gain for 1998–99, before the annual exemption

(13 marks)

Note: None of the above assets qualify for taper relief at the business rate.   **(Total: 22 marks)**

Section B – THREE questions ONLY to be attempted

94   (Question 4 of examination)

(a)   **You are required** to state:

    (i)   who is required to register for value added tax,   **(2 marks)**
    (ii)   when should the registration take place and what is the date of registration,   **(4 marks)**
    (iii)   the practical consequences of late registration.   **(3 marks)**

(b)   When may a person de-register for value-added tax?   **(2 marks)**
(Total: 11 marks)

95   (Question 5 of examination)

You are required to briefly discuss the criteria to be considered when deciding whether an individual is 'employed' or 'self-employed'.   **(11 marks)**

96   (Question 6 of examination)

You are a practising chartered certified accountant and have a large number of personal tax clients.

You are required to prepare a check-list to send to clients, other than clients who are self-employed, shortly after 5 April 2000. This will act as an aide-memoir for them when sending you the relevant information to include in their Tax Returns for the year ended 5 April 2000. The check-list should have 3 main headings - Income, Payments and Allowances.   **(11 marks)**

97   (Question 7 of examination)

(a)   Malcolm started in business as a self-employed builder on 1 August 1997. His adjusted trading results, after capital allowances, were:

		£	
Period ended 30.11.97		(10,000)	Loss
Year ended 30.11.98		(20,000)	Loss
Year ended 30.11.99		14,000	Profit

Prior to being self-employed Malcolm was employed as a builder when his earnings were:

	£
1997–1998 (to 31 July 1997)	5,000
1996–1997	8,000

He received annual dividend income of £3,000 (net) from 1996–97 onwards and in 1997–98 realised a capital gain of £10,000, after indexation but before annual exemption.

You are required to show how Malcolm's trading losses can be utilised most effectively, giving your reasoning.

NB You may assume the rates and allowances provided apply to all years relevant to this question. All apportionments should be made in days.   **(9 marks)**

(b)   **You are required** to state by what date(s) the claims you are proposing in part (a) should be submitted to the Inland Revenue.   **(2 marks)**

(Total: 11 marks)

98   (Question 8 of examination)

Josephine, who is not contracted out of the state pension scheme, receives a weekly salary of £400. Josephine is provided with a company car by her employer. Until 5 December 1998 the car was a 1900 cc diesel car which was first registered on 1 September 1994 with a list price of £12,000. On 6 December 1998 the car was exchanged for a new 2,500 cc petrol car with a list price of £21,000. Josephine's employer provided fuel for both cars for both business and private motoring. The car mileages were.

6.4.98 – 5.12.98
20,000 of which 11,000 were business
6.12.98 – 5.4.99
9,000 of which 7,000 were business.

You are required to calculate the national insurance contributions payable by Josephine and her employer for the year 1998–99.

NB Apportionments should be made in months.   **(Total: 11 marks)**

ANSWERS TO DECEMBER 1998 EXAMINATION

91   (Answer 1 of examination)

A Corporation Tax question testing:
(a)   the calculation of corporation tax where there is small company marginal relief.
(b)   the calculation of capital allowances, both plant and machinery and industrial buildings,
(c)   the treatment of charges on income, and
(d)   the calculation and set-off of income tax.

Unashamedly Upmarket Limited
Corporation Tax Computation

Chargeable accounting period to 31 January 1999		£
Trading profit		390,000
Capital allowances	– Plant and machinery (W1)	(86,250)
	– Industrial buildings allowance (W2)	138,000
		441,750
Chargeable gain (W3)		55,800
Debenture interest		60,000
		557,550
Patent royalties		(35,000)
Chargeable profits		522,550
Corporation tax payable (W4)		147,730
Income Tax (W5)		(2,750)
		144,980

WORKING 1

Capital Allowances
Plant and Machinery

		Main Pool 25%	Car Pool 25%	Expensive Car(1) 25%	Expensive Car(2) 25%	Claim
WDF b/f 1.2.98		75,000	23,000	11,000		
Sales		(20,000)	(4,000)	(9,000)		
		55,000	19,000	2,000		
Additions			11,000		24,000	
			30,000			
WDA		13,750	7,500		3,000 (R)	24,250
B.Allce				2,000		2,000
		41,250	22,500	–	21,000	
Additions qualifying for FYA	150,000					
FYA (40%)	60,000	90,000	–	–	–	60,000
WDV c/f 31.1.99		131,250	22,500	–	21,000	
						86,250

(R) Maximum allowance is at the rate of £3,000 pa.

WORKING 2

Capital Allowances
Industrial Buildings Allowances

	£	£
Cost		200,000
CAP to 31.1.86		
Initial allowance – 25%	50,000	
WDA – 4%	8,000	
4 CAP's to 31.1.90 – 4 × 4%	32,000	
2 CAP's to 31.1.92 – 2 × 4%	16,000 (notional)	
(The building was not in industrial use on 31.1.91 and 31.1.92)		
6 CAP's to 31.1.98 – 6 × 4%	48,000	154,000
Residue of expenditure before sale		46,000
CAP to 31.1.99		
Balancing charge (restricted to allowances actually given)		£138,000

WORKING 3

Chargeable gain on disposal of
industrial building

	£
Sale proceeds	400,000
Cost	200,000
Unindexed gain	200,000
Indexation allowance $\dfrac{163.9 - 95.21}{95.21} = 0.721 \times £200,000$	(144,200)
	55,800

WORKING 4

Corporation Tax payable	£
'T' (Chargeable profits)	522,550
Franked investment income $10,000 \times \dfrac{100}{80}$	12,500
	535,050

As 'P' is between the upper and lower limits for both financial years 1997 and 1998 the marginal rate of corporation tax applies. As there has been no change in the rate of corporation tax, the small companies rate or the taper relief fraction, it is not necessary to separately calculate the corporation tax payable for each financial year.

Financial years 1997 and 1998	
552,550 at 31%	171,290
Taper relief $(1,500,000 - 535,050) \times \dfrac{522,550}{535,050} \times \dfrac{1}{40}$	23,560
	147,730

WORKING 5

Income Tax

	£	£
Income tax deducted on payment		
Royalties – £35,000 at 23%		8,050
Income tax suffered on receipt		
Debenture interest – £54,000 at 20%		10,800
To set off against corporation tax		2,750

---

92   (Answer 2 of examination)

A two-part income tax question testing:

(a)   the calculation of Schedule D, Case 1 income for the first four years of a business incorporating a change of accounting date with utilisation of overlap profit created at the commencement of trading.

(b)   an income tax computation including savings and non-savings income and the calculation of age allowances where the income limit for age-related allowances is exceeded.

(a)

Otto
Business Profits chargeable to income tax

		£	£
1995–96	(1.6.95–30.11.95)	7,000	
	(1.12.95–5.4.96)	5,523	12,523
	(126/135 × £16,000) (note 1)		
1996–97	(1.12.95–30.11.96)		16,000
1997–98	(1.12.96–30.11.97)		19,000
1998–99	(1.12.97–28.2.99)	25,000	
	(overlap profit – note 2)	(3,945)	21,055

Note 1   Overlap profit on commencement
           1.12.95 – 5.4.96 £5,523

Note 2   Utilisation of overlap profit on change of accounting date

	Overlap Profit £	*Overlap days*
b/f	5,523	126
released	3,945	90*
c/f	1,578	36

* days in account (1.12.97 – 28.2.99)   455
  days in assessment (1998 – 99)   365
                                          90

(b)

Jeremy
1998–99 Income tax liability

		£
Non-savings income		
Retirement pension		8,100
Schedule A (W1)		3,680
		11,780
Savings income		
Purchased Life Annuity (12 × £25)	300	
Dividends $\left(£6,000 \times \dfrac{100}{80}\right)$	7,500	7,800
Total income		19,580

Personal allowance (W4)		4,195
Taxable income		15,385

	£	£
Tax on non-savings income		
£4,300 at 20%		860
£3,285 at 23%		756
£7,585		1,616
Tax on savings income		
£7,800 at 20%		1,560
		3,176
Married couple's allowance (W5)		
£3,060 at 15%		459
		2,717
Income tax suffered:		
Dividends (£7,500 at 20%)	1,500	
Annuity (£300 at 20%)	60	1,560
		1,157

WORKING 1

	£	£
Schedule A		
Rent		5,000
Insurance (W2)	370	
Water rates and council tax	500	
Wear and tear allowance (W3)	450	1,320
		3,680

WORKING 2

	£
Insurance	
¾ × £360	270
¼ × £400	100
	370

WORKING 3

Wear and tear

The wear and tear allowance is 10% of the rent less the items which are tenant's responsibility ie, water rates and council tax:

$$£5,000 - £500 = £4,500$$
$$10\% = £450$$

WORKING 4

	£
Calculation of personal allowance	
Total income	19,580
Allowance limit	16,200
Excess	3,380
Higher personal allowance	5,600
50% of excess	1,690
	3,910

As this reduction takes the level of personal allowance below £4,195 it is restricted to an amount (£1,405) to leave the allowance at £4,195, the basic personal allowance.

WORKING 5
Calculation of married couple's allowance.
The reduction of £1,405 in the person allowance will be taken into consideration.

	£	£
Married couple's allowance		3,345
50% of excess (W4)	1,690	
reduction in personal allowance	1,405	285
		3,060

This is in excess of the basic married couple's allowance £1,900, and no further adjustment is necessary.

93   (Answer 3 of examination)

A three part capital gains tax question testing:

(a)   calculation of a capital gain on the assignment of a short lease
(b)   the treatment of part-disposals of land and
(c)   calculation of a capital gain on the sale of quoted shares following rights and bonus issues.

(a)

Nigel

	£
Proceeds	75,000
	(14,953)
Unindexed gain	60,047
Indexation allowance	
	10,362
	49,685

* remaining life of lease on disposal
**remaining life of lease on acquisition

WORKING

17 years	66.470	66.470
16 years	64.116	
	2.354 ÷ 2	1.177
		65.293

(b)   The disposal proceeds of land by Kay in 1998–99 of £18,000 are less than £20,000 but the consideration of £18,000 exceeds 20% of the value of the land immediately prior to the sale [(£18,000 + £60,000) × 20% = £15,600]. The sale proceeds cannot therefore be deducted from the cost of the land under the small disposals procedure.

		£
Sale proceeds		18,000
Cost	× 40,000	9,231
Unindexed gain		8,769

Indexation allowance

$$\frac{161.2 - 138.8}{138.8} = .161 \times 9,231 \qquad\qquad\qquad 1,486$$

	£
Indexed gain	7,283
Annual exemption	6,800
Capital gain chargeable at marginal rate	483

(c)

Shirley
Wingfield plc

(i)

	£
Sale from FA 1985 pool	
Sale proceeds $\dfrac{4,500}{7,000} \times £56,000$	36,000
Indexed cost (W1) (£24,000 + indexation £1,826)	25,826
Indexed gain	10,174

(ii)

Sale from 1982 holding

	Cost £	MV at 31.3.82 £
Sale proceeds $\dfrac{2,500}{7,000} \times £56,000$	20,000	20,000
Cost/MV (W2)	7,667	13,000
Unindexed gain	12,333	7,000
Indexation allowance		
– original shares and bonus issue		
$\dfrac{161.2 - 79.44}{79.44} = 1.029$		
on $\dfrac{2,500}{7,500} \times £32,000$	(10,976)	(10,976)
– rights issue		
$\dfrac{161.2 - 139.3}{139.3} = 157$		
on $\dfrac{2,500}{7,500} \times £7,000$	(366)	(366)
Restriction of indexation allowance		4,342
	991	NIL

As there is no gain on 'MV', the sale of shares results in a 'no gain/no loss' situation.

Summary

	£
FA 1985 pool	10,174
1982 holding	NIL
	10,174

WORKING 1

FA 1985 pool

	No of Shares	Unindexed pool	Indexed pool
November 1995 – bought	3,000	24,000	24,000
January 1998 – bonus issue	1,500	-	-
	4,500	24,000	24,000
Indexation to April 1998			
$\dfrac{161.2 - 149.8}{149.8} \times £24,000$	–	–	1,826
	4,500	24,000	25,826
Sale	4,500	24,000	25,826
	–	–	–

WORKING 2

1982 holding

	No of shares	Cost	MV at 31.3.82
January 1981	4,000	16,000	32,000
March 1993 - rights issue	1,000	7,000	7,000
January 1998 - bonus issue	2,500	–	–
	7,500	23,000	39,000
March 1999 - sold	2,500*	7,667	13,000
Carried forward	5,000	15,333	26,000

*7,000 – FA 1985 pool (4,500)

---

94   (Answer 4 of examination)

(a)   (i)   A person making or intending to make taxable supplies of goods or services whilst carrying on business in the UK is required to register if annual taxable turnover exceeds or is expected to exceed £50,000.

(ii)   A - Customs and Excise should be notified within 30 days of the end of the month in which the annual threshold is exceeded: registration is then effective from the beginning of the next month, or earlier if agreed.
B - If taxable supplies in the next 30 days are expected to exceed the annual registration threshold Customs and Excise should be notified within 30 days of that date and registration then takes place from the beginning of that 30-day period.

(iii)   Unless there is 'reasonable excuse' for late registration the registration will be back-dated and penalties charged. The penalty will range from 5% to 15% of the VAT due from the date when registration was due until the actual date of registration depending on the delay in registering. The minimum penalty is £50. In addition VAT will, of course, have to be accounted for from the due date of registration and this may prove difficult to obtain from customers/clients.

(b)   A person may de-register for value-added tax when the value of taxable supplies (excluding VAT) in the following twelve-month period will not exceed £48,000, unless the expected fall in the value of taxable supplies is occasioned by the cessation of taxable supplies or the suspension of taxable supplies for a minimum period of 30 days in the following twelve-month period.

95   (Answer 5 of examination)

The following criteria will be considered when deciding whether an individual is employed or self-employed.

1   **Control.** Whether the individual is under the complete control and supervision of the business in the manner in which the work is carried out.

2   **Place of work.** Whether the individual can decide when and where the work is to be done or whether this is decided by the person for whom the work is being carried out

3   **Payment.** Whether the payment for the work consists of a fixed salary element, payable at regular intervals, and is accompanied by such things as holidays with pay and provision of pension rights or whether payment is made on an ad hoc basis at the completion of a particular job ie, on an invoice basis.

4   **Circumstances of engagement.** Whether the circumstances outlined at the beginning of the engagement require the individual to be provided by the business with a specified amount of work for which he will be paid and that he is obliged to accept and perform.

5   **Exclusivity and integration.** Whether the individual works for the business for the greater part of his time and whether he is integrated in the structure of the business.

6   **Work performance and correction of unsatisfactory work.** Whether the individual can engage someone else to do the job for him, and whether unsatisfactory work must be corrected before payment is made.

7   **Provision of equipment.** Whether the individual provides the tools and equipment necessary to carry out the work.

8   **Financial risk.** Whether the individual risks his own money which in extreme circumstances could result in a loss being made and profits from sound management.

9   **Insurance.** Whether the individual takes out professional indemnity and/or public liability insurance.

10   **Service contract/Contract for services.** Whether an individual works within the framework of a service contract or a contract for services.

11   **All relevant factors.** All relevant factors will need to be taken into account and a common-sense approach adopted.

96   (Answer 6 of examination)

(a)   **Income**

1   Dividends from shares in UK companies, UK authorised unit trusts and UK open-ended investment companies.

2   Interest received from UK banks, building societies and deposit takers, UK authorised unit trusts and UK open-ended investment companies.

3   Income received from UK National Savings including National Savings Bank ordinary accounts.

4   State Retirement Pension.

5   Other taxable state benefits — widow's pension, widowed mother's allowance, industrial death benefit pension, jobseeker's allowance, invalid care allowance, statutory sick pay and statutory maternity pay.

6   Other pensions and retirement annuities.

7   Income from employment(s) and benefits in kind (these details will be supplied by your employer(s)).

8   Income (and outgoings) from property.

9   Capital disposals, including dates of acquisition and disposal, proceeds, acquisition and transaction costs.

10   Any other income not included above.

(b)   **Payments**

1   Interest paid on a mortgage or loan for your main home (other than under the MIRAS scheme).

2   Payments under charitable deeds of covenant and gift aid payments.

3   Additional voluntary contributions (AVCs) to a pension scheme and payments into personal pension plans.

4   Payments to professional bodies.

(c)   **Allowances**

1   Marital status.
2   Date of birth.
3   Name of qualifying child where additional personal relief is being claimed.

---

97   (Answer 7 of examination)

(a)

Malcolm

(i)   Calculation of loss relief 1997-98

	£
Period ended 30.11.97	10,000
Year ended 5.4.98 (1.12.97–5.4.98) 126/365 × £20,000	6,904
	16,904
1998-99	
Year ended 30.11.98	20,000
less period 1.12.97-5.4.98	(6,904)
	13,096

(ii)   Allocation of loss relief 1996-97

	£
Schedule E income	8,000
Dividends	3,750
	11,750
1997-98 loss (s.380)	11,750
	–

1997-98	£
Schedule E income	5,000
Dividends	3,750
	8,750
1997-98 loss (s.380)	5,154
	3,596

1999-00	£
Schedule D income	14,000
1998-99 loss (s.385)	13,096
	904

Loss memorandum 1997-98	£
Loss	16,904
1996-97 (s.380)	(11,750)
	5,154
1997-98 (s.380)	(5,154)
	–

1998-99	£
Loss	13,096
1999-00 (s.385)	(13,096)
	–

(iii)   Rationale 1996-97 – s.380

Although there is a loss of relief for personal allowances this claim is considered worthwhile because of the repayment of income tax already paid, with repayment supplement, and the absence of a viable alternative.

1997-98 – s.380

The utilisation of the balance of the 1997-98 loss leaves in charge £3,596 which will absorb most of the year's personal allowance.

1998-99 s.385

The whole of the 1998-99 loss of £13,096 has been carried forward against the 1999-00 Case I income. This leaves the dividend income in charge which will absorb most of the year's personal allowances for 1998-99. For 1999-00 the income left in charge, £904, together with the dividend income of £3,750, will absorb the year's personal allowance

The alternative would have been to claim s.380 relief of £3,596 against the remaining income of the previous year, 1997-98, which would then have facilitated a claim under s.72, FA 1991 against the capital gain of £10,000 for the remaining loss of £9,500 (£13,096–£3,596):

	£
Capital gain	10,000
s.72 loss	9,500
	500
Annual exemption	500
	–

In doing this, losses of £13,096 would have been utilised to save capital gains tax of £640 (£10,000 – £6,800 = £3,200 at 20%).

(b)   **Loss relief claim time limits**

(i)   For claims to set-off losses against income of the year of the loss and income of the preceding year (s.380) the claim must be submitted within 12 months from 31 January next following the year of assessment in which the loss was sustained.

(ii)   There is no statutory time limit on claims to carry forward losses against future trading income (s.385). The claim must however be submitted within 5 years from 31 January next following the year of assessment in which the loss was sustained.

---

98   (Answer 8 of examination)

Josephine
1998-99 National Insurance Contribution

(a)   Class 1A – payable by employer only
       Benefits in kind (working)
       £3,545 at 10% =   354.50

(b)   Class 1 – payable by employer
       52 × £400 = £20,800 at 10% =   2,080

(c)   Class 1 – payable by employee

	£	£
Weekly	64 at 2%	1.28
	336 at 10%	33.60
		34.88
Annual 52 × £34.88 =	£1,813.76	

WORKING – Car and fuel benefit	£	£
Car 1		
35% × £12,000	4,200	
Mileage reduction	(1,400) (1/3)	
(equivalent of more than 2,500 but less than 18,000 pa)		
	2,800	
Age reduction	(933) (1/3)	
(over 4 years old on 5.4.99)		
	1,867	
Time reduction (4 months)	(622) (1/3)	1,245
Car 2		
35% × £21,000	7,350	
Mileage reduction	(4,900) (2/3)	
(equivalent of more than 18,000 pa)		
	2,450	
Time reduction (8 months)	(1,633) (2/3)	817
Fuel – Car 1		
1400 cc to 2000 cc (diesel)	1,280	
Time reduction (4 months)	(427) (1/3)	853
Fuel -		
Fuel – Car 2		
2001 cc and over (petrol)	1,890	
Time reduction (8 months)	(1,260) (2/3)	630
		3,545

Certificate Examination – Paper 7(U)   **Marking Scheme**
Tax Framework (UK Stream)

This marking scheme is given as a guide to markers in the context of the suggested answer. Scope is given to markers to award marks for alternative approaches to a question, include relevant comment, and where well reasoned conclusions are provided. This is particularly the case for essay based questions where there will often be more than one definitive solution.

		Marks
1	Corporation tax computation – Patent royalties	1
	Working 1 - Plant and machinery	
	First-year allowance	1
	WDA on 2 pools	1
	Balancing allowance	1
	WDA on expensive car (2)	1
	Carry forward of residue after FYA	1
		— 5
	Working 2 - Industrial buildings allowance	
	CAP to 31.1.86 – Initial allowance	1
	– WDA	1
	4 CAP's to 31.1.90 – WDA's	1
	2 CAP's to 31.1.92 – notional WDA's	1
	6 CAP's to 31.1.98 – WDA's	1
	CAP to 31.1.99 – Balancing charge	1
		— 6
	Working 3 - Chargeable gain	
	Unindexed gain	1
	Indexation allowance	1
		— 2
	Working 4 - CT payable	
	Calculation of 'P'	1
	Significance of 'P'	1
	CT calculation	3
		— 5
	Working 5 - Income tax	
	£35,000 at 23% = £8,050	1
	£54,000 at 20% = £10,800	1
	Set-off against MCT	1
		— 3
		22

2	(a)	1995–96	2	
		1996–97 and 1997–98	1	
		1998–99	1	
		Note 2	2	
			—	6
	(b)	Schedule A –		
		Insurance	1	
		Water rates and council tax	1	
		Wear and tear allowance	1	
		Purchased Life Annuity	1	
		Dividends	1	
		Personal allowance (W4)	3	
		Tax on non-savings income	1	
		Tax on savings income	1	
		Married couple's allowance	3	

			Income tax suffered	1	
				—	14
					20

3	(a)		16.5 years	1	
			65.293	1	
			30 years and 87,330	1	
			Indexation	1	
				—	4

	(b)		2 tests for 'small disposals'	2	
			Calculation of cost	1	
			Indexation allowance	1	
			Annual exemption and charged at marginal rate	1	
				—	5

	(c)		FA 1985 – Sale proceeds £36,000	1	
			1982 holding – Sale proceeds £20,000	1	
			Indexation – original shares and bonus issue	2	
			Indexation – rights issue	2	
			Restriction of indexation allowance resulting in 'no gain/no loss' situation	1	
			Summary	1	
			Working 1		
			Bonus issue – 1,500 shares	1	
			Indexation	1	
			Working 2		
			Rights issue – 1.000 shares	1	
			Bonus issue – 2,500 shares	1	
			Attributable cost on sale £7,667/£13,000	1	
				—	13
					22

4	(a)	(i)		2	
		(ii)	A	2	
			B	2	
		(iii)		3	
				—	9
	(b)				2
					11

5	1 mark for each point				11

6   1 mark for each correct item stated up to a maximum of 11.

7	(a)	(i)	1997-98	1
			1998-99	1
		(ii)	1996-97	1
			1997-98	1
			1999-00	1
		(iii)	1996-97 (s.380)	1
			1997-98 (s.380)	1

1998-99 (s.385)	1	
1997-78 why no s.72 claim	1	
	—	9

(b)   2
                                                                                            ——
                                                                                            11
                                                                                            ——

8   Class 1A – benefits in kind   1

Working
  Car 1
  35%   ½
  Mileage reduction   1
  Age reduction   1
  Time reduction   1
                                                                                            —   3½

  Car 2
  35%   ½
  Mileage reduction   1
  Time reduction   1
                                                                                            —   2½

  Fuel - Car 1   1
  Fuel - Car 2   1
  Class 1 - employer   1
  Class 1 - employee   1
                                                                                            —
                                                                                            11
                                                                                            ——

RATES AND ALLOWANCES (up to and including Finance Act 1998)

(A) INCOME TAX

(1) **Rates**

	1997/98			1998/99	
Rate %	Band of income £	Cumulative tax £	Rate %	Band of income £	Cumulative tax £
20	1 - 4,100	820	20	1 - 4,300	860
23	4,101 - 26,100	5,060	23	4,301 - 27,100	5,244
		5,880			6,104
40	26,101 -		40	27,100 -	

(2) **Personal allowances and reliefs**

	1997/98 £	1998/99 £
Personal allowance	4,045	4,195
Married couple's allowance	1,830*	1,900*
Age allowance (65 - 74)		
personal	5,220	5,410
married couple's	3,185*	3,305*
income limit	15,600	16,200
Age allowance (75 or over)		
personal	5,400	5,600
married couple's	3,225*	3,345*
income limit	15,600	16,200
Additional personal allowance	1,830*	1,900*
Widow's bereavement allowance	1,830*	1,900*
Blind person's allowance	1,280	1,330

* Relief restricted to 15%

(3) **Pension contribution limits**

Age at start of tax year	Personal pension schemes (%)
35 or less	17½
36 - 45	20
46 - 50	25
51 - 55	30
56 - 60	35
61 and over	40

(4) **Daily apportionment calendar**

Month	No of days	Month	No of days
January	31	July	31
February	28	August	31
March	31	September	30
April	30	October	31
May	31	November	30
June	30	December	31

(5)   **First year allowance rates**

Date expenditure incurred on plant and machinery	*FYA rate*
2 July 1997 - 1 July 1998	50%
2 July 1998 - 1 July 1999	40%

(B)   CORPORATION TAX

	FY 1994	*FY 1995*	*FY 1996*	*FY 1997*	*FY 1998*	*FY 1999*
Rate	33%	33%	33%	31%	31%	30%
Small companies rate (up to £300,000)	25%	25%	24%	21%	21%	20%

Section 13(2) ICTA 1988 relief

(M-P) ×   × fraction

where M is £1,500,000

Fraction

Advance corporation tax

N/A

The amounts of dividends received or paid represent the actual amounts without any adjustment for tax credits or advance corporation tax.

(C)   CAPITAL GAINS TAX

(1)   **Annual exemption**

	£
1993/94	5,800
1994/95	5,800
1995/96	6,000
1996/97	6,300
1997/98	6,500
1998/99	6,800

(2)   **Retail price index (RPI)**

	1982	*1983*	*1984*	*1985*
January	-	82.61	86.84	91.20
February	-	82.97	87.20	91.94
March	79.44	83.12	87.48	92.80
April	81.04	84.28	88.64	94.78
May	81.62	84.64	88.97	95.21
June	81.85	84.84	89.20	95.41
July	81.88	85.30	89.10	95.23
August	81.90	85.68	89.94	95.49
September	81.85	86.06	90.11	95.44
October	82.26	86.36	90.67	95.59
November	82.66	86.67	90.95	95.92
December	82.51	86.89	90.87	96.05

	1986	*1987*	*1988*	*1989*	*1990*	*1991*
January	96.25	100.0	103.3	111.0	119.5	130.2
February	96.60	100.4	103.7	111.8	120.2	130.9
March	96.73	100.6	104.1	112.3	121.4	131.4
April	97.67	101.8	105.8	114.3	125.1	133.1
May	97.85	101.9	106.2	115.0	126.2	133.5
June	97.79	101.9	106.6	115.4	126.7	134.1
July	97.52	101.8	106.7	115.5	126.8	133.8
August	97.82	102.1	107.9	115.8	128.1	134.1
September	98.30	102.4	108.4	116.6	129.3	134.6
October	98.45	102.9	109.5	117.5	130.3	135.1
November	99.29	103.4	110.0	118.5	130.0	135.6
December	99.62	103.3	110.3	118.8	129.9	135.7

	1992	*1993*	*1994*	*1995*	*1996*	*1997*	*1998*	*1999*
January	135.6	137.9	141.3	146.0	150.2	154.4	159.5	e164.8
February	136.3	138.8	142.1	146.9	150.9	155.0	160.3	e165.1
March	136.7	139.3	142.5	147.5	151.5	155.4	e160.7	e165.3
April	138.8	140.6	144.2	149.0	152.6	156.3	e161.2	e165.7
May	139.3	141.1	144.7	149.6	152.9	156.9	e161.3	
June	139.3	141.0	144.7	149.8	153.0	157.5	e161.8	
July	138.8	140.7	144.0	149.1	152.4	157.5	e162.6	
August	138.9	141.3	144.7	149.9	153.1	158.5	e162.2	
September	139.4	141.9	145.0	150.6	153.8	159.3	e163.3	
October	139.9	141.8	145.2	149.8	153.8	159.5	e163.8	
November	139.7	141.6	145.3	149.8	153.9	159.6	e163.9	
December	139.2	141.9	146.0	150.7	154.4	160.0	e164.1	

e - estimated

(3)   **Lease percentages**

Years	*Percentage*	*Years*	*Percentage*	*Years*	*Percentage*
50 or more	100.000	33	90.280	16	64.116
49	99.657	32	89.354	15	61.617
48	99.289	31	88.371	14	58.971
47	98.902	30	87.330	13	56.167
46	98.490	29	86.226	12	53.191
45	98.059	28	85.053	11	50.038
44	97.595	27	83.816	10	46.695
43	97.107	26	82.496	9	43.154
42	96.593	25	81.100	8	39.399
41	96.041	24	79.622	7	35.414
40	95.457	23	78.055	6	31.195
39	94.842	22	76.399	5	26.722
38	94.189	21	74.635	4	21.983
37	93.497	20	72.770	3	16.959
36	92.761	19	70.791	2	11.629
35	91.981	18	68.697	1	5.983
34	91.156	17	66.470	0	0.000

(4)   **Taper Relief**

Number of complete years after 5/4/98 for which asset held	*Business Assets*	*Non-business Assets*
	Percentage of Gain chargeable	
0	100	100
1	92.5	100
2	85	100
3	77.5	95
4	70	90
5	62.5	85
6	55	80
7	47.5	75
8	40	70
9	32.5	65
10 or more	25	60

(D)   CAR AND FUEL BENEFITS

(1)   **Car scale benefit**

35% of list price when new including accessories, delivery charges and VAT (subject to £80,000 maximum). Reductions in the charge are as follows:

Business mileage
2,500 to 17,999 pa

18,000 or more pa

Then, cars 4 years old and over at end of tax year

Second car 18,000 or more pa

Cars over 15 years old at tax year end with an open market value of more than £15,000 (which is also higher than the original list price) taxed by reference to the open market value.

(2)   **Van scale benefit**

Vans (under 3.5 tonnes) including fuel	*Under 4 years* £	*4 years and over* £
1998/99	500	350
1997/98	500	350
1996/97	500	350

(3)   **Car fuel benefit (petrol)**

	1997/98 £	*1998/99* £
Cylinder capacity		
Up to 1400 cc	800	1,010
1401 - 2000 cc	1,010	1,280
over 2000 cc	1,490	1,890

(E)   INHERITANCE TAX

(1)   **The nil rate band**

6 April 1991 to March 1992:	£140,000
10 March 1992 to 5 April 1995:	£150,000
6 April 1995 to 5 April 1996:	£154,000
6 April 1996 to 5 April 1997	£200,000
6 April 1997 to 5 April 1998	£215,000
6 April 1998 onwards	£223,000

(2)   **Tax rates**

	Rate on gross transfer	*Rate on net transfer*
Transfers on death	40%	
Chargeable lifetime transfers	20%	¼

(F)   NATIONAL INSURANCE CONTRIBUTIONS 1998/99

(1)   **Class 1 employed**   From 6 April 1998

Employee
£ per week earnings

	Contracted in	Contracted out
Up to £63.99	Nil	Nil

Rates for earnings between
£64.00 and £485.00

		Contracted in	Contracted out
(a)	on first £64.00 plus	2%	2%
(b)	£64.01 to £485.00	10%	8.4%

Employer
£ per week earnings

	Contracted in	Contracted out	
Select earnings band		*First £64*	*Balance*
Up to £63.99	Nil	Nil	Nil
£64.00 to £109.99	3%	3%	Nil
£110.00 to £154.99	5%	5%	2%
£155.00 to £209.99	7%	7%	4%
£210.00 to £485.00	10%	10%	7%
Over £485.00	10%	£35.87 plus	10%
		on excess over £485.00	

(2)   **Class 2 Self-employed**

Weekly rate £6.35

Small earnings exemption £3,590 pa

(3)   **Class 3 Voluntary**

Weekly rate £6.25

(4)   **Class 4 Self-employed**

6% on annual profits £7,310 – £25,220

ACCA
AT FOULKS LYNCH

HOTLINES
Telephone: 0181 844 0667
Enquiries: 0181 831 9990
Fax: 0181 831 9991

AT FOULKS LYNCH LTD
Number 4, The Griffin Centre
Staines Road, Feltham
Middlesex TW14 0HS

Examination Date:
☐ June 99
☐ December 99

	Textbooks	Revision Series	Lynchpins	Distance Learning — Include helpline & marking	Open Learning
Module A – Foundation Stage					
1 Accounting Framework	£17.95 [UK] [IAS]	£10.95 [UK] [IAS]	£5.95 ☐	£85 ☐	£89 ☐
2 Legal Framework	£17.95 ☐	£10.95 ☐	£5.95 ☐	£85 ☐	£89 ☐
Module B					
3 Management Information	£17.95 ☐	£10.95 ☐	£5.95 ☐	£85 ☐	£89 ☐
4 Organisational Framework	£17.95 ☐	£10.95 ☐	£5.95 ☐	£85 ☐	£89 ☐
Module C – Certificate Stage					
5 Information Analysis	£17.95 ☐	£10.95 ☐	£5.95 ☐	£85 ☐	£89 ☐
6 Audit Framework	£17.95 [UK] [IAS]	£10.95 [UK] [IAS]	£5.95 ☐	£85 ☐	£89 ☐
Module D					
7 Tax Framework FA98	£17.95 ☐	£10.95 ☐	£5.95 ☐	£85 ☐	£89 ☐
8 Managerial Finance	£17.95 ☐	£10.95 ☐	£5.95 ☐	£85 ☐	£89 ☐
Module E – Professional Stage					
9 ICDM	£18.95 ☐	£10.95 ☐	£5.95 ☐	£85 ☐	£89 ☐
10 Accounting & Audit Practice	£22.95 [UK] [IAS]	£10.95 [UK] [IAS]	£5.95 ☐	£85 ☐	£89 ☐
11 Tax Planning FA98	£18.95 ☐	£10.95 ☐	£5.95 ☐	£85 ☐	£89 ☐
Module F					
12 Management & Strategy	£18.95 ☐	£10.95 ☐	£5.95 ☐	£85 ☐	£89 ☐
13 Financial Rep Environment	£20.95 [IAS]	£10.95 [IAS]	£5.95 ☐	£85 ☐	£89 ☐
14 Financial Strategy	£19.95 ☐	£10.95 ☐	£5.95 ☐	£85 ☐	£89 ☐
P & P + Delivery UK Mainland	£2.00/book	£1.00/book	£1.00/book	£5.00/subject	£5.00/subject
NI, ROI & EU Countries	£5.00/book	£3.00/book	£3.00/book	£15.00/subject	£15.00/subject
Rest of world standard air service	£10.00/book	£8.00/book	£8.00/book	£25.00/subject	£25.00/subject
Rest of world courier service†	£22.00/book	£20.00/book	£14.00/book	£47.00/subject	£47.00/subject

SINGLE ITEM SUPPLEMENT: If you only order 1 item, **INCREASE** postage costs by £2.50 for UK, NI & EU Countries or by £10.00 for Rest of World Services

TOTAL
Sub Total £
Post & Packing £
Total £

†*Telephone number essential for this service* — *Payments in Sterling in London* — Order Total £

DELIVERY DETAILS
☐ Mr ☐ Miss ☐ Mrs ☐ Ms Other
Initials ___ Surname ___
Address ___
Postcode ___
Telephone ___ Deliver to home ☐

Company name ___
Address ___
Postcode ___
Telephone ___ Fax ___
Monthly report to go to employer ☐ Deliver to work ☐

PAYMENT
1 I enclose Cheque/PO/Bankers Draft for £_____
Please make cheques payable to AT Foulks Lynch Ltd.

2 Charge Mastercard/Visa/Switch A/C No:
Valid from: ☐☐☐☐ Expiry Date: ☐☐☐☐
Issue No: (Switch only) ☐☐
Signature ___ Date ___

DECLARATION
I agree to pay as indicated on this form and understand that AT Foulks Lynch Terms and Conditions apply (available on request). I understand that AT Foulks Lynch Ltd are not liable for non-delivery if the rest of world standard air service is used.
Signature ___ Date ___

Please Allow:
UK mainland — 5-10 w/days
NI, ROI & EU Countries — 1-3 weeks
Rest of world standard air service - 6 weeks
Rest of world courier service - 10 w/days

Notes: All delivery times subject to stock availability. Signature required on receipt (except rest of world standard air service). Please give both addresses for Distance Learning students where possible.

Form effective at Jan 99 — *All details correct at time of printing.* — Source: ACRSF9